THE
PORTSMOUTH
BOOK
OF
DAYS

JOHN SADDEN

Acknowledgements are due to the authors of the books and magazines and newspaper articles, that have been plundered for this volume. It is hoped that those who are curious or intrigued by the brief stories, facts, ephemera and trivia presented here will seek out the sources, the majority of which are available for consultation in the Local Studies section of the Portsmouth Central Public Library. Thanks are due to the staff at Portsmouth City Council Libraries and Museum service, Portsmouth Grammar School Library, Hampshire County Library service and to M.C. Sadden and Tim Reynolds.

The Julian Calendar was in use up until Wednesday 2 September 1752. The following day the Gregorian Calendar was adopted making the date Thursday 14 September 1752. The dates in this book before and after this shift correspond to the respective calendars.

John Sadden, 2011

First published 2011

The History Press
The Mill, Brimscombe Port
Stroud, Gloucestershire, GL5 2QG
www.thehistorypress.co.uk

British Library Cataloguing in Publication Data.
A catalogue record for this book is available from the British Library.

ISBN 978 0 7524 5765 9

Typesetting and origination by The History Press
Manufacturing managed by Jellyfish Print Solutions Ltd.
Printed in India

January 1st

1831: On this day the name Landport was used for the first time. The area was formerly known as Halfway Houses, named after some houses that stood halfway between Portsea and St Mary's Church. (City of Portsmouth Records of the Corporation [1827-1979], ed. W. Gates, G. Singleton Gates, G.E. Barnett and V. Blanchard, Dr R. Windle, Dr R.C. Riley)

———◆———

1856: Portsea (later Kingston) Cemetery was opened. Among the first people interred were six Dockyard workers killed when a steam-engine boiler exploded. The greater part of the red-hot boiler, which weighed a ton, was hurled 100ft and then rebounded another 100ft towards the building slip. The force of the explosion demolished the boiler shed, sending the roof 60ft into the air, and burst the wall of the adjoining building, causing wounds 'of a most frightful description'. The funeral was attended by an estimated 20,000 people, and the deceased were buried in a communal grave. (*Daily News*, *Hampshire Telegraph*)

———◆———

1805: The Hampshire Library opened its doors in St George's Square to the Portsmouth gentry, who paid a 2 guinea joining fee and an annual subscription of £1 2s. The rest of the population had to wait seventy-eight years before a public library service was established. (*Hampshire Telegraph*)

January 2nd

1887: On this bitterly cold winter's day, soldiers of the 2nd Battalion Worcestershire Regiment were sitting around the fire in the basement of Cambridge Barracks. At nine o'clock, leaking gas ignited and the men were blown to pieces. Above them, the explosion took out a side of the barracks, sending men and debris onto the parade ground. The upper two floors collapsed, trapping others. Men from other barracks hastened to help in the attempt to dig out survivors by lantern light. Ambulances were summoned but frozen roads prevented the horses getting a footing and so the soldiers pulled the ambulances themselves, to and from the hospital, on Lion Terrace.

The coroner's inquest recorded a verdict of accidental death on the five men killed, but the jury added a rider that the military authorities' procedures over the supervision of gas were 'most unsatisfactory'. A subsequent military court of inquiry blamed the Quartermaster and a non-commissioned officer, who were both demoted. The under-floor gas pipes were found to be corroded with rust and the Portsea Island Gas Company was found negligent for not maintaining them properly. (*Pall Mall Gazette; A History of Cambridge Barracks* by C. Smith, 2001)

January 3rd

1801: A new flag, the Union Jack, was hoisted on the saluting platform for the first time. (*Annals of Portsmouth* by W.H. Saunders, 1880)

---•◆•---

1961: Heckling at the King's Theatre forced the closure of the gallery for the season as 'teenage hooligans' upset the actors at the pantomime. (City of Portsmouth Records of the Corporation, ed. Gates, Singleton-Gates, Barnett, Blanchard, Windle, Riley)

---•◆•---

1665: Commissioner of the Dockyard, Thomas Middleton, wrote to Samuel Pepys:

> Great want of seamen. The new ship is to be launched next month and not one man belonging to her except the officers whose work is to look upon them. It is hard to make bricks without straw but am content, the small time I have to live to serve my King and country, though I would rather be buried alive than put upon impossibilities.

Middleton appeared to dislike Portsmouth, later writing:

> For my part to you as a frinde I declayre I intend not to make Portsmouth my habitation if I can avoid it. 'Tis Trew if the Kinge command me to live underwater if it weare possible I would and must do it, but if I can anyway with the preservation of my reputation avoid it, I shall not live heare for the rent of Hampsheere.

(*Portsmouth through the Centuries* by W. Gates, 1931)

January 4th

1907: An inquest was held on the death of two lifeboatmen who were washed up on Southsea beach after the Ryde lifeboat capsized in a heavy squall. (*The Times*)

1958: Sir Edwin Alliott Verdon-Roe, aircraft designer and manufacturer, died in St Mary's Hospital, Portsmouth, having resided at Rowlands Castle.

On learning of the successful flight of the Wright brothers in 1903, Roe decided to devote himself to powered flight.

By 1910, he had set up one of the world's first aircraft building manufacturers, A.V. Roe & Co.(AVRO), in Manchester. In 1911 he designed the first enclosed cabin aeroplane and established a British flying record of seven and a half hours. The following year he designed and built the famous *Avro* 504, which in its improved form became the best-known military aeroplane of the First World War. In 1917 it became the standard trainer and was used in Gosport at the pioneering School of Special Flying at Grange airfield. It was also used as a bomber, carrying out the first ever air raid on Zeppelin sheds at Friedrichshafen in 1914. (*Oxford Dictionary of National Biography*)

January 5th

1834: The *Marianne* docked at Portsmouth, carrying 212 Polish soldiers who had escaped Tsarist Russian aggression. The refugees were housed in local barracks and were 'determined to make the best of their situation, seeking out employment, companionship and a degree of independence'. Sympathy for their plight was widespread, helped by explanatory newspaper articles headlined: 'The Suffering, Brave Poles'. Each man was given a small government allowance until, it was explained, they might achieve 'the dearest object of their existence, the liberty of their country'. When one refugee died, the Royal Marine Band played in the procession to Mile End Cemetery (now the site of the Continental Ferryport), and sympathetic crowds turned out.

Novelist Walter Besant, who spent his early years in Portsmouth at this time, later described their poverty in *By Celia's Arbour*, and how they survived on bread and cabbage soup. Over time, many of the men found employment and became self-sufficient, integrating into the local community, a number marrying into Portsmouth families. (*Settlers, Visitors and Asylum Seekers* by P. MacDougall, 2007; *Hampshire Advertiser; Hampshire Telegraph*)

———— ◆ ————

1816: The last remaining French prisoners, captured during the Napoleonic wars, were sent home from Portchester Castle. (*History of Portsmouth* by W. Gates, 1900)

January 6th

1800: The borough's bakers went on strike over the price of bread. At that time, the price was controlled by the magistrates, and, bowing to the pressure, they revoked the Assize of Bread, allowing the bakers to charge whatever they liked. The price immediately shot up, and meetings were held by local people unable to feed their families at which there were at least seven arrests. Posters appeared, calling on the rich to, 'Repent before too late, the time is drawing nigh ... You grind us so our children can't get bread, consider this before you lose your head ... The halter's made, The time is near at hand, That you must make, Your exit from this land.'

Three halters were suspended at the Lion Gate in Portsea, with a notice proclaiming, 'A caution. To the farmers, millers and bakers ... Each of you take your choice. The greatest rogue, May have the greatest hoist.'

By August the price of bread had gone up again and 'formidable demonstrations' took place in St George's Square. (*see* September 1st) By October, following a successful harvest, the price was reduced. (*Portsmouth* by A. Temple Patterson, 1976; *History of Portsmouth* by W. Gates, 1900)

January 7th

1919: On this day in 1919, 300 Portsmouth men who had just been released from enemy POW camps during the First World War were entertained in the Town Hall by local people, who had organised food and clothing parcels to be sent to the men during their incarceration.

Stories had appeared in the press during the war that POWS were being systematically starved by their German captors and immediately a 'comforts fund' was set up to pay for food parcels. By the end of 1916 there were 180 POWs from Portsmouth who were receiving these parcels, including survivors who had been picked up after the Battle of Jutland. Parcels continued to be sent throughout 1917 and 1918 when there were severe food shortages. In all, nearly 17,000 parcels were dispatched containing, amongst other things, OXO cubes, tinned meat and Huntley & Palmer biscuits. (*Keep the Home Fires Burning* by J. Sadden, 1990; City of Portsmouth Records of the Corporation, ed. Gates, Singleton-Gates, Barnett, Blanchard, Windle, Riley)

———◆———

1688: Following a petition from the Mayor and Corporation, William of Orange ordered that no soldiers were to be billeted with inhabitants until the barracks were full, and that 8*d* a week should be paid for their accommodation and upkeep. (City of Portsmouth Records of the Corporation, ed. Gates, Singleton-Gates, Barnett, Blanchard, Windle, Riley)

January 8th

1869: Following an eight-year life of crime centred on the Marylebone area of Portsmouth, just east of the Town Hall, a notorious 'rough' who went by the name of 'Punch Cubby' was sentenced to seven years' imprisonment for stealing potatoes. The potatoes had disappeared from a field in Elm Grove cultivated by Josiah Simmons, a market gardener, and were valued at 5s. John Tilbury, aka 'Punch Cubby', and an accomplice were arrested by a policeman on the beat.

Born in around 1846, John Tilbury had tried the patience of local magistrates since he was a boy, having been convicted on numerous occasions for the theft of food, including bread, pork and rabbits. Two years earlier, Tilbury had served twelve months in prison with hard labour for his part in the 'tin-kettle' killing (*see* May 30th), but was back before the Bench within two months of his release. (*Hampshire Telegraph*)

———— • ◆ • ————

1923: Wireless research workers were reported to be searching for an explanation as to why broadcasts in the new medium from Manchester were heard with ease in Portsmouth, but those from London were lost in the ether. (*The Times*)

January 9th

1450: The Bishop of Chichester, Adam de Moleyns, Keeper of the King's Privy Seal, completed a service at the Domus Dei (later the Garrison Church).

The Bishop had been dispatched to the town to pay soldiers and sailors a part of their outstanding wages, but a group of angry sailors arrived at the church, not having had anything to live on for some time. They remonstrated with the Bishop, also accusing him of being partially responsible for the recent loss of Normandy, which had been given away as part of Henry VI's marriage negotiations. They dragged him out of the church and beat him so severely that he died. Before being killed, the Bishop is said to have alleged that the King's Chief Minister, the Earl of Suffolk, had embezzled large amounts of money which is why the men had not been paid. For this heinous crime against the church, the town was excommunicated by the Pope, and it was nearly sixty years before this was lifted after an elaborate ceremony of penance. (*War of the Roses* by M. Miller, 2003)

January 10th

1941: At seven o'clock, the thirty-first air raid on the city began. Incendiaries and high explosive bombs fell in waves over the next seven hours, dropped by 300 raiders. Three batches of incendiaries fell on the Guildhall and a high explosive bomb hit the roof, which collapsed. The Electricity Station was hit, cutting off all power to the city, and sixty-three water mains were broken. The main shopping areas in Palmerston Road, King's Road and Commercial Road were in ruins and other buildings that were destroyed included six churches, three cinemas, the Eye and Ear Hospital, part of the Royal Hospital, Clarence Pier, the Hippodrome, the Dockyard School, Connaught Drill Hall, Central Hotel, the Royal Sailors' Rest and the Salvation Army Citadel in Lake Road. Three thousand homes were made uninhabitable. Altogether, there were 2,314 fires. A direct hit on an underground air-raid shelter killed forty-seven people. Several ARP Wardens' Posts were damaged or destroyed. A total of 171 people were killed and 430 injured in those seven hours. (City of Portsmouth Records of the Corporation, ed. Gates, Singleton-Gates, Barnett, Blanchard, Windle, Riley)

January 11th

1660: Samuel Pepys wrote:

> This day comes news, by letters from Portsmouth, that the Princess Henrietta is fallen sick of the measles on board the London, after the Queen and she was under sail. And so was forced to come back again into Portsmouth harbour; and in their way, by negligence of the pilot, run upon the Horse sand. The Queen and she continue aboard, and do not intend to come on shore till she sees what will become of the young Princess. This news do make people think something indeed, that three of the Royal Family should fall sick of the same disease, one after another.

(*The Administration of the Navy from the Restoration to the Revolution* by J. Tanner, English Historical Review Vol. XII, 1897)

———•◦•———

1905: John Jacques was born. He was Chief Executive of the Portsea Island Mutual Co-operative Society (PIMCO) from 1945 to 1965, during which time he helped double membership and increase sales six-fold. His forward thinking led to the introduction of Britain's first self-service store at Albert Road in 1948, three years before Tesco caught on. This enabled customers to choose their own products from shelves rather than rely on an assistant to retrieve them from behind a counter. (*A Pictorial History of Portsea Island Mutual Co-operative Society Ltd* [1873-1998] by Community Link Associates)

January 12th

1948: Popular Edwardian music hall comedienne and singer, Daisy Dormer, who had been born Kezia Stockwell in 1883, the daughter of a Portsmouth Dockyard worker, died in 1947. On this cold January morning, the details of her will were published. To the Commanding Officer of the RN Barracks she left 'my largest theatrical hamper containing my glamorous clothes, character and comedy dresses for the use of the ratings of any ship based in Portsmouth.' She added, 'And I express the hope that they will be useful in connection with the amateur theatrical entertainments which they provide.' (*The Times*)

———•◆•———

1740: Mary Lacy, lesbian sailor and shipwright, was born. In 1759 she went to sea as William Chandler and, in 1763, began an apprenticeship as a shipwright at the Dockyard. According to her autobiography, rumours forced Mary to admit to two fellow workers, who had been chosen to check out her manhood, that she was a woman, but the men swore to keep her secret, and told a crowd of Dockyard workers that 'he is a man-and-a-half to a great many'. A voice from the crowd said, 'I thought Chandler could not be so great with his mistress if he was not a man.'(*Female Tars* by S. Stark, 1998)

January 13th

1869: Janet Steel, a girl of around fourteen years of age, went shopping in Arundel Street and Commercial Road. She visited ten shops, and by the end of her spree was laden with goods, including a box of figs, a silk necktie and an ermine muff. On this day in 1869, the 'extensive swindling of Landport tradesmen' was reported in the local press. On visiting the shops, Steel had ordered lengthy lists of goods to be delivered to a respectable resident at a local address, to whom the bill was to be charged. Before leaving, she asked to carry one item with her. Subsequently, the deliveries were returned to the traders, the addresses, if not the respectable residents, being fictitious. (*Hampshire Telegraph*)

———— ◆ ————

1871: The first Portsmouth School Board was elected, its mission being to provide schools 'for children who at an early age are compelled to earn their own living and to amend the consequences of past neglect'. At the core of 'the system of instruction' were the compulsory subjects of Bible Reading, Reading and Grammar, Writing and Arithmetic. Boys were to have Drill, girls and infants Needlework. (*Portsmouth's Schools 1750-1975* by P. Galliver, 2011)

January 14th

1944: Lieutenant Worth and Surgeon-Lieutenant Fowler of the Royal Naval Volunteer Reserve attended a séance in a darkened room above Homer's Drug Store at No. 301 Copnor Road. The medium was a Scottish woman, Helen Duncan, who had previously been prosecuted as a fake. She had come to the attention of the Navy after having suggested she had knowledge of the sinking of HMS *Barham* before it had been officially announced.

A white figure appeared from a cabinet, purporting to be Duncan's spirit guide, Albert, who summoned up what was claimed to be Lieutenant Worth's sister. This surprised Lieutenant Worth as his sister was an ambulance driver in London. Another spirit guide called Peggy appeared and sang Loch Lomond before producing an ectoplasmic cat, which meowed, an ectoplasmic parrot, which said 'Pretty Polly', an ectoplasmic rabbit and various human spirits, including that of a policeman. After the séance, Lieutenant Worth was given four photographs which purported to show spirits. He took the photographs to a real policeman, who began an investigation that led to Duncan being tried at the Old Bailey and imprisoned under the Witchcraft Act of 1735. (*The Trial of Mrs Duncan* by C. Bechhofer Roberts, 1945)

January 15th

1948: Foreign Secretary Ernest Bevin, who supported the creation of an Arab-ruled state in western Palestine, signed a treaty with Iraq on board HMS *Victory* in the Dockyard. Bevin undertook to withdraw British troops from Palestine to allow for immediate Arab occupation of the territory. This became known as the Portsmouth Treaty. Bevin was also reported to have sold the Iraqi foreign minister 50,000 tommy-guns, and the meeting ended with optimism about the future of Palestine. (*Ernest Bevin, Foreign Secretary* by A. Bullock, 1967)

1841: Children's author and hymn writer Sarah Doudney was born at Portsea. Her father ran a candle and soap manufacturing business at Mile End. She began writing verse and prose as a child and, when she was fifteen, wrote The Lesson of the Water-Mill, a song which became well known in Britain and the United States. From 1871 she published a series of pious children's novels, including *The Great Salterns* (1875), which was set on Portsea Island. Some of her hymns are still occasionally sung, including 'Sleep on, beloved, sleep and take thy rest and Saviour, now the day is ending'. She died in 1926. (*Portsmouth Novelists* by D. Francis, 2006, *Oxford Dictionary of National Biography*)

January 16th

1699: Mr Henry Seager complained about the conduct of Mr Thomas Ridge in a written deposition:

> Henry Seager, gent, one of the justices of the Peace for ye said Burrough maketh oath. That severall days and times within Three months last past att Portesmouth aforesd Mr Thomas Ridge hath abused this deponent (Seager) by bidding him this deponent kiss his breech, and after giving him the lye that he said Mr Ridge did not give a f--t for this deponent and that this deponent might goe and acquaint the Society of itt, and further this deponent maketh oath that about Wednesday night last …
> [he] told this deponent that … he was a Rascall and a Villaine, and then gave this deponent opprobeious languadge.

What had upset Mr Ridge is not known. He was the son of a local brewer and Mayor and the Ridge family were described as 'of very ancient and respectable standing in the Borough', a status that was seemingly unaffected by Thomas's behaviour (*see* February 15th).There is no record of Mr Seager having kissed Mr Ridge's bottom. (Extracts from 'Records in the possession of the Municipal Corporation of the Borough of Portsmouth' by Robert East, 1891)

———◆———

1772: Charles Chubb was born in Fordingbridge. He set up a business in Portsea as a locksmith and patented the detector lock in 1818. (*Oxford Dictionary of National Biography*)

January 17th

1906: Successful author, journalist, illustrator and eccentric, Fred T. Jane, stood as an independent 'Navy before Party' candidate for the Portsmouth seat in the General Election. He came last. In 1899, Jane was commissioned by Pictorial World to cover naval manoeuvres and an inspection of the combined fleets at Spithead by the German emperor Wilhelm II. Jane was able to sketch nearly 100 ships. Nine years later, he published *Jane's All the World's Fighting Ships* (shortened to *Jane's Fighting Ships* in 1905), with details of all major surface warships; this was to be used as a ship recognition and intelligence aid by all sides in many future naval conflicts.

Aircraft, television, and laser holograms were recognisably foreshadowed in a series of Jane's illustrations in the *Pall Mall Magazine* in 1894-5. He also became a successful novelist with *Blake of the Rattlesnake* (1895), followed by several science-fiction titles, including *The Incubated Girl* (1896), *To Venus in Five Seconds* (1897), and *The Violet Flame* (1899), which featured an armament with the characteristics of a nuclear weapon. Fred T. Jane died of a heart attack following severe influenza at No. 26 Clarence Esplanade on 8 March 1916. (*Oxford Dictionary of National Biography*, City of Portsmouth Records of the Corporation, ed. Gates, Singleton-Gates, Barnett, Blanchard, Windle, Riley)

January 18th

1876: Charles Sewell, aged twelve, appeared before magistrates charged with stealing a pair of boots from Mr Budden's bootshop in Commercial Road. At a time when many children went barefoot through poverty, the temptation to acquire footwear in the middle of winter must have been great, a fact perhaps recognised by the court. The Clerk expressed surprise when it emerged that not only had the boots been displayed outside the shop, but that nobody was employed to watch over them. The case was reported under the headline, 'Another theft through the exposure of goods'. However, less than two hours after stealing the boots, the boy returned to Commercial Road to try to pawn them, which was to be his undoing. Whether this was his intention all along, or whether they didn't fit (they were men's) is not known.

Barefoot children were a common sight on the streets of Portsea well into the twentieth century. In the Portsmouth-based novel, *Mudlark*, set during the First World War, the theft of boots by two barefoot mudlarks sparks a tragicomic chain of events. And even into the 1920s, the Portsmouth Brotherhood, based at Arundel Street Wesleyan Church, was running a charitable Boot Fund. (*Mudlark* by J. Sedden, 2005; *Hampshire Telegraph*)

January 19th

1901: Elizabeth Rowland of No. 24 Prince Albert Street, Eastney received this letter from George Hill, aged twenty-two, whom she had been seeing while her soldier husband was serving in India. Hill was a marine at Eastney Barracks until he was convicted of stealing there. He was later arrested for murdering a man on a train during an armed robbery.

Dearest Lizzie,

It makes my heart bleed, as I am writing these few lines, to think I shall never see you again, and that you will be alone and miserable now ... I always loved you dearly ... I am truly sorry and penitent for having, in an evil moment, allowed myself to be carried away into committing ... murder ... I went and purchased a revolver, so that when I came down to Portsmouth ... I could end both our lives if I had not been successful in obtaining money from my father. I know you were not happy at home, nor I either, for I have been very unhappy of late, mostly on account of the false charges brought against me at barracks. God knows I was as innocent as the dead. I shall get hung now ... I believe I was mad; I know I was drunk. God help me! My days are numbered, but I will bear it unflinchingly.

Your wretched and broken-hearted sweetheart,

Geo. H. Hill

Hill was hanged at Wandsworth Prison on 19 March 1901. (Old Bailey Proceedings, *The Times*)

January 20th

1899: Portsmouth magistrates petitioned Parliament, urging them to repeal a law which had just been passed enabling people to opt out of being vaccinated. The petition stated that the outcome would be to 'nullify the incalculable benefits [that] have resulted in the prevention of the dangerous, loathsome and disfiguring disease, Small Pox'. (*Hampshire Telegraph*)

———— • ◆ • ————

1934: *The Times* reported that two submariners who had just returned from China had missed their train from Waterloo to Portsmouth because they had left their group to 'seek refreshments'. Their group, which numbered 150, were due back at the submarine depot at Fort Blockhouse in Gosport.

The two submariners immediately hailed a cab and drove to Croydon, where they chartered an aeroplane which flew them to the newly-opened Portsmouth Airport. They then phoned Portsmouth Harbour Station to hear that their fellow submariners had just arrived and were about to cross the harbour. They then engaged a taxi to drive them the 6 miles from Portsmouth Aerodrome to Gosport 'and had the satisfaction of joining their comrades as they marched into Fort Blockhouse'. (*The Times*)

January 21st

1899: It was reported that there was at least one dog poisoner at large in Portsmouth. Though 'thoroughly reprehensible and cruel', the *Hampshire Telegraph* blamed irresponsible dog owners for keeping 'half-bred brutes that bark and snap at everyone they meet' and howl through the night, provoking other residents. (*Hampshire Telegraph*)

1895: On this busy day for Mayor Thomas King in 1895, he opened the town's first public museum in the High Street (previously the Town Hall). In his speech he said that Portsmouth had lost out because of its tardiness in starting the museum, suggesting that many artefacts had been lost to other towns because of the delay. The first curator, local historian William Saunders, thanked the Mayor before he left for his next engagement. Arriving in Arundel Street, the Mayor opened the new Technical Institute, where it was reported that 800 students had already enrolled for courses. In his speech, he expressed regret that a larger, purpose-built building had not been commissioned. The local MP added that, through education, 'they were affording the poorest boy in the land the opportunity of rising to the highest position'. The day ended with a banquet at the Town Hall to celebrate the launches. (City of Portsmouth Records of the Corporation, ed. Gates, Singleton-Gates, Barnett, Blanchard, Windle, Riley; *Hampshire Telegraph*)

January 22nd

1805: Jane Austen wrote a letter addressed to her brother, Captain Francis Austen on HMS *Leopard*, at Portsmouth:

> My dearest Frank,
> I wrote to you yesterday, but your letter to Cassandra [Jane's sister] this morning, by which we learn the probability of you being by this time at Portsmouth, obliges one to write to you again, having unfortunately a communication so necessary as painful to make to you. – Your affectionate heart will be greatly wounded, and I wish the shock could have been lessened by a better preparation; – but the event has been sudden, and so must be the information of it. We have lost our Excellent Father. An illness of only forty hours carried him off yesterday morning between ten and eleven...

At this time, Jane was living in Bath and working on a novel, *The Watsons*, about an invalid clergyman with little money and his four unmarried daughters. Austen appears to have stopped work on the novel after her father's death because her personal circumstances resembled those of her characters too closely for her comfort.

(*Jane Austen's Manuscript Letters in Facsimile*, ed. J. Modet, 1990)

January 23rd

1821: At ten to seven in the morning, the valet of Portsmouth's Commander-in-Chief, entered his dressing room. Admiral Sir George Campbell was lying on the floor. Beside him was a discharged pistol.

Campbell had been appointed Commander-in-Chief in 1818 and was coming to the end of his term of office. His abilities were highly rated by Lord Nelson and he was a friend of the Prince Regent. At the coroner's inquest, a verdict of 'lunacy' was returned. (*Gentleman's Magazine*)

———◆———

1875: Mr Baker was a speculative builder who began erecting houses at Stamshaw. Unfortunately, Baker did not deposit plans for his development with the Sanitary Authority and was fined £1 by magistrates. The local authority then maintained that the site was not fit to build on because it had been used as a tip and lacked drainage. They demanded that the work be stopped. This prompted Baker to speed up development, which was only stopped by legal embargo. Prolonged litigation ensued which was only finalised two years later. At stake was the issue of the power of a local authority against the freedom of an individual to do what he wished to make money. In an editorial on this day in 1878, the *Hampshire Telegraph* made clear that 'the battle was worth fighting, and the public, for whose protection alone the bye-laws are framed, have good reason to rejoice at the victory that has been won'. (*Hampshire Telegraph*)

January 24th

1826: A 'numerous and respectable meeting of the inhabitants of the Borough of Portsmouth' took place at the Beneficial Society's Hall in Kent Street, Portsea. Built in 1784 as a free school for boys, the building was also used for meetings, social functions and entertainments.

The meeting, with Mayor David Spice in the chair, resolved to petition the Houses of Lords and Commons with an issue that troubled many people across the country. 'Slavery,' the meeting decided, 'under any form or circumstance, however mild or plausible, is contrary to the dictates of justice, as well as repugnant to sound and enlightened policy and that the principles and benign spirit of Christianity are equally opposed to its inhumanity.'

Though slave trading had been abolished in 1807, 'a state of the most rigorous and cruel slavery' still continued in the British colonies in the West Indies. The condition of the slave population, the meeting heard, 'remains as wretched and merciless as ever'.

Perhaps mindful that some people are blind to moral imperatives that lack an economic justification, the meeting added to its petition that 'free labour is more productive and advantageous than slave cultivation'. (*Hampshire Telegraph*)

January 25th

1881: The *Evening News* published this editorial, prompted by some inhabitants' reactions to the great snowstorm which brought 5ft-deep snowdrifts, the suspension of all public transport and an appeal for money to help those in distress:

> There still exist numbers of ignorant and exasperating fanatics, thick-headed men with leather lungs and the epidermis of a rhinoceros, who set common sense, science and the Register General's returns equally at defiance, and bellow forth their delight in this 'good old-fashioned weather'... it never strikes them ... that those who suffer from insufficient food or clothing, the aged, the very young, the delicate, the ailing can feel no such pleasant reaction, but succumb to the icy touch of winter as do flowers and vegetation. Cold is death.

The Council spent £1,100 in helping to clear the roads of snow, and troops from local barracks assisted in transporting essential mail. Over £700 was raised by public subscription for those in need. However, this was not enough to prevent the local coroner having to deal with an increase in cases of hypothermia. (*Evening News, Portsmouth*; City of Portsmouth Records of the Corporation ed. Gates, Singleton-Gates, Barnett, Blanchard, Windle, Riley)

January 26th

1941: Mr George Balfour, who was born in Portsmouth in 1872, and founded the company Balfour, Beatty & Co. Ltd in 1909, died on this day in 1941. Balfour played an important role in the development of the electrical industry in the UK, and served as Conservative and Unionist MP for Hampstead from 1918 until his death. (*The Times*)

———— ◆ ————

1923: Mary Pelham was murdered in her home off Queen Street. Mary lived in one of the numerous slum homes in Portsea. During the day she was a familiar figure selling flowers in the streets, and at night she sold the use of her body. Her body was found on her blood-soaked bed with head injuries, and a scarf around her neck with which her murderer had tried to strangle her.

Mary Pelham had been seen with a sailor shortly before her death and a ticket for the Royal Sailors' Rest was found near her body. The Navy arranged an identity parade of 3,500 sailors and, perhaps not surprisingly, the witness was unable to identify the killer. (*History in Hiding* by A. Triggs, 1989)

January 27th

1913: Michael Ripper was born in Portsmouth, the son of Dockyard worker Harold Ripper. In his spare time Ripper senior was an elocutionist, who published a book, *Vital Speech* in 1928.

Michael Ripper attended Portsmouth Grammar School and took part in school productions. The family became close friends with a man who was to become one of Britain's greatest character actors, Alastair Sim. The Ripper's Alhambra Road house was regularly filled with Sim's talk and love of poetry, drama and the theatre. In 1928, Michael successfully auditioned at the Central School of Speech and Drama.

In 1952, Michael's promising theatrical career was brought to an end when he underwent an operation for a thyroid condition which left him unable to project his voice. He devoted himself to film and television work and appeared in over 200 films and television series, but is most famous as a stalwart of the Hammer Horror studio's output, appearing in more of their films – thirty-four – than any other actor. (*Michael Ripper Unmasked* by D. Pykett, 1999)

———◆———

1932: Peter Cheeseman, described as one of the most influential theatre directors of the second half of the twentieth century, was born in Portsmouth. (*The Guardian*)

January 28th

1805: The first motor car was seen in Portsmouth. It was a steam carriage capable of carrying twelve people. (*History of Portsmouth* by W. Gates, 1900)

———•◆•———

1929: The first 'talking' film to be shown in Portsmouth, *The Singing Fool*, was screened on this date at the Plaza cinema at Bradford Junction. (*Cinemas of Portsmouth* by R. Brown, 2009)

———•◆•———

1956: An eighteen year old who had been called up for National Service, and had been in the Army for eight days, was found dead between the railway lines at Portsmouth. (*The Times*)

———•◆•———

1909: Lionel 'Buster' Crabb, naval frogman, was born in Streatham. During the war, Crabb was active on bomb disposal duties, combating underwater saboteurs and disabling weapons attached to ships' hulls. He was awarded the George Medal and the OBE and retired, but reappeared at Portsmouth on 17 April 1956 with a member of the Secret Intelligence Service and booked a room at the Sally Port Hotel. He went to HMS *Vernon* (on the site of Gunwharf Quays) where he prepared for a dive to investigate the Soviet cruiser Ordzhonikidze berthed in Portsmouth Harbour. He disappeared on this mission, prompting many imaginative theories as to what had happened to him. (*Oxford Dictionary of National Biography*)

January 29th

1909: Victor Grayson MP was attending the ninth annual national Labour Party Conference at Portsmouth Town Hall, alongside the socialist playwright George Bernard Shaw. After a packed morning which included discussions on the right to work, hereditary privileges, old age pensions and the problem of the unelected Lords, Grayson was summoned outside by two gentlemen who offered to take him for a spin around town in their motor car to take in the sights. Grayson relished the opportunity, but very soon became suspicious when he discovered he was being driven out of town and into the countryside 'at a dangerous speed'. At the wheel was Fred T. Jane, who had very effectively prevented Grayson from delivering a speech to the conference that afternoon.

Victor Grayson later went on to expose Lloyd George's selling of honours, which at that time was considered bad form as it was too brazen. Grayson continued to investigate high-level corruption and was beaten up in The Strand at the beginning of September 1920. This did not dissuade him from continuing to threaten to reveal the extent of the corruption, and it is widely believed that when he disappeared on the 28 September that he was murdered to prevent any more revelations. (*The Strange Case of Victor Grayson* by R. Groves, 1975; *The Times*)

January 30th

1910: Cosmo Lang, who had served as vicar of Portsea from 1896 to 1901, returned to St Mary's Church as ArchBishop of York. His rapid elevation to this position, within eighteen years of his ordination, was unprecedented and, in 1928, he was appointed ArchBishop of Canterbury. During Lang's visit he preached to a male-only congregation as President of the Church of England Men's Society and then spoke at a meeting in the Town Hall.

As vicar of Portsea, Lang supervised the construction of St Mary's Parish Institute, which opened in 1898. The size of the building had to be reduced when the estimated cost rocketed, but it had five classrooms and a hall which was used for temperance meetings, educational talks, fundraising bazaars and other parish activities. The Institute later became Northern Secondary School. Lang also served as chaplain to the local prison, the 2nd Hampshire Royal Artillery Volunteer Corp and Honorary Chaplain to Queen Victoria, whose funeral he helped arrange.

In 1936, as ArchBishop of Canterbury during the King's abdication, Lang took a hard line and was widely criticised for being uncharitable towards the departed king. (*The Times*)

January 31st

1805: Pioneering explorer of the African continent, Mungo Park, sailed from Portsmouth for the Gambia aboard the frigate *Eugenia*.

The full expedition that set off into the African interior comprised three officers and forty other Europeans, mostly British soldiers, plus local guides and slaves. The expedition reached the River Niger in August, by which time only eleven Europeans were still alive, the remainder having died of fever. In November, Park set sail downstream into the unknown reaches of the river in a large canoe with what remained of his expedition, one British officer and three soldiers (one by now was mad), a guide and three slaves. Park is believed to have sailed downstream for a further 1,000 miles, past Timbuktu, through Niger and into north-west Nigeria. Attacks by local tribes were successfully fought off with the available guns but, in Nigeria, the canoe became stranded and the party again came under attack from native tribesmen. It is believed that Park and the remaining three other Europeans were drowned trying to escape. In 1811, the *Hampshire Telegraph* reported that 'all hope of the safety of Mungo Park has been entirely abandoned...' (*Morning Chronicle*; *Hampshire Telegraph*)

February 1st

1957: The aircraft carrier HMS *Warrior* was due to leave Portsmouth for the British nuclear weapons tests at Christmas Islands in the Pacific, but was unable to leave because of heavy gales. She left the following day to act as flagship of the naval squadron taking part in the tests, with 130 soldiers on board. Many of the men who took part in the tests were conscripts.

An able seaman on board *Warrior*, Nicholas Wilson, wrote in his diary:

> We were seated and all dressed correctly for anti-flash on the flight deck. Amusing but uncalled for jokes were cracked about failure. It was not until five seconds before the burst that I was concerned; then I became nervous. 'Fire!' At the same time I felt my back warming up and experienced the flash, though I had my hands over my face and dark goggles on. Five seconds after the flash we turned round and faced the flash, but it was still bright so I replaced them … there in the sky was a brightly glowing seething ball of fire … the whole sight was most beautiful and I was completely filled with emotions.

(www.janesoceania.com; *The Times*)

February 2nd

1661: Colonel Richard Norton wrote a letter to Secretary Nicholas pleading for some pay for the Portsmouth garrison. 'It is twenty weeks since they received any, they are most undone by trusting, and a little pay would give them new life.'

Colonel Norton, described by a Royalist newspaper as 'the great incendiary of Hampshire' had been a staunch Parliamentarian and a friend of Oliver Cromwell, who apparently used to call him 'Idle Dick Norton'. Internal wrangling and growing disillusionment led to him 'dwindling ultimately into Royalism' and in 1660 he represented Portsmouth in the Parliament that invited Charles II to return to rule. Upon restoration, Norton was appointed 'Captain of the Town, Isle and Castle of Portsmouth', having served as Governor twice before.

Colonel Norton had succeeded to the Southwick estates on the death of his father, which was then passed to his son, also Richard. When Richard junior died he left a will leaving his estates in trust for 'the poor, hungry, thirsty and naked to the end of the world'. This was ignored, and the lands ultimately ended up in the possession of the Thistlethwayte family. (*The Puritan Gentry Besieged* 1650-1700 by J. Cliffe, 1993; *History of Portsmouth* by W. Gates, 1900)

February 3rd

1900: George Holdron's linen drapery shop in Commercial Road was one of the best appointed businesses in town, situated at the junction with Arundel Street. Perhaps it was competition from the Landport Drapery Bazaar, on the opposite corner, that prompted him to diversify. Holdron had acquired a new product, a lotion that was guaranteed to promote hair growth. Could this make his fortune? He decided to give it his best shot.

On this day in 1900, Holdron appeared before magistrates, summoned by police 'for that he, by means of the public exhibition of two females with long hair hanging down their backs and as an advertisement, seated in the window of his shop, did unlawfully cause such a number of persons to collect together on the footway as to obstruct free and uninterrupted passage'.

Holdron's solicitor pointed out to the Bench that similar advertisements had been used in London's Regent Street and other places and that police 'in none of these towns had thought it proper for them to interfere'. After some deliberation and concern that they should not interfere with trade, the Bench ruled that an offence had been committed, but imposed a nominal fine of 1s and 13s 6d costs, presumably easily covered by Holdron's profits for the day. (*Hampshire Telegraph*)

February 4th

1899: When the Portsmouth-born actress, Ada Ward, gave up acting in 1897 it made international headlines. The *L.A. Times* reported, 'A pretty actress renounces the stage forever. She gave her wardrobe and jewels away and has donned the uniform of General Booth and his band of valiant warriors.'

Since the 1870s, Ward had had a very successful career on the stage in the UK, Australia and the States. At the end of a local performance at the Prince's Theatre, she gathered the company together, distributed her theatrical belongings and announced her decision to join the Salvation Army. The next day she addressed an audience at the Salvation Army Barracks in Lake Road and it was reported that 'many were moved to tears'. However, it was reported that the former actress had given two talks in Portsmouth in which she attacked the morality of the theatre. She had, perhaps unwisely, invited members of the theatrical profession to attend, and so was heckled when, for example, she announced that, 'No mother who wished to keep her young daughter pure should allow her to take up the stage as a profession.' (*Hampshire Telegraph*)

February 5th

1881: It was reported that tensions and dissatisfaction were afflicting the Royal Marine Artillery Barracks at Eastney. Non-commissioned officers and gunners were up-in-arms after an old standing order had been revived that prohibited 'familiar association'. For many years it had been the custom for married men who did not have quarters in barracks to rent small houses in the neighbourhood, and in many instances it was reported that corporals and sergeants had shared houses with 'men occupying the humble position of gunner'. This was seen as a very beneficial arrangement for everybody 'with no evil results following'.

The issue of the mixing of ranks came to the fore again in 1899 when two sergeants of the Royal Artillery went into the saloon bar of the Parade Hotel in Southsea. The landlord refused to serve them in that particular bar, but they declined to leave, saying they were unable to use the public bar because privates were served there. The incident escalated, the police were called and the Lieutenant-Governor General, Sir Baker Russell, placed all 120 of Brickwood's pubs out of bounds to men of the garrison in protest. Very soon afterwards the landlord was sacked. (*Hampshire Telegraph*)

February 6th

1862: HMS *Britannia* ended its service as an officers' training ship at Portsmouth because of Admiralty concerns about 'the temptations to which boys were exposed when they went ashore'. These temptations were illustrated by the fact that, in the previous year, there were twenty-four reported cases of venereal disease amongst the sailors who trained the boys. Another concern was 'the emanations from the mud and sewer drains' in the harbour. ('Britannia at Portsmouth and Portland' by H. Dickinson, *The Mariner's Mirror, 1998*)

1963: Photographer and former chairman of Portsmouth FC, Stephen Cribb, was buried following a service at St Peter's Church, Somers Road. Cribb started his photographic career in 1893 and became the Club's official photographer, but is best known for his naval photographs which were reproduced in publications worldwide. (*Evening News, Portsmouth*)

2008: In a speech at the School of Science and Art, General Drayson said that he had 'heard from a friend that, thirty years ago, Portsmouth was stupid and Southsea frivolous. That might have been true then, for they had no Free Library, no Literary and Scientific Society and no School of Science and Art, but it could not be said of Portsmouth now.' (*A Portsmouth Canvas: the Art of the City and the Sea* by N. Surry, 2008)

February 7th

1852: Martha Loane was born in Plymouth to a naval father but, in the 1860s, she moved to Southsea. At the age of twenty-three, Loane decided to take up nursing, a profession that had gained respectability because of Florence Nightingale. By 1897 she had risen to the position of Superintendent of Queen's Nurses for the Borough of Portsmouth, having become a highly respected figure, renowned for her efficiency and concern for the poor. Ill health forced her early retirement but did not affect her well-established career as a writer on nursing and social topics.

Encouraged by Florence Nightingale, she made contributions to journals and the national press, and wrote six nursing handbooks. Of greatest significance were her six popular social commentaries which confirmed her reputation as a leading authority on the condition of the working-class poor in Britain. These appear to have been co-authored by her younger half-sister, Alice. (*Oxford Dictionary of National Biography*)

1812: Elizabeth Dickens, aged twenty-two, carefully did her hair by the dim light of candles, dressed herself in a silk gown and prepared herself for a ball at the Beneficial Society's Hall in Rope Walk. Early on the following morning, she gave birth to Charles Dickens at home at No. 387 Commercial Road. (*History of Portsmouth* by W. Gates, 1900)

February 8th

1964: A demonstration of nearly 20,000 people took place in the Guildhall Square in protest at council house rent increases. (City of Portsmouth Records of the Corporation, ed. Gates, Singleton-Gates, Barnett, Blanchard, Windle, Riley)

———◆———

1890: Daniel Ferbridge, aged twenty-four, lived in Stone Street and worked for Mr Page's bakery in Hambrook Street. After a hard day of working the ovens, he left the bakery to carry out his delivery round. Two hours later, Charles Hayward, who worked for Yearworth's bakery of Kingston Road, spotted him sitting in his cart in Melbourne Street. He knew Ferbridge well as they both belonged to the same club. As Hayward delivered some bread to Mrs Saunders in Melbourne Street, he said, 'It seems as if that chap has gone to sleep.' She replied that he had been there since six o'clock. By now it was dark and Hayward went up to Ferbridge's cart and shouted, 'Come on Dan, wake up! You won't get home tonight if you stay here!' He tried shaking and pulling him up, but without success. He fetched his cart lamp and realised that he was dead.

Leaving his own cart with Mrs Saunders, Hayward drove Ferbridge's body to Landport Police Station. The local newspaper headline, published on this day, read 'Dead Man Driving', suggesting that press sensationalism is not a modern phenomenon. (*Hampshire Telegraph*)

February 9th

1732: Dr William Smith lay in bed with a quill pen in his hand. As a doctor, he probably knew he was dying. Forty years earlier, he had been appointed physician to the town and garrison of Portsmouth and became involved in local politics. He was elected a burgess and served two terms as Mayor in 1713 and 1714. He bought himself one of the most prestigious houses in the town, No. 11 High Street (Buckingham House), and a coat of arms.

While the doctor was an Alderman of the Borough, the Grand Jury at the Portsmouth Quarter Sessions expressed strong regret at the town's lack of a grammar school. Without any suitable local schools, the gentry were sending their sons away to board at huge expense and 'to the prejudice of the Town in general'. Perhaps it was his memory of this that prompted Dr Smith to add a bequest to his will, two days before his death, to 'constitute and support a Grammar School'. It took over twenty years for his dying wish to be put into effect, the first Portsmouth Grammar School being opened in Penny Street in 1753. (*Early Days: PGS c. 1750-1870: The Penny Street School* by C. Smith, 2004)

February 10th

1817: A great reform meeting was held on Portsdown Hill, at which a petition to Parliament was adopted, pleading for universal suffrage (which meant men over twenty-one at that time) and annual elections. Twenty thousand people came from miles around to protest despite magistrates having posted warnings on toll gates and distributing handbills threatening all who valued their safety to keep away. Employers also warned their employees not to attend if they knew what was good for them. The Hampshire Yeomanry Cavalry was called out in force and ball cartridges issued. In town the garrison guns were loaded and the town placed under virtual siege.

In the event, it was reported that, 'no animosity, no riot disturbed the proceedings of the day' and the petition was presented to Parliament. If there had not been threats it was estimated that 100,000 people would have attended.

The town, and country, had to wait some fifteen years before the electoral franchise was extended, due to strong opposition from the Tories. The Reform Act of 1832 extended the vote to the middle classes, increasing the electorate to one in seven males. (*The Morning Post*; *History of Portsmouth* by W. Gates, 1900)

February 11th

1756: Pioneering oculist and surgeon James Ware was born at Portsmouth. He was educated at Portsmouth Grammar School and, during his medical apprenticeship, practised at Haslar Naval Hospital. Ware was noted for raising ophthalmic surgery from its reputation of quackery to serious medical science with effective surgical methods. He wrote extensively on ophthalmology and was a pioneer in techniques for the removal of cataracts. (*British Journal of Ophthalmology*)

———•◆•———

1779: The verdict in the court martial of Admiral Keppel was made known. The charge of cowardice was a result of an incident during a battle with the French in July 1778, when Keppel's bad management, and a failure to obey orders by Sir Hugh Palliser, led to the French escaping.

As a result, Keppel, a Whig, found himself charged with cowardice and Palliser, a Tory MP, 'displayed the greatest animus' towards him. Keppel was acquitted, the accusation described as 'malicious'. Dreading the local reaction, Palliser fled from Portsmouth in a post chaise at five o'clock in the morning. A crowd arrived at his house in St Thomas's Street and pelted it with mud and 'filth', breaking the windows. Celebrations at Keppel's acquittal resulted in several pubs immortalising his name on their signs. (*History of Portsmouth* by W. Gates, 1900)

February 12th

1848: George Turner was born at No. 12, Chapel Row, Portsea. Over sixty years later, and on a different continent, he was shaving when he noticed some marks on his hand. As a doctor who had worked for three years in his spare time at the Pretoria Leper Colony, he knew immediately what it was.

Turner had qualified at Guy's Hospital and, in 1873, was appointed first Medical Officer of Health for Portsmouth. He also held other positions at the Royal and Fever Hospitals, as well as campaigning for a continuous water supply, proper drainage and an Infectious Diseases Hospital. After seven years he was appointed Medical Officer for Herts and Essex and, in 1895, moved to South Africa where he helped develop and carry out a programme of inoculation for the prevention of cattle disease. In the first Boer War he was called on to supervise health care in military hospitals and in concentration camps. Despite his best efforts, 28,000 Boer women and children and at least 20,000 black people died in these camps.

Upon his retirement he continued his research into leprosy and ,when he was diagnosed as having the disease, was knighted. He died two years later in 1915. (*Hampshire Telegraph*)

February 13th

1946: It was reported that Portsmouth City Council approved a revolutionary post-war plan to reduce the population density of the city by re-housing 10,000 people at Paulsgrove, 35,000 at Leigh Park and 15-20,000 at Waterlooville and Purbrook. The implementation of a green belt around the city and a target of six acres of open space for 1,000 of the population was also approved. (*The Times*)

———— • ◆ • ————

1804: George Gregory, the last of the crew of *Centurion*, which circumnavigated the world with Lord Anson, died at Kingston at the age of 109. (*History of Portsmouth* by W. Gates, 1900)

———— • ◆ • ————

1948: An eleven-year-old boy who claimed to be British left St James's Hospital to return to Berlin. Jurgen Kuhl had arrived at Newhaven a year earlier claiming that his name was Richard Lawrence and that he had been taken to Europe by American troops. He kept up the pretence until December, when he admitted to a doctor that he was German. He was reported to be happy to be returning home, and went loaded with clothes, sweets and souvenirs. He went home cured of his habit of smoking sixty cigarettes a day. (*Yesterday*)

February 14th

1820: On this Valentine's Day, nineteen-year-old Frederic Madden recorded in his diary that he 'rose at eight and impatiently waited the postman's arrival with the letters. In doing so it was quite amusing to observe the confusion and bustle prevailing at the Post Office. A dense crowd was formed round it.'

Madden went on to be the Keeper of the Department of Manuscripts at the British Museum and the leading palaeographer of his day. (*Sir Frederic Madden and Portsmouth* by J. Webb, 1987)

———◆———

1720: The following decree was made in Portsmouth:

> Whereas riots, quarrels, and other mischiefs are often occasioned and do arise at and by the barbarous usuage of throwing at cocks, the Rt worshipfull the Mayor and His Majesties Justices of the Peace of the said Burrough Do therefore prohibit all persons wtsoever from assembling together ... for that purpose ... (anyone) found any way acting or assisting in throwing at Cocks shall be punished for such offence as severely as by law they may.

Cock throwing was a blood sport involving securing a rooster to a post and throwing special weighted sticks at it until it died. Pembroke Street was formerly known as Fighting Cock Lane, possibly named after the more popular activity. (Extracts from 'Records in the possession of the Municipal Corporation of the Borough of Portsmouth' by Robert East, 1891)

February 15th

1710: An investigation began in the House of Commons into the conduct of Alderman Thomas Ridge, the Queen's cooper at Portsmouth who also sat as the MP for Poole. The Ridge family were 'of a very respectable standing' in Portsmouth as landowners and brewers (on the site of the current Guildhall). The parliamentary investigation shed some light on the possible source of the wealth. Ridge had been contracted to supply 5,513 tons of beer, but had delivered only 3,313 tons. For the outstanding 2,200 tons he had paid compensation to the pursers at the rate of 30s a ton, whilst receiving 56s a ton from the Queen. Ridge had defrauded the Crown, in this instance, of £19,000. Unashamed, he said that it was a common practice, but was expelled from the House of Commons.

Other Portsmouth brewers were implicated in these frauds and fined. Being routinely corrupt was no hindrance to Ridge's political ambitions, however. He was re-elected as an alderman in 1711, and returned again to Parliament to represent Poole in 1722 (*see* January 16th). (*History of Portsmouth* by W. Gates, 1900)

February 16th

1971: With a growing problem of drug abuse in the city, a unit for former drug users was set up in Stubbington Avenue. (City of Portsmouth Records of the Corporation, ed. Gates, Singleton-Gates, Barnett, Blanchard, Windle, Riley)

———◆———

1693: William III reviewed the fleet at Spithead and dined at Portsmouth with Admiral George Rooke, whom he then knighted. In May 1692, Rooke had served at the Battle of Barfleur, and distinguished himself in a night attack on the French fleet at La Hogue, when he succeeded in burning twelve of their ships. In 1696 he was appointed Admiral of the Fleet. When William died in 1702, Rooke showed Queen Anne's husband, Prince George of Denmark, who she had just appointed Lord High Admiral, around Portsmouth Dockyard and the town. Prince George also visited Dutch troops stationed at Gilkicker and inspected soldiers in Newport and the Isle of Wight. Rooke records in his diary that Prince George 'rowed around the fleet' at Portsmouth.

Admiral Sir George Rooke is most famous for having captured Gibraltar and claimed it for Britain in 1704. (*The Journal of Sir George Rooke, Admiral of the Fleet, 1700-1702,* 1897)

February 17th

1899: The famous contralto, Clara Butt, starred in a Grand Evening Concert at a packed Town Hall. Tickets cost 7s 6d for the best seats and 2s for the worst. Sir Thomas Beecham once said of Butt that 'on a clear day you could have heard her across the English Channel', so perhaps no ticket was necessary. (*Hampshire Telegraph*)

———•◆•———

1787: The famous eighteenth-century actor, William Brereton, died in a lunatic asylum at Hoxton. It was while performing at Portsmouth in the summer of 1785 that his mental illness became apparent. Audiences were perplexed by his improvisation of 'ludicrous lines' and his abrupt departure off stage during a critical scene. His illness was said to have been prompted by his unrequited love for the actress Sarah Siddons, the best known tragedienne of the day, a situation not helped by excessive drinking. (*Oxford Dictionary of National Biography*)

February 18th

1840: John Wesley Judd was born in Bath Square, Portsmouth; he was to become one of the leading British geologists of his day. After working as a schoolmaster, Judd was involved in a serious railway accident which forced him to find an occupation out of doors. He joined the geological survey as a temporary field officer and mapped much of the Midlands.

At various times he served as President of the Geological Society, Dean of the Royal College of Science and Emeritus Professor of Geology at Imperial College. During his career, Judd published ninety-seven papers and books, including *Volcanoes: What They Are, and What They Teach* (1881) and *The Coming of Evolution: The Story of a Great Revolution in Science* (1910). He also co-authored works with, amongst others, Charles Darwin. (*Oxford Dictionary of National Biography*)

———•◆•———

1773: A murder that had been committed in Pesthouse Field (in the Charlotte Street area) a year earlier was explained. A prisoner who was confined in Portsmouth Jail on another charge confessed his involvement in the murder of Binsteed Goffry to a fellow prisoner, who informed on him. He was later executed at Winchester. (*History of Portsmouth* by W. Gates, 1900)

February 19th

1838: John Bonham-Carter died. Three days earlier *The Times* admitted that, 'The report of the death of Mr Bonham Carter, the member for Portsmouth, for which borough he has sat for twenty years, was premature. The hon. gentleman's illness is, however, of a very alarming nature.' The Portsmouth MP came from a family that had been closely connected with the history of the town since the seventeenth century, with various members having filled the office of Mayor on thirty-two occasions.

The son of Sir John Carter, he changed his name to Bonham-Carter to inherit his cousin's vast estates at Buriton. He was a Justice of the Peace and Deputy Lieutenant, High Sheriff of Hampshire in 1829 and MP for Portsmouth from 1816 to 1838. He died of an illness 'mainly induced by his exertions in the popular cause'. Florence Nightingale was a relative of the Bonham Carter family and Helena Bonham Carter, the actor (famous for her roles in the quirky films of her partner Tim Burton) is his great, great granddaughter. (*The Times*; *History of Portsmouth* by W. Gates, 1900)

February 20th

1973: Since 1966 there had been three proposals to fluoridate the water supply, all of which had been rejected. On this day the Health Committee recommended that the proposal be accepted and a concentration of fluoride of one part per million was agreed to improve the dental health of the borough. (City of Portsmouth Records of the Corporation, ed. Gates, Singleton-Gates, Barnett, Blanchard, Windle, Riley)

———•◆•———

1948: A complaint appeared in the *Evening News* with an issue that appeared to be on everybody's lips:

> Even high ranking and presumably well-educated residents of Portsmouth persist in pronouncing Cosham as Cosh'm. Yet they probably know as well as I that 'ham' is a suffix from the Anglo-Saxon meaning village or town (literally 'home'). Why not, therefore, Coss'm, with the h sounding lightly or not at all? The former pronunciation sounds decidedly uglier and is surely not popular among those who wear dentures.

Cosham, the name, is said to derive from the 'homestead or enclosure of a man called Cossa', so the writer was correct, though it is now even more unusual to hear the correct pronunciation. (*Oxford Dictionary of Place Names*; *Evening News, Portsmouth*)

February 21st

1882: Portsmouth High School opened its doors under the leadership of Headmistress Miss Ledger. Its premises at Marlborough House in Osborne Road were described as 'commodious and well situated', the classrooms were fitted with state-of-the-art desks and the walls adorned with 'Stanford's excellent maps'. The sanitary and ventilation arrangements were described as 'perfect'.

The school was set up to fill a need for the education of the daughters of businessmen. While the 'ladies' academies' in the town welcomed 'daughters of gentlemen', they demonstrated some snootiness about the daughters of fathers who were engaged in business or commerce. There was also an issue with the quality of the education offered by those elitist and increasingly detached establishments. The school opened with thirty-two pupils but soon expanded, moving to its present Kent Road site in 1885. Dovercourt, the junior school, was purchased in 1927. (*Portsmouth High School 1882-1957* by M. Howell)

1902: Arthur Darby Nock was born in Portsmouth. After attending and briefly teaching at Portsmouth Grammar School, he studied Classics at Cambridge and went on to become a professor of the history of religion and authored many books on the subject. (*The Times*)

February 22nd

1889: James Belsey, aged nineteen, of North Street, Portsea, had been courting Clara Figgins, a domestic servant, for three months. One evening they decided to go for a walk and headed off for Cosham. When they reached the Hilsea Lines, a black and tan collie came bounding out of the fields towards them. They walked on and the dog followed. When they reached Cosham, they went into a coffee house to have some refreshments. When they came out the dog was waiting; they continued walking but the dog suddenly seized Clara by her jacket. James attempted to separate them, but the dog leapt at him, biting him in the face. After being referred to five doctors, three chemists and hospital, James was eventually referred to the Infectious Diseases Hospital at Milton where he died an agonising death of rabies. At the inquest, held on this day, the police said that a dog of the type described had been found and shot in Fawcett Road.

Five weeks later, a thirteen-year-old errand boy, John Frampton, was also reported to have died of rabies after having been bitten in Somers Road by what was believed to be the same stray dog. (*Hampshire Telegraph*)

February 23rd

1846: Orientalist and MP, Sir George Staunton, inherited his father's baronetcy and land in Ireland, and bought Leigh Park in 1819. He added a 'gothick' library to the house, and hothouses for his rare flowers and exotic fruits. He travelled and wrote extensively on China. After losing his seat as an MP for South Hampshire, he was re-elected without opposition for Portsmouth three times between 1838 and 1852.

On this day, he wrote:

> My first eight years in Parliament was an affair of money ... My present advantages in respect to wealth, rank, and station, and, I trust, character, would probably have made my social position higher than it is, if I knew how to make the most of them, but, still, it is a very good one, and ought to satisfy my reasonable ambition.

Staunton's ambitions as an MP were modest. He spent a lot of his time travelling or in his library, 'I have seldom been called upon to speak in Parliament, since my election for Portsmouth, except in reference to China.' He also spoke to oppose extending the franchise and in favour of a 'Bill for the Suppression of Dog-carts'. A creek in Hong Kong was named Staunton Creek in his honour, but became a cesspool. (*Memoirs of Sir George Thomas Staunton, Bart*, 1856)

February 24th

1942: Paul Jones, lead vocalist and harmonica player of Manfred Mann (1962-66), was born in Portsmouth (as Paul Pond). He attended Portsmouth Grammar School and was a chorister at the cathedral. Jones wrote and played the harmonica on the theme tune, 5-4-3-2-1, for the television pop show *Ready Steady Go!*

He went solo and had several hits before taking up acting. He starred in the cult film *Privilege* and went on to appear in many television series before embarking on a successful stage career. By the 1990s, Jones was a familiar face on children's television in the series *Uncle Jack*, and a familiar voice on radio, presenting a weekly show on Radio 2. He is also a member of The Blues Band and The Manfreds. (*Debrett's People of Today, 2010*)

———◆———

1762: Friedriche von Kielmanslegge recorded a visit to Portsmouth in his diary:

Of the town of Portsmouth it may be said, without doing it any injustice, that it is one of the worst towns in England; the houses are bad, the streets narrow, and the inns especially are dirty and bad. This is the reason why hardly any strangers who have friends here, lodge in the town ... there is no beauty or society in the place to attract anyone.

(*Diary of a Journal to England* by F. Kielmanslegge, 1902)

February 25th

1762: Susanna Rowson, novelist and actress, was baptised at St Thomas's parish church. The only child of Lieutenant William Haswell RN and his wife, Susanna – who died soon after her daughter's birth.

Susanna lived in Portsmouth, possibly in Penny Street, before moving to Massachusetts where her father collected customs revenue for the Royal Navy. During the American War of Independence, the family were POWs. After a prisoner exchange, they returned to England in 1778. In 1786 Susanna Haswell published her first novel, *Victoria*. In the same year she married William Rowson, an occasional actor with connections to the Covent Garden Theatre. She and her husband probably worked provincial circuits before moving to the United States. In 1791, after several unsuccessful novels, *Charlotte: a Tale of Truth* became popular in America; the title was later changed to *Charlotte Temple*, by which it is best known today. The novel, whose frail protagonist is seduced and abandoned by a British soldier, went through more than 200 editions and was enjoyed by an estimated half a million people by the mid-nineteenth century. Today, her work is praised as pioneering for introducing new types of fictional women, characterised as 'independent-minded adventurers'. (*Portsmouth Novelists* by D. Francis, 2006; *Oxford Dictionary of National Biography*)

February 26th

1916: The first plea of conscientious objection was reported before an 'impartial' local tribunal set up to hear appeals from men who objected to fighting in the First World War on religious, political, humanitarian or self-preservation grounds. During the first six months of tribunal sessions, the *Evening News* reported on twenty-one appeals from men of diverse beliefs, occupations and classes.

Twelve maintained they were 'absolutist', asserting that they would carry out no work associated with the military, including the Medical and Non-Combatant Corps. Members of the tribunal asked questions like, 'What would you do if a German hit you on the nose?', and 'If a child was struggling in the sea as a result of a German shell being fired at South Parade Pier, would you make no effort to save it?' The tribunal granted no 'absolute exemptions' in the first six months, and the Chairman, Mr Corke, was knighted for his services to recruitment. (*Evening News, Portsmouth*)

———— ◆ ————

1915: The Army Service Corps, based in the High Street, placed an advertisement in the classified ads section of a local newspaper inviting tenders for 'Military Funerals and Window Cleaning' for the following year. (*Hampshire Telegraph*)

February 27th

1868: Like many holidaymakers, the Revd Benjamin Speke was attracted to the south coast, though his arrival in Portsmouth on a January day in 1868 was out of season. A brother to the late explorer, John Hanning Speke, who is credited as having traced the source of the Nile, the clergyman was seemingly less adventurous. A keen reader, he braced the elements, taking his book to the seashore in between embarking on excursions to the Isle of Wight, Southampton and Netley Abbey. At the end of the month he set off for Plymouth to continue his coastal tour.

While at Portsmouth, newspaper articles appeared country-wide concerning the clergyman's whereabouts. He had set off to officiate at a friend's wedding in London but went missing. On the day he left Portsmouth, it was reported in the *Hampshire Telegraph* that Speke's hat had been found in St James's Park and that a reward of £500 was being offered.

Out this day, the *Daily News* reported the reverend's discovery. He had been arrested in Cornwall having been mistaken for another man wanted by police. Various theories were suggested for Speke's 'Reggie Perrin' moment. One was that he had felt the pressure of family expectations and had developed a 'morbid fear of marriage'. (*Hampshire Telegraph*; *Daily News*)

February 28th

1842: Queen Victoria visited Portsmouth for the first time since her accession. She was led through crowds to the Lion Gates, where the keys of the garrison were presented. On passing through the gates, the ships in harbour and shore batteries thundered out their Royal salute. The procession then made its way to the Dockyard where Prince Albert inspected the blockmills and watched an anchor being forged.

The following day, the royal party reviewed the fleet at Spithead. The Queen 'desired to taste the grog' and declared it 'very good'. It was reported that, 'with a tear in her eye', she said, 'I feel today that I am indeed Old Ocean's youthful Queen, and that I am indeed surrounded by those who will uphold that title in the battle and the breeze.' (*History of Portsmouth* by W. Gates, 1900)

———•◆•———

1922: Peter Taylor, film editor, was born in Portsmouth. He won an Academy Award for his work on *Bridge on the River Kwai*, and also worked with David Lean on *The Sound Barrier* and *Hobson's Choice*. Among his many other credits are Lindsay Anderson's *This Sporting Life* and Carol Reed's *The Third Man*. (*The Independent*)

February 29th

1804: The *Hampshire Telegraph* advertised the following:

Wants a situation as WET NURSE, a good wholesome Young Woman, with a full Breast of Milk, can be recommended by the Person who attended. Enquire of Mr Judd, Victualling Office, Portsmouth.

If the Man, who on Friday the 17th instant, accidentally run against the Lamplighter's ladder on Common Hard (through which a child was a little hurt) will call at No 20 Glamorgan Street, Portsea will greatly oblige a much injured person. EBENEZER WITHERS. The person is assured that no ill consequences will attend his calling.

A cargo of very fine Lisbon and China oranges just landed, to be sold on reasonable terms at Mr Samuel Redward's, No 101 Queen Street, Portsea.

(*Hampshire Telegraph*)

March 1st

1829: Jack Stacey was a twenty-one-year-old barber's apprentice, employed at Thomas Weeks' shop in Warblington Road. He visited customers in their homes to shave or cut their hair. One of his customers was a seventy-five-year-old retired bricklayer and plasterer, Samuel Langtry, who lived with his housekeeper, Charity Jolliffe in a small house in Prospect Row near the Blue Bell Tavern. On this day, Stacey killed them both with a plasterer's hammer, cut their throats from ear to ear and rifled through Langtry's bedroom, pocketing savings of over £600.

Handbills offering a reward for the discovery of the murderer were circulated around the town. The Governor of Portsmouth Jail, Edward Hunt, suspected Stacey because of his access to the house and some scratches on his hands he had noticed while being shaved by him. When Stacey was found to have gone to Portchester, flush with money and two prostitutes, the game was up. He was sentenced to death and executed at Winchester on 3 August 1829. (*Annals of Portsmouth* by W.H. Saunders, 1880)

———— ◆ ————

1819: Owing to scarcity of work in the borough, 500 inhabitants emigrated to America. (*History of Portsmouth* by W. Gates, 1900)

March 2nd

1908: Olivia Manning, the novelist, was born at No. 134 Laburnum Grove, North End, the elder child and only daughter of Lieutenant-Commander Oliver Manning RN, and his wife, Olivia. With a womanising father and nagging mother, childhood insecurity and unhappiness shadowed her personality and later work. Her happiest memories were of holidays on the Isle of Wight.

Manning spent some time at Lynton House School in Kingston Crescent, and later studied art at the technical college with the ambition of being a painter, but her parents could not afford the fees. She went to work in a local architect's office and began writing in her spare time.

Her 1953 novel, *A Different Face*, describes a thinly disguised Portsmouth where:

> ...respect was not for the naval families cheeseparing on low pay, and less for widows with their mouse-meal pensions, but for the business men who ran the city in their own interests and each year bought a bigger car, or a bigger house, and took it in turns to be Mayor...

Manning is best known for the two trilogies that were collectively known as *Fortunes of War*. Anthony Burgess described the series as 'the finest fictional record of the war produced by a British writer'. (*Portsmouth Novelists* by D. Francis, 2006; *Oxford Dictionary of National Biography*)

March 3rd

1970: 'There is a full awareness of the problems of unorganised vice that are associated with any naval port,' reported *The Times* on this day, 'though Portsmouth has its fair share of these.' The reporter got into his stride, 'It has something of a reputation for homosexuality. Drugs are an anxiety, though no more so than in any comparable community. The illegitimacy rate is high, and prostitution has assumed alarming proportions in the past.' There was some reassurance. 'Today, however, when a fleet is in port most of the prostitutes seem to come flocking in from other cities.' (*The Times*)

———•◆•———

1941: A letter written by the Commander-in-Chief of Portsmouth, Admiral Sir William James, makes mention of an air attack during 1941: 'By the greatest luck bombs that fell on the 3rd [March] near the Portsbridge did not explode, else our communications would have been cut.'

The importance of Portsbridge was not lost on the Royalists, 300 years earlier during the Civil War. They built 'a little fort or bulwark of earth' to defend the island but the Parliamentarians, with 500 foot soldiers and 250 horses, gave it short shrift and the Royalists retreated to within the town ramparts on 12 August 1642. (*Portsmouth Letters* by W. James, 1946; *The Civil War in Hampshire* by G. Godwin, 1973)

March 4th

1890: Arthur Fage, aerodynamicist, was born in Portsmouth. He attended Portsmouth Secondary School and became a shipwright apprentice in the Dockyard, but also continued his studies at the Municipal College. During 1914 he wrote, *The Aeroplane*, in which he managed to explain aeronautical engineering in an accessible way. The book was immediately popular, running into many editions. After the war, Fage continued his investigations into the theory and practical engineering of airscrews and published extensively, becoming a world authority on the subject. (*Oxford Dictionary of National Biography*)

———•◆•———

1972: Twenty-six people were travelling across the Solent on the hovercraft SR.N6 when, just before reaching Southsea, she overturned, killing four people. Doubts were raised in the House of Commons about the safety of this new form of transport. (*The Times*)

March 5th

1864: A letter appeared in the *Hampshire Telegraph* drawing attention to 'the monstrous evil which has been permitted to exist for a considerable time past without any effectual attempt being made to check it'. The writer referred to 'the nightly assembly on the main roads crossing Southsea Common of prostitutes of the most vile and abandoned character' who 'assail every passenger, even in the hearing of the guardian policeman, with their filthy invitations, couched in language the most revolting and obscene'.

The power of the pen appears to have had some effect; the following week the newspaper reported that 'we understand that the authorities have given instructions to the police to remove these creatures from all places where they are a nuisance to passengers, and more particularly from Southsea Common'. In the country's major naval ports and garrison towns, a blind eye was normally turned to such activities. What appears to have provoked concern and prompt action in this case was that it was happening in Southsea, which had aspirations of being a respectable and high-class seaside resort, rather than the slummy backstreets of Portsea. (*Hampshire Telegraph*)

March 6th

1841: A civil rights protest meeting was reported to have taken place in Portsea. The meeting had been held at the Synagogue Chambers in White's Row (now Curzon Howe Road), at which petitions to the Houses of Commons and Lords were adopted, calling for the 'removal of civil disabilities which, as citizens and British-born subjects they [Jews] labour under'. (*Hampshire Telegraph*)

———•◆•———

1898: Annie Gammans was born at No. 61 Marmion Road, Southsea, Hampshire, the daughter of Frank, a master grocer, and his wife, Annie. She was educated at Portsmouth High School. On 21 November 1917 she married Leonard Gammans, who had attended Portsmouth Grammar School. In 1941 he was elected Conservative MP for Hornsey, Middlesex, and later served as assistant postmaster-general from 1951 until 1955, when he was created a baronet. Annie assumed most of his constituency duties and she was chosen to stand in the by-election necessitated by Leonard's death in 1957. She served the constituency in a hands-on role until 1966, but retired because she was less comfortable with the political aspect of being an MP. Lady Gammans died in 1989. (*Oxford Dictionary of National Biography*)

March 7th

1930: Television writer Brian Hayles was born in Portsmouth. He took up writing while working as a schoolteacher in Birmingham, and is best known for contributing to the original *Doctor Who* series in the 1960s and '70s. He also wrote for the groundbreaking police series *Z-Cars*, as well as *Barlow at Large*, *Public Eye*, *Doomwatch* and *The Regiment*.

Hayles also contributed occasional television plays and wrote for the radio series *The Archers*. His credits include the screenplays for three feature films, *Arabian Adventure* and *Nothing but the Night* (both starring Christopher Lee and Peter Cushing) and *Warlords of Atlantis*.

Hayles penned a novel based on *The Archers*, as well as novelisations of his Doctor Who stories *The Curse of Peladon* and *The Ice Warriors*, an adaptation of his scripts for the BBC drama *The Moon Stallion* and two plays for children, *The Curse of the Labyrinth* and *Hour of the Werewolf*. Hayles died in 1978 and his original novel *Goldhawk* was published posthumously. (www.imdb.com)

———— ◆ ————

1958: In supporting a bill in the Commons to increase the penalty for using abusive language, Portsmouth MP Geoffrey Stevens insisted that the measure was not solely aimed at Teddy Boys. (*The Times*)

March 8th

1919: Three hundred soldiers gathered on the steps of Portsmouth Town Hall and asked to see the Mayor. Throughout the country, many men who had fought in the First World War were still awaiting demobilisation several months after the Armistice. This situation led to unrest, confrontation and mutiny. Two months earlier, 5,000 troops had mutinied in Southampton after being informed that they were being demobilised, only to be ordered to board troop ships for France.

Eight soldiers were invited to talk to the Mayor, Councillor John Timpson. They argued that they were former prisoners-of-war and should receive preferential treatment as they had already been incarcerated for a long period. They also thought it unfair that some of them were to be drafted to look after German prisoners, having suffered at their hands. Mayor Timpson praised the men's 'splendid service' and said he would pass on their complaints if they marched back to barracks and 'behaved as soldiers were expected to behave'. (*Yesterday*)

1784: Mary Bagley was burnt at Portsmouth for the murder of her husband. (*Portsmouth Parish Church* by H.Lilley & A. Everitt,1921)

March 9th

1802: A boy made a discovery in the trunk of an old tree at Wish Farm on Southsea Common. He pulled out an old stocking and found, tied up inside, a bundle of damp banknotes, wet from recent rain. As the boy made his way along the road from Southsea to Portsmouth, happily clutching the money in his fist, a man approached him and asked to see what he was holding. The boy half-recognised the man, who instantly snatched most of the notes and ran off.

The boy went to local magistrate, Sir John Carter, and identified the thief as a man he had seen at an address in St Thomas's Street. Constables caught Hurlock, a shoemaker, drying the notes over a fire, and he was arrested and jailed. The banknotes, it emerged, were forgeries.

Five years earlier, Carter was commended for his conduct during the Spithead mutiny. The sailors, whose three comrades had been killed, wished to carry their bodies in procession through Portsmouth. As the Governor of the local garrison refused to allow this, further fighting looked certain. Carter allowed the men to march through the town and also negotiated the release of an Admiral who the mutineers were holding. (*Lancaster Gazetteer*)

March 10th

1996: A national newspaper revealed that Portsmouth City Council had 'called on the town's women to leave their boyfriends behind and go to a hospitality disco to welcome 500 French sailors in port for the weekend'. The Council 'distributed hundreds of leaflets, mostly at Portsmouth University, urging 'girls, girls, girls' to extend a traditional British welcome to the matelots'. It was reported that 'menfolk did not approve, not because they were concerned about Gallic charm, but because they were concerned about the reputation of the city's women'. (*The Observer*)

1777: James Hill, alias Hind, alias Aitkins, alias John or Jack the Painter, was paraded around the Dockyard in an open cart and then drawn by pulleys to the top of a gibbet, 65ft above the Dockyard Gates. Hill was said to have visited America at an early age where he 'imbibed principles opposed to the interests of his own country'.

On 7 December 1776, a fire broke out in the rope-house of the Dockyard, totally destroying it and Hill was arrested for arson. On the day of his execution, Hill was reported to have looked at the ruins of the rope-house and said, 'I acknowledge my crime and am sorry for it.' (*History of Portsmouth* by W. Gates, 1900)

March 11th

1948: Twin Screw Motor Vessel (TSMV) *Southsea* was launched to help replace wartime losses from the old Solent paddle fleet. Along with her sister ship MV *Brading*, she was launched at Denny's Yard in Dumbarton and offered accommodation for 1,331 passengers. At this time, Portsmouth was the destination for tens of thousands of holidaymakers, who arrived in the city by rail and coach, en route to the Isle of Wight.

TSMV *Southsea* was 182ft long and had a top speed of 14.5 knots. She was the first Solent ferry to be fitted with radar, enabling a more reliable service in the foggiest conditions.

Initially, passengers were divided into first and third class, but, in the spirit of the egalitarian age, they were combined in 1951. In 1967, the upper bridge deck was extended, providing a popular platform for magnificent sea views, enabling thousands of holidaymakers to appreciate that the journey could be as enjoyable as the destination. (*Solent Passages and their Steamers* by K. Davies, 1982; *Yesterday*)

March 12th

1962: The ferry service to Hayling Island was taken over by Portsmouth Corporation. The following month, a proposal by a private company to construct a chair-lift across the entrance of Langstone Harbour to connect the city to Hayling was dropped. (City of Portsmouth Records of the Corporation, ed. Gates, Singleton-Gates, Barnett, Blanchard, Windle, Riley)

———•◆•———

1926: It was reported that Southsea was 'the third sunniest place in the Great Britain'. Statistics showed that Southsea had 1,923.3 hours of bright sunshine during 1925, no doubt pleasing the newly-formed Southsea Beach Committee. Following the purchase of Southsea Common from the War Office in 1922, the Committee set about providing tearooms, a bandstand and the Rock Gardens, and the record sunshine was an added attraction for potential holidaymakers. The 1929 Southsea holiday guide describes the Common as 'the greatest pleasure garden on the south coast'.

At this time, the vicar of St Mark's Church in North End, Revd Eric Southam, also sang the praises of Portsmouth at a Rotary meeting, 'Accessible to beautiful countryside, the most concentrated amusements outside of London, fine and cheap shops, splendidly run public services and the people and public servants are so polite.' 'The town,' he declared, 'is one of a thousand romantic delights.' (*Portsmouth Times*)

March 13th

1774: Urgent orders were received at Portsmouth for the immediate despatch of four ships of the Royal Navy to Boston where, three months earlier, revolting Americans had thrown three shiploads of tea into Boston Harbour. (*History of Portsmouth* by W. Gates, 1900)

———— • ◆ • ————

1853: Roger Charles Tichborne, heir to the Tichborne Baronetcy, sailed from Portsmouth for Chile, leaving England for the last time. From Chile he visited Brazil but he was lost at sea the following year while sailing to New York.

Arthur Orton, who became known as the Tichborne Claimant, attempted to impersonate him to get his hands on the family fortune. After a long trial he was convicted and imprisoned. He served the latter part of his sentence at Portsmouth Convict Prison, where, because of his obesity and celebrity, he appears to have received preferential treatment. He was allocated a quarter more food than other convicts and was employed in the hospital, the tailor's shop, and, at his own request, labouring in the stacking ground of Portsmouth Dockyard where he resented being gazed at by workers. He settled in the carpenter's shop where he showed some skill. His conduct was deemed 'exemplary' prior to his release, after serving ten years, in 1884. (*The Tichborne Claimant* by D. Woodruff, 1957)

March 14th

1757: Admiral John Byng had a reputation as a loyal and reliable naval officer, but he became famous on this day for another reason:

> Admiral John Byng [*sic*] spent most of the time between eleven and twelve o'clock standing in the stern-walk of the Monarque watching the crowd with a telescope. He said to one of his friends, 'I fear many of them will be disappointed – they may hear where they are, but they can't all see!'... on the stroke of eight bells, noon, he was informed that all was ready. To that he only replied by saying he was glad that the tide would serve for his body to be taken ashore in the afternoon, adding that he was also glad to understand that there was no disposition on the part of the Portsmouth people to insult it ... The Admiral continued on his knees for rather more than a minute, amid an awful silence all round. He was quite composed, and kept his head bent, apparently in earnest prayer. Then he gave the signal to 'fire', by dropping a second handkerchief which he had held in his hand. The fatal volley went off on the instant. Five bullets struck Byng. The sixth passed over his head. He fell forward stone-dead.

Byng appears to have been executed to cover up the Admiralty's incompetence in providing him with an inadequate fleet to relieve Minorca. (City of Portsmouth Records of the Corporation, ed. Gates, Singleton-Gates, Barnett, Blanchard, Windle, Riley)

March 15th

1911: Pro and anti-vivisectionists 'had a rare field day' at a packed Portland Hall in Southsea when speakers expressed their opinions on scientific experimentation on animals. In the afternoon, a Mr Paget gave a lantern lecture with the title 'Research for the Defence of Society', though it soon became clear that many in the audience were not in agreement with him. Mr Paget contended that there was no cruelty involved, and listed scientific and medical advances made as a result of experimentation. This was met by opposing views from the floor, but the presence of a policeman helped maintain order. In the evening, a Mr Reed gave harrowing accounts of the maltreatment of animals. He argued that:

> Disease arose from sin, dirt and ignorance, and if people had regard to the food they ate, drank pure water and less beer, and lived in healthy homes, they would be free from illness. Man had no moral right to inflict cruelty upon the lower creation for his own benefit. Let vivisectionists experiment upon themselves, especially with their filthy inoculations.

(*Portsmouth Times*)

———◆·———

1971: Three thousand Council tenants marched to the Guildhall in protest at a 15 per cent rent increase. (City of Portsmouth Records of the Corporation, ed. Gates, Singleton-Gates, Barnett, Blanchard, Windle, Riley)

March 16th

1878: Mayor William Pink was criticised for describing working people as having 'Communistic tendencies'. An outraged correspondent in the *Hampshire Telegraph* argued that Portsmouth workers were 'industrious, sober and frugal'. 'The state of their homes, their social habits, the care they bestow upon the education of their children and the extent to which they strive to become owners of their own habitations entitle them to better treatment...The working men of Portsmouth are the last men of their class in the country to be branded as Communists.' (*Hampshire Telegraph*)

———— •◆• ————

1896: A telephone line enabling communication with London was opened for public use for the first time. The charge was ninepence (4p) for three minutes. Two days earlier, an Ericson Table Instrument had been installed in the Mayor's banqueting room in the Town Hall and the town's top businessmen and civic dignitaries gathered for the ceremonial opening of the line, prior to it going public. After preliminary speeches, during which the commercial applications of the new device were emphasised, the Mayor solemnly took one of the receivers and 'exchanged compliments and congratulations' with the Lord Mayor of London. Satisfied that the thing worked, the group retired to the Mayor's parlour to toast its success. (*Hampshire Telegraph*)

March 17th

1900: As the twenty-five-strong company of the 1st Hampshire Engineers, dressed in khaki, marched out of the Drill Hall into Commercial Road, the huge crowd cheered. A detachment of cyclists headed the procession as it proceeded down Edinburgh Road and into Queen Street. As they turned the corner by the Dockyard they were met by a crowd of 10,000 waiting at the Hard where 'the footpaths and roadway were black with cheering humanity'. Mounted policemen struggled to control the crowd. The men eventually reached the railway station and took their seats in a third class carriage.

A band struck up *Old Lang Syne* as the train moved away. With brown helmets waving from the windows they slowly disappeared round the curve of the track and the crowd slowly dispersed. The men were going to Chatham for training and then, embarking from Southampton for South Africa and the Boer War. (*Hampshire Telegraph*)

———◆———

1974: Alex 'Hurricane' Higgins celebrated St Patrick's Day by visiting the Playboy Casino Club where he charmed an employee who was dressed as a rabbit. The Southsea club relieved punters of their money between 1973 and 1982 and employed Joe Jackson as a pianist at one time. (*From the Eye of the Hurricane: My Story* by A. Higgins, 2007)

March 18th

1750: Portsmouth was subjected to the shock of an earthquake which hit in the early evening, accompanied by 'a hollow rustling sound'. Several houses were reported to have been damaged but there were no casualties. (*History of Portsmouth* by W. Gates, 1900)

———◆———

1868: Thomas Marlowe, journalist, was born at No. 39 St James's Street. In 1899, Marlowe was appointed news editor of the new *Daily Mail*. He very soon established himself as a significant figure in Fleet Street and was given most credit for the *Daily Mail*'s burgeoning circulation. After Lord Rothermere took over as proprietor, Marlowe was closely involved in two historic events. In 1924 he published the infamous Zinoviev letter four days before the General Election, which falsely associated the Labour Party with armed communist insurrection. Though later exposed as a forgery, the Labour Government was undermined and lost the election.

In 1926, his provocative actions led to negotiations between the Cabinet and trade unionists to be called off, precipitating the General Strike. Marlowe resigned soon afterwards, and later wrote that 'Journalism has been killed by newspaper owners'. Marlowe died in 1935, at a time when the *Daily Mail* was supporting Oswald Mosley's fascists and publishing articles supportive of Adolf Hitler. (*Oxford Dictionary of National Biography*)

March 19th

1904: News of Britain's first submarine disaster was announced. The *A1* submarine had failed to return from naval manoeuvres the previous day and divers were sent down where a circle of bubbles revealed she had gone down, near the Nab Lightship. It is believed that the 100ft-long submarine had been positioning itself to fire a dummy torpedo at the cruiser HMS *Juno*, with its conning tower a few feet from the surface, when the *Berwick Castle*, sailing from Southampton to Hamburg, ran her down. The ship reported a dull bang, but it was assumed that a practice torpedo had been struck and nothing was thought of it. Seven of the eleven-man crew had been from the Portsmouth area.

A month later, the *A1* was raised by a salvage company and brought into dry dock, and the bodies were recovered and buried. The inquest revealed that the conning tower had been damaged, the periscope bent and a ventilator damaged. It was believed that the force of the collision had thrown the men against the sides of the vessel, rendering them unconscious before they drowned. A message of sympathy, referring to 'the natural brotherhood of sailors', was received from the German Admiral von Tirpitz. (*Yesterday*)

March 20th

1977: At the Locarno in Arundel Street, the glam rock band T. Rex performed their final gig. Formed in 1967 as a folk rock group, they achieved success in the early 1970s as a glam band with hits such as *Get it On*, *Ride a White Swan*, *Jeepster*, *Telegram Sam* and *Metal Guru*. However, with the advent of punk, the band's success waned and in 1977 they went on tour supported by The Damned, the final date being at the Locarno.

Six months later, lead singer Marc Bolan, whose real name was Mark Feld, was killed in a car crash at the age of twenty-nine. Bolan had often said that he expected to die young. On the death of Elvis, a month earlier, he had said 'at least it meant that he won't end up like Bing Crosby'.

Marc's elder brother, Harry Feld, who worked in Portsmouth as a bus inspector, didn't see his brother in concert until the band's final Locarno gig. Interviewed for the *Daily Telegraph* in 2002, Harry said that Mark was actually 'very quiet, very introverted'. Becoming Marc Bolan was, 'like Clark Kent going into the telephone box and putting on his swimming trunks and cape'. (*The Daily Telegraph*; The *Observer Music Monthly*)

March 21st

1896: The *Hampshire Telegraph* reported that a local inventor, W.R. Barridge of Fratton Road, had applied for two patents, one for a telescopic vapour flue and the other a double-flanged pan. (*Hampshire Telegraph*)

———◆———

1950: Roger Hodgson, songwriter, vocalist and musician of Supertramp fame, was born in Portsmouth. The son of a lieutenant-commander in the Royal Navy, his first guitar was a parting gift from his father at age twelve when his parents divorced. He was brought up in Oxford and boarded at Stowe School.

Hodgson co-founded the band in 1969, and was the writer of most of their hits which feature his distinctive high-pitched voice, including The Logical Song, Dreamer, Give a Little Bit and Breakfast in America. His lyrics often have a spiritual or philosophical theme. The band's first success was the album, *Crime of the Century*, released in 1974, followed by, *Crisis? What Crisis?* and *Even in the Quietest Moments*. In 1979, they released their most successful album, *Breakfast in America*, which sold over 20 million copies. Hodgson left the band in 1983 to spend more time with his family in California. (*The Sunday Times*)

March 22nd

1957: The shocking smoking habits of schoolboys hit the headlines when *The Lancet* published research suggesting that many fourteen year olds were regular smokers.

At Paulsgrove Modern School, Headmaster Mr Tribe admitted that there were 'a fair number' of secret smokers amongst his pupils, but that only a small proportion smoked regularly. Mr Tribe said that smokers were barred from out-of-school activities, like football, though the biggest deterrent was 'the fact that records of indiscipline are taken into account when recommending boys for jobs'.

In 1970, the Medical Officer of Health reported that despite the fall in the population of Portsmouth, the number of deaths from lung cancer in the city was the largest ever recorded, totalling 170. (*The Times*; City of Portsmouth Records of the Corporation, ed. Gates, Singleton-Gates, Barnett, Blanchard, Windle, Riley)

———◆———

1882: A runaway horse belonging to the Southsea Laundry Company careered down Highland Road one evening, having, it was said, been alarmed by some boys playing. Mrs Cleveland of St Andrew's Road, was being pushed in her bath chair when the horse collided with it, throwing Mrs Cleveland out. The inquest into her death was held in a local pub – the Elms Tavern in Elm Grove – as was the custom of the day. In 1902, the law was changed to prevent inquests on licensed premises. (*Hampshire Telegraph*)

March 23rd

1820: Two men were sent by a local magistrate to the Red Lion pub to investigate a report from a local woman who had become suspicious of a man who she had been sleeping with. The two men sent on the mission were the town jailer, Mr Hunt, and the turnkey. When they approached the man in the pub he immediately drew a loaded pistol from his waistcoat pocket. Mr Hunt sprang at him and managed to grab the pistol, causing the flint to fall out, but the man pulled another pistol and tried to shoot the turnkey. Luckily the gun misfired. Mr Hughes, the landlord, joined in and seized the suspect from behind while Mr Hunt hit him several times with his staff. He was handcuffed and taken to jail for questioning.

It emerged that the man, John Nesbitt, had confessed to the woman that he had committed murder. He was staying in Portsmouth whilst en route to France. Among Nesbitt's possessions were a quantity of burnt money, silver cutlery and a watch engraved with the initials 'T.P.' Several weeks earlier, Thomas Parker and his housekeeper, Sarah Brown, had been murdered in Woolwich and his house set alight to conceal the crime. Nesbitt was tried, found guilty and publicly executed. (*Freeman's Journal*; *The Times*)

March 24th

1878: The training ship *Eurydice* was returning from the West Indies with a crew of young seamen and some passengers, including court-martialled prisoners being sent to Portsmouth to serve their sentences. Upon reaching the Isle of Wight at noon she clung to the coast but, at half past three, she was struck by a snow squall. The order was given by Captain Hare for the sails to be taken in, but the snow was so thick it was impossible to carry out the order. The vessel heeled over, water poured through the open ports onto the main deck and in a few minutes she sank. The freezing waters claimed the lives of 364 crew; only two men survived.

The tragedy shocked the nation, and inspired poets. Gerald Manley Hopkins wrote, 'Death teeming in by her portholes, raced down decks round messes of mortals...' Dr Arthur Conan Doyle, who practised as a G.P. in Southsea between 1882-1890, wrote the lines, 'Give help to the women who wail by the water, Who stand on the Hard with their eyes past the Wight...'

The sinking prompted the Royal Navy to abandon sail-training, final recognition that the days of the traditional man-o'-war were at an end. (*Naval Heritage of Portsmouth* by J. Winton, 1989; *History of Portsmouth* by W. Gates, 1900)

March 25th

1884: Princess Edward of Saxe-Weimar ceremoniously turned the first sod, signalling the beginning of the building of the Southsea Railway; the Saxe-Weimar Road was named in her honour. At a ceremony afterwards, the vision of a new railway was celebrated with a specially composed march entitled *Southsea Railway*.

The line cost £55,000 but, by 1903, the trains were replaced by a motor service. The bridges at Goldsmith Avenue, Jessie Road, Albert Road and St Ronan's Road were removed in 1925-26. Princess Edward's honour was withdrawn during the First World War because of anti-German feeling, and the road was renamed Waverley Road after Sir Walter Scott's novel, *Waverley*. (*Railway Magazine*)

———◆———

1843: What is believed to be the first tunnel to have been successfully constructed under a navigable river was opened, using technology invented by pioneering engineers Marc Brunel and Portsmouth-born Isambard Kingdom Brunel. The Thames Tunnel, from Wapping to Rotherhithe, took nearly twenty years to build.

In 1828, following a flood in which six workmen drowned and Brunel narrowly escaped death, the project was suspended for seven years. Designed for horse-drawn carriages, it now serves the London Overground railway network. (*The Times*)

March 26th

1653: At the Easter Sessions, the court heard from a witness that Stephen Eddin had Lydia Jackman on his lap at a house in Portsmouth on 14 March. Eddin asked Jackman to 'come into the bakehouse' but Jackman refused, pointing out that the baker's boy was there. Eddin 'thereupon lay with her there on the floor and used her body'.

Jackman complained that 'she was so hurt that she was sore for three days after'. She confessed to fornication and was sentenced to 'be whipped at the cart's tail out of Town and sent to Whiteparish' (her birthplace). (Borough Sessions Papers, 1653-1688)

———◆———

1840: Dame Agnes Weston, founder of the Royal Sailors' Rest was born. In 1881 she opened a new Sailors' Rest in Commercial Road. The idea was to provide Bluejackets with wholesome and clean entertainment and accommodation, an alternative to the many pubs and prostitutes of the town. (City of Portsmouth Records of the Corporation, ed. Gates, Singleton-Gates, Barnett, Blanchard, Windle, Riley)

———◆———

1895: A sailor was charged with 'committing an act of gross indecency with a seaman gunner' in Dame Agnes Weston's Sailors' Rest in Commercial Road. (*Hampshire Telegraph*)

March 27th

1834: The Tolpuddle Martyrs were moved from the Dorset County Jail to the notorious convict hulk *York*, moored in Portsmouth Harbour, prior to being transported. Their 'crime' was to take an oath of solidarity in forming a trade union. Mass public protest led to their pardon two years later. (*Dorset Evening Chronicle*)

———◆———

1912: Former Prime Minister James Callaghan was born in Portsmouth and lived at No. 38 Funtington Road. His father, who had been a Chief Petty Officer in the Royal Navy, died suddenly when the boy was nine, leaving his mother to struggle on without the aid of a pension. His education, ending at Portsmouth Northern Secondary School (opposite St Mary's Church), was patchy and inadequate, a fact of which he sometimes spoke bitterly and which made the right to a decent education one of his great political passions.

Callaghan was the only person in the twentieth century to hold the four most important offices of government: Chancellor of the Exchequer, Home Secretary, Foreign Secretary and Prime Minister. According to the *Financial Times*, Callaghan was the last Prime Minister to believe in a welfare state that would help the needy and give opportunity to all. (*The Guardian*; *Financial Times*)

March 28th

1891: In 1836, the responsibility for protecting the people of Portsmouth from fire shifted from 'big society' style amateur volunteers to the police. The efficiency of the police, whose priority was naturally fighting crime not fire, appears to have been only marginally better, with Portsmouth being reckoned to be 'the worst force in the country, year after year' there being 'criminal neglect of fire cover'.

An example of this occurred on this day in 1891, when a fire broke out at Carter Brothers' drapery store in Commercial Road. A shortage of police officers meant that the fire machines took twenty minutes to arrive. The appliances had to be partly used by well-meaning but untrained passers-by and drunken sailors. Tragically, a fourteen-year-old housemaid and three-year-old child died. The jury at the inquest concluded 'the force of police at disposal for fire brigade purposes is deplorably inadequate'. (*Go to Blazes* by P. Smith, 1986; *Hampshire Telegraph*)

1981: *The Times* reported that nine sailors from the *Royal Yacht Britannia* were tried at HMS *Nelson* in Queen Street for taking part in homosexual acts while ashore at Portsmouth. They were jailed and dismissed the service. In 1999 the law was changed, permitting homosexuality in the Armed Services. (*The Times*)

March 29th

1784: The first local balloon flight set off from White Swan Fields behind the short-lived Sadler's Wells Theatre (behind the current White Swan and New Theatre Royal). The balloon was blown out to sea and later recovered at Niton, on the Isle of Wight. It was one of a number launched at different times across the South by 'an itinerant lecturer in experimental philosophy', James Dinwiddie (1746-1815), who was reported to be charging 2s 'for admittance to the balloon and other apparatus' at an earlier launch. (*History of Portsmouth* by W. Gates, 1900)

———— ◆ ————

1871: A Royal Marine Artillery gunner, James Harrald, who reportedly 'wooed and won a female keeping an Eastney beerhouse' felt himself unable to stay at Eastney Barracks in the few days before their wedding and went absent without leave. As the happy pair, accompanied by the best man and bridesmaids, exited St Thomas's Church, the groom caught sight of a policeman, ran back into the church and tried to escape from another door – but was met by another policeman. A 'regular chase took place between the tombstones to the great amusement of a small crowd of persons who had congregated'. He was caught and charged. (*Hampshire Telegraph*)

March 30th

1936: The D'Arcy Exploration Company set up an oil rig and drilled into the chalk at the base of the south side of Portsdown Hill, in what they claimed was the first test for oil in England. The test hole was over a mile deep but no oil was found. Another attempt in the 1950s was also unsuccessful. (*Portsdown Panorama* by A. Triggs, 2005)

———•◆•———

1963: The clocks changed for British Summer Time and The Beatles played for the first time in Portsmouth. The two shows, at the Guildhall, included the American singers Chris Montez and Tommy Roe each of whom had had big hits in 1962 with Let's Dance and Sheila respectively. The *Evening News* headline read, 'Britain Wins Pop Tussle at Guildhall' and that the Americans were 'overshadowed' by The Beatles. The band's first hit single, *Please, Please Me* had been released just eight days before the gig. (*Here Comes the Sixties* by D. Allen, 2009)

———•◆•———

1966: The BBC showed a play entitled *The Portsmouth Defence*, referring to a ploy used by criminals accused of robbery with violence. This involved alleging that the victim had made a homosexual pass at him and that he was obliged to defend himself with violence. (*The Times*)

March 31st

1966: Olympic runner Roger Black was born in Portsmouth. He was head boy at Portsmouth Grammar School where his first love was rugby, not running. He went on to win gold medals at the European Championships, the World Championships and the Commonwealth Games, and silver medals at the Olympic Games. He is now a television presenter and corporate motivational speaker. (*How Long's the Course?* by R. Black, 1999)

———— • ✦ • ————

1804: A Mr Henry Clear, having served three months in prison for stealing hemp from the Dockyard, was publicly whipped 'from the Dockyard to the north corner of the Gunwharf' to complete his punishment. An accomplice was transported for seven years.

Another man, having stolen three iron bolts weighing 10lbs, was ordered to receive forty lashes at the Dockyard Gate with the bolts tied around his neck throughout. Between 1698 and 1781, records show that 120 men and ninety-eight women were whipped as part of their sentences. A few were punished for begging, but the vast majority had been conviced of theft. (Extracts from 'Records in the possession of the Municipal Corporation of the Borough of Portsmouth' by Robert East, 1891; *Hampshire Telegraph*)

April 1st

1882: Two boys entered the premises of Ginnett's Circus in Bow Street to sweep the place out. It was nine o'clock in the morning. The season had ended, but the building was being run as a variety theatre. Almost immediately, a fire behind the stage was discovered. The boys raised the alarm and released some performing dogs from their kennels. Fire steam engines were sent, but by the time they arrived, the wooden building was completely ablaze, a stiff breeze helping to fan the flames. The narrowness of the street and intensity of the heat made fighting the fire difficult and, before long, seven houses opposite were ablaze, though the occupants managed to escape.

The town railway station looked at serious risk. Railway carriages were shunted away from the low level platform, against which the rear of the circus building abutted. Burning embers were carried for miles, some falling in the Dockyard, where they were 'stamped out by constables', and others fell down Alderman Pink's chimney, causing him some alarm. (*Isle of Wight Observer*)

---◆---

1961: Portsmouth ceased to be a garrison town after 700 years. (City of Portsmouth Records of the Corporation, ed. Gates, Singleton-Gates, Barnett, Blanchard, Windle, Riley)

April 2nd

1982: The first round of redundancy notices was issued to Portsmouth Dockyard workers as part of Margaret Thatcher's Government defence cuts. On the same day, the Falklands War began with the Argentinian invasion and occupation of the Falkland Islands. Seven weeks earlier, Portsmouth-born MP and former Prime Minister James Callaghan had stood up in the Commons and asked Margaret Thatcher to change her mind about withdrawing HMS *Endurance* from the South Atlantic, saying that 'it is an error that could have serious consequences'. Thatcher refused to do a U-turn; the war lasted seventy-four days and resulted in the deaths of 257 British and 649 Argentine soldiers, sailors, and airmen, and three civilian Falkland Islanders. (*The Times*)

———— •◆• ————

1932: Mike Vernon was born in Portsmouth to a naval family. In his early twenties, he emigrated to Australia where he became a leading consumer activist. He held many positions on Government boards and committees and is best known for banning lead and cadmium in house paint and children's toys, regulating pesticides, stopping the dumping of unsafe products in third world countries and improving condom reliability in Australia. He died in 1993. (*Who's Who in Australia*)

April 3rd

1883: H. Percy Boulnois was elected Borough Engineer of Portsmouth. Born in 1847 of a Huguenot family, as a young man Boulnois was articled to the civil engineer Joseph Bazalgette. Bazalgette was also of Huguenot descent and is most famous for planning Central London's sewer network, which put an end to cholera epidemics in the capital. On taking up the post, Boulnois very soon learnt that the War Office and Admiralty 'had a good deal to say before any improvements could be carried out'. Boulnois wrote in his memoirs:

> I had an instance of this some little time after my appointment, when the Commanding Royal Engineer of that date said to me one day, 'Mr Boulnois, you lay a good many eggs, but they are not all hatched.' In reply I said, 'I'm afraid, sir, that is because you sometimes addle them.'

In the seven years Boulnois served the Borough, he hatched many eggs, including the building of Southsea promenade, the laying of many miles of arterial sewers, coastal protection, the laying out of North End Recreation Ground, improvements in paving and the construction of the Canoe Lake. (*Reminiscences of a Municipal Engineer* by H.P. Boulnois, 1920)

April 4th

1933: Nine people appeared before the Police Court accused of being involved in the staging of a cock fight in the rifle range of a local concern. Cocks were fitted with sharp steel spurs and set to fight, according to witnesses. The aftermath of a fight was described, with one bird having twenty puncture wounds, an injured eye and blood pouring from its head and neck. All but one of the defendants were convicted and fined. (*A History of the Police of Portsmouth* by J. Cramer, 1967)

———— • ◆ • ————

1653: Elizabeth Alkin, nurse and spy, spent some time working at Portsmouth, as evidenced by a payment she received for caring for the sick and wounded from the First Anglo-Dutch War. Known as 'Parliament Joan', she was the wife of Francis Alkin, who was hanged by the Royalists as a spy during the Civil War. She was described as an 'old Bitch' who could 'smell out a Loyall-hearted man as soon as the best Blood-hound in the Army'. She was involved mainly in the detection of Royalist newspaper publishers and printers. (*Oxford Dictionary of National Biography*)

April 5th

1898: A meeting took place at No. 12 High Street at which Portsmouth Football Club was born. A syndicate was formed with the intention of acquiring a piece of land in Goldsmith Avenue at £1,100 an acre, which was to become Fratton Park. (*Pompey: History of Portsmouth Football Club* by M. Neasom, 1984)

———•◆•———

1825: The *Union* steamer began a ferry service from Portsmouth to Ryde, to be joined a few weeks later by the *Arrow*. Both vessels used tow boats for the carriage of cattle and horses across the Solent (*see* May 19th). (*Early Solent Steamers* by F. O'Brien, 1973)

———•◆•———

1982: HMS *Hermes*, HMS *Invincible* and other ships of the Task Force steamed out of Portsmouth Harbour for the Falkland Islands amid 'an extraordinary display of national fervour', with noisy farewells from ships and well-wishers crowded onto docks, jetties, beaches and rooftops to wave their Union Jacks and cheer. 'We normally get two men and their dogs walking on the beach who might give us a glance,' commented one naval officer. (*The Times*)

April 6th

1931: The marine artist William Lionel Wyllie died. Born in London in 1851, Wyllie first exhibited at the Royal Academy in 1868. In the early 1870s, he started work as an illustrator for the *Graphic*, producing illustrations of maritime subjects. Wyllie moved to Tower House, overlooking the entrance to Portsmouth Harbour and, at the suggestion of Lord Baden Powell, organised a Sea Scouts troop and also co-founded Portsmouth Sailing Club. He became closely involved with the Royal Navy and depicted First World War scenes and events. Late in life, Wyllie became increasingly interested in naval history and campaigned for the restoration of HMS *Victory*.

In 1923, he laid the foundation stone for the Royal Naval Museum, and painted a panorama of the Battle of Trafalgar there, which was unveiled by King George V. (*Oxford Dictionary of National Biography*)

———•◆•———

1869: Two boys were looking for birds' nests on the ramparts at the back of Colewort Barracks when one of them thrust his arm up a gulley hole and pulled out a box containing two gold Albert chains, twenty gold finger rings and twenty-three gold earrings. They were from a haul from a burglary the previous year for which a man had been imprisoned. (*Illustrated Police News*)

April 7th

1808: Eleven French prisoners cut a hole and escaped from the prison hulk *Vigilant* that was permanently moored in Portsmouth Harbour. They swam to the nearby *Amphitrite,* stole some clothes and a rowing boat, then, in the semi-darkness, came across the Master Attendant's buoy boat, 'one of the finest unarmed crafts in the harbour, valued at £1,000'. They boarded her and immediately got away at about five in the morning, successfully navigating the Channel crossing.

They sold the boat for £700 and it was fitted out with eight six-pounders and used as a privateer under the name *Le Buoy Boat de Portsmouth*; her career was shortlived, however. Six months later she was captured by HMS *Coquette* and repatriated.

Four years later two French hulk prisoners, Dubois and Benry, were condemned to be hanged at Winchester for forging a £1 banknote. While awaiting execution they tried to take their lives 'by opening veins in their arms with broken glass and enlarging the wounds with rusty nails', declaring they would die as soldiers, and not as dogs. They were restrained and their lives saved. At the moment they were hanged, they cried, 'Vive l'Empereur!' (*Prisoners of War in Britain 1756-1815* by F. Abell, 1914)

April 8th

1710: Four Indian kings, three Mohawks and a Mohican, arrived at Portsmouth from Canada en route to see Queen Anne. They were in England to make an appeal for military and economic aid but, having been converted to Christianity, also appealed for more missionaries, chapels, Bibles and prayer books. Their address to the Queen was widely printed and disseminated, inspiring chapbooks and ballads. On 3 May they left London by coach, the ride to Portsmouth being part of a grand tour of the country. They stopped at Hampton Court, Windsor Castle and Southampton before arriving at Portsmouth. On 8 May they sailed from Spithead aboard HMS *Dragon*, laden with a cornucopia of souvenirs and merchandise supplied by Queen Anne, including fancy clothes, looking glasses, brass kettles, six kinds of knife, four dozen pairs of scissors, tobacco boxes, a gross of necklaces, razors, combs, Jew's harps, swords, pistols, lead, one hundred pounds of gunpowder and much more. (*Transatlantic Encounters: American Indians in Britain* by A. Vaughan, *Annals of Portsmouth* by W.H. Saunders, 1880)

———◆———

1949: Film director John Madden was born in Portsmouth. His television work includes *Inspector Morse* and *Prime Suspect*, and his films include *Mrs Brown*, *Shakespeare in Love*, *Captain Corelli's Mandolin* and *The Debt*. (*Debrett's People of Today 2010*)

April 9th

1960: Douglas Bader, famous Second World War air ace who lost both his legs in a plane crash, opened a new extension of the Blind and Limbless Ex-Servicemen's Association home in Bruce Road. (City of Portsmouth Records of the Corporation, ed. Gates, Singleton-Gates, Barnett, Blanchard, Windle, Riley)

——•◆•——

1806: 'On the 9th April and at five minutes before one o'clock in the morning my dear Sophia was brought to bed of a boy.' And so, Marc Brunel recorded the birth of his son, Isambard.

Marc taught the young Isambard Kingdom to draw and instructed him in geometry. He took an avid interest in his father's plans and achievements, including the revolutionary block machinery in Portsmouth Dockyard. He was also encouraged to routinely 'measure and draw with neat precision' buildings of note by his father.

In 1831, the young Brunel's design for the suspension bridge at Clifton was accepted and, two years later. he was appointed engineer to the Great Western Railway. His other achievements included the *Great Britain*, the first large iron steamship, and the first that used a screw propeller. Brunel died in 1859, one of the great engineers of the 'heroic age' of British engineering (*Brunel: The Life and Times of Isambard Kingdom Brunel* by R. Angus Buchanan, 2006; *Isambard Kingdom Brunel* by L. Rolt, 1957)

April 10th

1899: An unnamed witness saw two men with a bag going up Flint Street, Southsea, heading towards Landport. The men's boots, he observed, were not fastened and they had slippers sticking out of their pockets. He reported the sighting to the police.

At this time, Southsea's well-to-do was the target of burglars who, on at least two occasions, left a calling card. A house in Yarborough Road had been robbed, and the intruders helped themselves to 'a bounteous feast of bread, beef and liquid refreshment' before slipping away with their haul. On a plate they left the message, 'A visit from the midnight demon'.

Then, No. 43 Kent Road was hit. The burglars removed their boots, wiped them on the housekeeper's mackintosh, closed the shutters, lit a lamp and proceeded to test the silver collection with acid, separating out the real silver from the plate. Before leaving they visited the larder and washed a large jam tart and a plate of shrimps down with a bottle of Bass Ale. A card was left reading, 'A visit from the Night Demon'. After the local press suggested that residents were keeping loaded firearms in readiness, there were apparently no more similar burglaries. (*Hampshire Telegraph*)

April 11th

1801: Six thousand French prisoners-of-war were returned to France. The problem of what to do with the men captured in the Napoleonic Wars was a recurring one. In 1813, there were about 18,000 men in the Portsmouth area, 4,000 at Forton in Gosport, 5,000 at Portchester and around 9,000 distributed among fourteen hulks in the harbour. (*Annals of Portsmouth* by W.H. Saunders, 1880)

———•◆•———

1814: 'Grey or Carrotty Whiskers are a great disfigurement to Gentlemen,' maintained an advertisement published on this day. Fortunately for gentlemen suffering from this disfigurement, Mr Belam, druggist of 'opposite the Parade', Portsmouth was available to help. The remedy was Prince's Dye, the magical properties of which were not limited to the benefit of gentlemen. 'Several ladies ... have been obliged to wear false hair' to cover up the presence of grey, but the application of Prince's Dye gave them 'the youthful appearance as when twenty years of age'. Mr Belam also announced, on the same day, that he had received 'a fresh supply of strengthening pills' which was 'a sovereign remedy' for 'female weaknesses of every description' as well as, miraculously, 'seminal weakness in the male sex'. (*Hampshire Telegraph*)

April 12th

1743: One day in around 1740, Lot Cavenagh decided to go it alone and carry out his trade, as he put it, 'in a more Gentlemanlike Manner'. He hired a bay mare and rode to Portsmouth to start his new life. He stayed in town for a couple of days before riding out towards Portsdown Hill:

'I spied two Gentlemen coming over the Down towards me; I rode up to them with my Pistol in my Hand, and bid them immediately deliver their Money and Watches, with the usual Compliment of God damn you stand, or else you are dead Men...'

Cavenagh returned to the same spot a week later and robbed a gentleman and his servant, though when the servant begged for the return of his ten shillings, saying, 'you see what Station I am in,' Cavenagh returned the cash, taking his shirts instead. He cut the girths and bridles of their horses and rode back to Portsmouth. Two weeks later, on the same road, Cavenagh held up a coach and relieved three ladies and a gentleman of their money and jewellery. He then left the area for Plymouth to continue his profession. The morning of 12 April 1743 saw him hanged at Tyburn. (Account of the Ordinary of Newgate, 1743)

April 13th

1926: Portsmouth Town Council voted to allow ante-natal clinics to provide information on birth control 'in cases they consider warrant the giving of such information'. The following week, a letter from Marie Stopes, the family planning pioneer, campaigner for women's rights and advocate of eugenics, appeared on the front page of the *Portsmouth Times* asking that such information be provided 'to all mothers desiring it'. The measure was strongly opposed by some councillors. Alderman Dr J. Mulvany described contraception as 'contrary to the laws of nature, and immoral'. Another argued that public money should not be spent 'to instruct mothers how to evade the natural consequence of the sexual act'. It was pointed out by Cllr Avens that, 'The educated class had free access to the advice which it was suggested should be denied to other people.' (*Portsmouth Times*)

———— • ◆ • ————

1957: The Golden Barque, which served as a weather vane for nearly 200 years on the cathedral, was placed on permanent display in the nave. (City of Portsmouth Records of the Corporation, ed. Gates, Singleton-Gates, Barnett, Blanchard, Windle, Riley)

April 14th

1953: Portsmouth-born author Frederick 'Lawrie' Green died. He was most famous for his novel, *Odd Man Out*; which was made into a successful film starring James Mason. Green was born in 1902 of Irish and Huguenot descent. His father was a headmaster of St John's Roman Catholic School. He attended St Luke's School and the Salesian College at Farnborough.

As a boy he was prone to illness, and spent much of his time swimming and fishing at Southsea, while in the winter, he roamed around the town's docks and factories. His working life started at an accountancy firm but he soon tired of it, embarking on a nomadic life, taking work where he could get it in hotels, breweries, factories and theatres. He settled in Northern Ireland in 1929 and published his first novel, *Julius Penton*, in 1934. From 1939 he published a novel every year but was described as 'a novelist of promise rather than achievement'. He died in Bristol at the age of fifty-one and is buried in Havant Cemetery. (*Portsmouth Novelists* by D. Francis, 2006; *The Times*)

———◆———

1800: Richard Dart, a grocer in St James's Street, Portsea, was found murdered behind his counter. (*History of Portsmouth* by W. Gates, 1900)

April 15th

1972: Portsmouth Polytechnic students were evicted from Ravelin House following a 'sit-in' protest lasting fifty days. (City of Portsmouth Records of the Corporation, ed. Gates, Singleton-Gates, Barnett, Blanchard, Windle, Riley)

———— • ◆ • ————

1786: Jane Austen's brother, Francis William Austen, entered the Royal Navy Academy in Portsmouth Dockyard. (*A Naval Biographical Dictionary* by W. O'Byrne, 1861)

———— • ◆ • ————

1703: This Leet or Grand Jury presentment was dated this day:

we doe present that the throwing of Bloude an ffilth which comes from the Queens slauter house downe the slipe at Towne Keye, And over the said Keye is a common nusance and a prejudice to her Majesties Subjects coming to the said Keye with their ships and vessels.

(Extracts from 'Records in the possession of the Municipal Corporation of the Borough of Portsmouth' by Robert East, 1891)

April 16th

1926: A riot took place in Commercial Road involving Australian sailors and police armed with batons. Ten sailors of HMS *Melbourne* subsequently appeared in court charged with being drunk and disorderly, assaulting the police and using obscene language and of inciting their comrades to resist arrest. According to the evidence of PC Sainsbury, who was kicked and bitten in the fight, the trouble started by the Albert Hall when the crowd of Australians emerged 'like mad', shouting the Australian 'war whoop', 'Up the Aussies'. They then proceeded to assert their national identity and pride in a physical manner, a fight ensued and a crowd of 500 people gathered to watch the mêlée.

The magistrates expressed regret that they had to fine four of the defendants and caution six others, saying that 'Everyone wished to make the Australians welcome in England.' (*Portsmouth Times*)

April 17th

1833: George Vicat Cole, landscape painter, was born in Portsmouth to George Cole and Eliza Vicat. He was the eldest of their five children. George junior adopted his mother's French Huguenot maiden name to distinguish it from his father's name.

As a boy, Cole was taught by his father, who was also a landscape painter, and accompanied him on journeys round country houses, where they would paint portraits of the owners, their horses, and dogs. By the age of twenty, two of his works were accepted for exhibition at the Royal Academy. His works were described as being 'marked by the same general character of sunlight, peace and English air'.

George Cole senior was born in 1810 and was a self-taught artist. Some of his earliest studies were of animals in Wombwell's travelling menagerie (*see* July 18th). Impressed with his work, Wombwell commissioned a large canvas nearly seven metres square depicting a tiger hunt in the jungle with elephants, and it proved a great success. Cole continued making show-cloths to advertise the menagerie at fairs. Later he studied animal painting in Holland and gained awards for his landscape painting, though he never achieved the success enjoyed by his son. (*Oxford Dictionary of National Biography*; *History of Portsmouth* by W. Gates, 1900)

April 18th

1890: Major Lionel Langley of the Royal Engineers went on a shooting expedition. He was the son of General Sir George Colt Langley of the Royal Marines and, at the age of forty, had served his Queen in defending her empire for many years. During the expedition at Kullur Madras Presidency in India, Major Langley was killed by a tiger. His remains were returned home and interred in Highland Cemetery, and a memorial was erected in St Jude's Church. (*Hampshire Advertiser*)

———◆———

1683: Edward Chapman, a glover, was in court accused of 'regrating' the market by buying 10lbs of butter at 5*s* a lb and then re-selling it at a higher price in the public market.

In 1679, Thomas Damarum, a ropemaker, was charged with the same offence having bought twenty salt fish to the value of 10*s* and immediately sold them, making a profit which was 'contrary to the statute'. Chapman paid a fine of 13*s* 4*d*, while Damarum went unpunished. (Borough Sessions Papers, 1653-1688)

April 19th

1882: Roderick McLean, a twenty-seven-year-old grocer's assistant, visited a Portsmouth pawnbroker and paid 5s 9d for a Colt revolver. He then visited Warrill & Son, gunsmiths, and bought some cartridges. He then walked from Portsmouth to Windsor.

McLean found lodgings in a poor area of Windsor. A week later, at twenty-five past five in the afternoon of 2 March 1882, Queen Victoria arrived at Windsor railway station and mounted her carriage. As the carriage left the station to loud cheers, John Brown, the Queen's personal assistant, saw a shabbily-dressed man aim a revolver and fire.

McLean was arrested. A number of Eton boys, it was reported, 'were desirous of lynching him'. It emerged that McLean had sent the Queen a poem and it had not been received as he had wished. On this date in 1882, McLean was tried and found not guilty due to insanity. (*The Morning Post*; *Illustrated London News*)

1895: Mary Cotten of No. 19 Clarendon Road, Buckland found herself in the dock of the Police Court. Twelve days earlier she said she had been lying in bed when her chimney caught fire. It seemed that wood had been put on the fire and that a spark had ignited the soot. As the chimney had not been cleaned for eighteen months, she was charged with neglect. (*Hampshire Telegraph*)

April 20th

1869: With heavy hearts. 175 local men, women and children boarded a troopship, the *Crocodile* in Portsmouth Harbour, joining over 200 other emigrants who were being forced to leave their home country because of unemployment and poverty. On 1 May a further 776 joined the *Serapis*. Both ships were bound for Canada, where there was a shortage of labour.

The men were mainly skilled Dockyardmen who the Admiralty had decided were surplus to requirements. Many had resorted to selling clothes and furniture to survive and were 'suffering the pangs of positive starvation'.

The *Hampshire Telegraph* campaigned for the emigration, arguing 'as we cannot bring remunerative labour to Portsmouth, means must be taken to convey our deserving poor to the places where it might be had'. It argued that charity was inadequate to finance their passage, and the Admiralty eventually agreed to cover the cost. Large crowds of friends, family, former Dockyard workmates and visitors assembled on the Hard and along the walls of the fortifications and gave a great roar of cheers as the vessels departed. It was later reported that 'most, if not all the emigrants did well and prospered in their Canadian homes'. (*Hampshire Telegraph; Penny Illustrated Paper*)

April 21st

1958: It was reported that 'the presence of swans on the Canoe Lake' had 'reached serious proportions'. Officials, accompanied by the press, arrived at the lake to carry out a 'thinning out' process, but instead of the hundreds of swans that had been there, only nine birds were on the lake. After nearly two hours, three swans had been bagged and, after some discussion about what to do with them, the birds were released in Langstone Harbour. It was not realised that swans regularly flew between the two locations. (City of Portsmouth Records of the Corporation, ed. Gates, Singleton-Gates, Barnett, Blanchard, Windle, Riley)

———◆———

1927: Gerald Flood, the actor whose face became familiar in television series in the 1960s and '70s, was born in Portsmouth of a naval family. In an interview, he said:

> I'd wanted to be an actor from about sixteen but my parents didn't think it was good idea; but they never thought anything was a good idea. During the War, I was known as a 'runner'. I'd run from air-raid precaution to air-raid precaution post or the scene of an emergency during the air raid. In Portsmouth, I nearly got killed by a piece of shrapnel from a shell. It missed my head by about 3 inches.

Before he took up acting, Flood had a clerical job with the National Cash Register Company in Commercial Road. (www.imdb.com, www.eyeofhorus.org.uk)

April 22nd

1899: It was reported that 'the biggest betting raid' for many years took place in Portsmouth, netting fourteen people who were charged with either 'keeping a betting house' or 'resorting to a place for the purposes of betting'. The raids were carried out simultaneously so that nobody could be alerted, and on a day when the popular City and Suburban horse race was being run. The raid on Rigler's tobacconist and newsagent at No. 63 Commercial Road netted two men, who were accused of running the betting, and five punters, two of whom were Royal Marines. A hairdresser's in Queen Street, where a bet had been observed being placed on the Oxford and Cambridge boat race, and George Clue's newsagent shop in Marmion Road, were also hit.

Police officers had had the premises under surveillance for some time, and had even placed bets themselves, Detective Smith's 'racing speculations proving very successful'. However, when asked what he was wearing while placing the bets, Smith replied that he wore the uniform of the Royal Engineers. It was pointed out to him that he, himself, was committing an offence by wearing it. Nevertheless, those running the betting shops were heavily fined, while the punters were discharged. (*Hampshire Telegraph*)

April 23rd

1893: Five-year-old Emma Downton left Sunday School and waited for her sister to take her home. An older girl walked by, pushing a baby in a pram, and Emma joined them for a walk. The girl pushing the pram, fourteen-year-old Elizabeth Whiting, was later seen making dolls' clothes from Emma's bonnet.

Over a week later, Emma's body was discovered in a well in Highland Road. The well was next to a building site where four houses were under construction between Exeter Road and Festing Road. She had been strangled with a handkerchief that was still around her neck. A witness came forward saying that he had seen Elizabeth tying a handkerchief around Emma's neck.

Emma Downton's funeral and the trial were reported extensively in the press. The judge, Mr Justice Day, in considering a sentence for wilful murder, expressed some difficulty in deciding upon an appropriate sentence, because of the defendant's age. He acknowledged that she had 'decoyed away a young child and it met its death at her hands' but believed that it was a case of manslaughter. He sent her to prison for five years, and 'she was led away crying'. (*Hampshire Advertiser*)

April 24th

1882: Shortly after four in the morning, PC White was on duty in Lake Road when he became aware of smoke and the flicker of flames. 'By means of the telephone,' it was reported, 'the man in charge of the Corporation stables was aroused and horses got ready'. Not long after, Mrs Gillam of Lake Road went to her window and saw flames in the top window of The New Prince's Theatre opposite her house. By six, the roof was ablaze and soon collapsed. The heat was such that she could no longer stand at her window.

Horse-drawn appliances arrived, closely followed by the steam fire engine, but it was too late to save the theatre. Hydrants were located and seven jets of water were used to prevent the fire spreading to its neighbours, including the Sultan Tavern next door.

Three urchins, who were sleeping in the theatre yard, sheltering amongst the sandwich boards, had a rude awakening and were taken to safety. The press commented that this was the third place of entertainment that had been destroyed by fire in the town in the last four years. (*The Era*; *Hampshire Advertiser*)

April 25th

1801: The first ever census took place. The population of Portsmouth was 3,148 males, 4,691 females. Portsea had 11,161 males and 13,166 females. (*History of Portsmouth* by W. Gates, 1900)

———◆———

1741: An Act was passed to enable Thomas Smith, Lord of the Manor of Farlington, to supply the town and neighbourhood of Portsmouth with water. Smith was said to have been granted it as a reward for reclaiming Farlington Marshes and other areas by erecting a sea wall. Smith died before he was able to take advantage of the right, which was sold on to Peter Taylor, who later became Member of Parliament for Portsmouth (1774-77).

In around 1770 Taylor sank a well in Crookhorn Copse, on the north side of Portsdown , and drove a tunnel, half a mile long, through the hill to a point uphill from Farlington Church, on the south side. He hoped to discover the springs in the chalk which could be piped, under gravity, to Portsmouth. However, hardly any water was found. It was to be another forty years before water was piped into the town (*see* September 28th). (*A History of the Portsmouth & Gosport Water Supply* by D. Halton Thomson, 1957)

April 26th

1883: Flushed with civic pride, Mayor William Pink opened the town's first public library. Standing on the corner of Commercial Road and Park Road, the building had formerly been occupied by the Commanding Officer of the Royal Artillery. In 1886 it was demolished to make way for the new Town Hall and the library was transferred to its basement, where it shared facilities with the Sanitary Authority.

The spread of education and literacy as a result of free, universal education led to a burgeoning demand for libraries. Branches were opened in Southsea (1893) and North End (1897), Milton (1925), Cosham (1935), Paulsgrove (1954) and Copnor (Alderman Lacey) (1964). An endowment from philanthropist Andrew Carnegie paid for the library in Fratton (1906). By 1908, a new central library was opened as part of the new prestigious Municipal College and served as the city's main library until 1976. During the Second World War demand for engineering books increased, reflecting the work of national importance that many civilians were engaged in, and the reference library did its bit as an Emergency Information Service. (*At the Heart of the Community: A History of the Public Library Service in Hampshire & the IOW* by J. Sadden; *Hampshire Magazine*)

April 27th

1877: The Portsmouth *Evening News* (later *The News*) was first published as a four-page broadsheet. The editor was a Scotsman, James Graham Niven, who had developed his entrepreneurial skills in Australia. Six compositors handset the type in a small upstairs bedroom above a disused butcher's shop in Arundel Street, and the paper was printed in a former slaughterhouse to the rear of the premises.

The press could produce 2,000 copies an hour and each was folded by hand before being transferred to a dogcart for distribution. In 1892, William Gates became editor, a post he held for thirty-four years at the same time as working as a local historian and author. (*The News*)

———◆———

1941: Two land-mines were dropped on Portsmouth and Southsea (Town) Station, causing several fatalities and much damage. Thousands of rail tickets were scattered amongst the debris. 'If this brought anyone hope of free travel,' they were to be disappointed because 'the tickets were all most carefully retrieved under the travelling auditor's eye and withdrawn from stock'. (*War on the Line* by B. Darwin, 1946)

———◆———

1965: Burrfields Road and bridge was opened. (City of Portsmouth Records of the Corporation, ed. Gates, Singleton-Gates, Barnett, Blanchard, Windle, Riley)

April 28th

1916: A bull, which was being taken through Portsmouth streets to a slaughterhouse in Hyde Park Road, was alarmed by a motor car in Stanhope Road. The bull's drover, Leonard Bart, was pinned against a wall and the bull broke away, charging through the streets and into Spickernell's furniture shop in Lake Road. Windows were smashed and much damage done before the bull was put down. Spickernell took full advantage of the publicity, running advertisements with the heading, 'Spickernell's Furniture is Indestructable – will resist attack of Bulls or the roughest usage.' (*Evening News, Portsmouth*)

———— •◆• ————

1954: Hertha Ayrton (born Phoebe Marks), electrical engineer and suffragist, was born above a glass merchant's shop at No. 6 Queen Street. She was the granddaughter of a Polish refugee who had escaped the Tsarist persecutions of Jews.

Ayrton specialised in arc lamp technology and wrote the standard work on the subject. She patented anti-aircraft searchlights, and her interest in vortices inspired the Ayrton fan, used extensively in the trenches to dispel poison gas.

Ayrton nursed Mrs Pankhurst and other suffragettes when they were recovering from hunger strike and she was 'very proud' when her daughter went to prison in 1912. (*Hertha Ayrton* by E. Sharp, 1926; *Oxford Dictionary of National Biography*)

April 29th

1993: The surrealistic novel *Pompey* was published. Written by Jonathan Meades, the city is portrayed as 'a dystopian little England, a rocking cradle of disease, sleaze, venality and lubricity' populated by 'garish freaks'. Meades emphasises that he was not describing Portsmouth as it is, but that he 'grafted the noxious detritus of countless other cities while adhering (mostly) to cartographic actuality'. (*The Times*; *The Independent*)

1815: A newly-installed steam engine in St James's Street was the subject of an arson attack, possibly by someone fearful of new technology. (*History of Portsmouth* by W. Gates, 1900)

1895: Keir Hardy, leader of the Independent Labour Party, gave a speech to a packed People's Hall in Lake Road. Dressed in a 'homely tweed suit' with a flower in his buttonhole, he explained that the average earnings of the working man was £75 a year, the middle class £400 and the unoccupied (upper) class £2,000 a year. He then explained how socialism is real Christianity. (*Hampshire Telegraph*)

1939: Pompey won the FA Cup. The players were paid £20 each and shared a win bonus of £550. Jimmy Guthrie, the captain, discovered that the band that played at half-time were on better money. (*Soccer Rebel* by J. Guthrie, 1976)

April 30th

1878: The Borough Gaol in Penny Street was closed. Opened in 1808, it was 'not fully in accordance with contemporary principles of reform', charging exploitative fees and taking the Borough allowance but not actually spending the money on prisoners' upkeep. This was contrary to the recommendation that those running prisons should never have the opportunity to profit from their prisoners.

In 1832, a treadmill was installed which raised water for the jail, but in 1843 a pipe was installed returning it to the well, reinforcing the pointlessness of inmates' existence. Female prisoners sentenced to hard labour picked oakum. One night in 1843, while the guards guarded their prisoners, 2cwt of lead was picked from the jail roof.

By the 1850s, overcrowding was becoming a serious problem, with three to a single cell, two sleeping on the floor. A growing number of soldiers were being sentenced to imprisonment, rather than suffering a flogging, which added to the problem. Following its closure, prisoners were transferred to Winchester and, the following year, Kingston Prison was opened. (*Portsmouth Borough Gaol in the 19th Century* by P. Thompson, 1980)

———— • ◆ • ————

1230: Henry III sailed with his army from Portsmouth for St Malo. (*History of Portsmouth* by W. Gates, 1900)

May 1st

1661: Samuel Pepys and his wife arrived by coach at the Red Lion. He had recently been appointed Clerk of the King's Ships and this was his first visit to Portsmouth.

Pepys was not impressed by the accommodation, although he was pleased and flattered when several officers from the Dockyard visited him. The following morning, Pepys walked around the town walls and earthworks and noted in his diary that Portsmouth seemed 'a very pleasant and strong place'. He also visited Buckingham House in the High Street, where the Duke of Buckingham had been murdered in 1628. (*Pepys in Portsmouth* by D. Dymond, 1977)

———◆———

1795: The ship HMS *Boyne* caught fire at Spithead. All her guns were loaded and, as the fire reached them, they went off and shot fell amongst other ships and reached the shore. She started to drift, still ablaze, until she was opposite Southsea Castle. Suddenly, at around five o'clock in the evening, the magazine exploded, shaking the town to its foundations, with doors and windows in Portsmouth and Portsea being blown in; shot, iron and burning timbers were flung in all directions. Southsea Castle suffered considerable damage. Several men who had been removing copper sheathing from the grounded ship, along with about fourteen seamen, were killed. (*Annals of Portsmouth* by W.H. Saunders, 1880)

May 2nd

1194: Richard the Lionheart signed Portsmouth's first charter. He had gathered his army and fleet at Portsmouth to prepare for the expedition and needed money to finance it. To do so he sold privileges in the form of charters.

Inhabitants purchased the charter enabling them to hold an annual fair lasting fifteen days (which later became known as the Free Mart Fair), a weekly market every Thursday, the right to try minor offences and tax local residents. Richard also gave orders for houses and a royal residence to be built – King's Hall at the upper end of a thoroughfare, which later became St Nicholas Street, and later became part of the site of the Cambridge Barracks (now the site of the Portsmouth Grammar School). (*Portsmouth: A History* by A. Temple Patterson, 1976)

———•◆•———

1844: Katie Magnus, writer and schoolteacher and daughter of Alderman Emanuel Emanuel, who was the first Jewish Mayor of Portsmouth, was born at No. 101 High Street. Her literary output was largely educational in intent. She published her first books for children between 1865 and 1869 under the *nom de plume* H.N., and wrote a number of school textbooks on both Jewish and English historical themes. She died in 1924. (*Oxford Dictionary of National Biography*)

May 3rd

1979: Portsmouth North voters elected Peter Griffiths as their Member of Parliament. Griffiths was a Conservative who had fought for the Smethwick seat in the 1964 General Election when he ran an explicitly racist campaign, adopting the infamous slogan: 'If you want a nigger for a neighbour, vote Labour'; he won.

In 1979, Griffiths beat the sitting Labour MP, Frank Judd. Judd, who had been an MP in the city since 1966. Judd is recognised throughout the city by people of all political persuasions as being the most hard-working MP Portsmouth has had. His accessibility, both at his advice centre and on his regular visits to offices, factories, clubs and hospitals is legendary. He championed the cause of the underpaid, homeless and unemployed and was a great believer in community values. Ennobled in 1991, Lord Judd is an expert on issues related to the developing world and human rights. He was made a Freeman of the City in 1995.

Following his election defeat, the following day's news reported 'Poll Triumph for Thatcher' on the front page, heralding the end of Portsmouth-born James Callaghan's Labour Government. (*The Times, The News,* Portsmouth)

May 4th

1840: Portsmouth Harbour's first steam-powered ferry, a 'floating bridge', made its way from Portsmouth to Gosport on its maiden crossing. Two years earlier, 1,100 harbour watermen, fearful for their livelihoods, had petitioned Parliament, urging the rejection of the enabling act for the floating bridge, but failed.

The floating bridge was run by two 16hp steam engines and ran along two chains which had balance weights attached to each end, so that 'in the roughest weather no motion is perceptible to those on board'. After the twelve-minute crossing, enthusiastic passengers praised the 'smooth and noiseless operation'. The first week of operation exceeded all expectations, with 12,466 passengers, 568 vehicles, 20 oxen and 117 sheep, as well as mail packages. Passengers were charged a penny to cross, though entrance to the 'best room or cabin' cost 2*d*. A horse-drawn carriage was 6*d*, while livestock was three farthings a head. During the cholera epidemic of 1849, bodies were ferried across on the bridge to be buried at Browndown in Gosport, though it is not known what fare was charged. (*Crossing the Harbour* by L. Burton and B. Musselwhite, 1987; *Hampshire Advertiser*)

May 5th

1888: It was reported that a 'monument to bravery' had been erected in Highland Cemetery on the grave of a Mrs Fox.

Annie Fox had accompanied her husband, a Sergeant Major in the Connaught 94th Regiment of Foot, to the Transvaal during the first Boer War in 1880. An attack by the Boers cut the Connaughts to pieces and Mrs Fox was seriously injured. The Boers were reported by the British Commanding Officer to have been 'very sorry at having wounded a woman, and the minute after the arms were laid down they became most obliging and civil. They offered to get us everything they could for our comfort and it was not a hollow promise.' Mrs Fox was held prisoner for four months, during which time she acted as a nurse to her wounded fellow prisoners despite her own serious injuries. For this she was decorated by Queen Victoria with the Royal Red Cross.

In Cambridge Barracks, eight years later, Mrs Fox succumbed to her wounds. The funeral procession went from the barracks to Highland Cemetery, with many local people lining the route to pay their respects. The monument to her bravery was later erected in her memory by the soldiers of the barracks. (*Hampshire Telegraph*; *The Times*; *The Star*)

May 6th

1926: A local demonstration in support of the General Strike took place, at which 'about 500 men and 200 women' protested. The march was headed by a man with a Davy lamp and a pit pony. Coal miners' wages had been cut by up to 25 per cent and their working hours extended by the coal owners, who were anxious to maintain their profits. Other trade unions wanted to help defend their fellow workers; local tramway workers, railwaymen, engineers, firemen, woodworkers and bricklayers were amongst those taking part in the march, which set off from the Trades Hall in Fratton Road. Thousands of people lined the route through Fratton, Lake Road, Commercial Road, Town Hall Square and the Terraces to Southsea Common, where there was a mass meeting of nearly 4,000 people. There was reported to be 'one red flag, silk and embroidered and carried by a small girl', but the demonstration was 'conducted in an orderly fashion'.

One hundred and fifty local tramway workers lost their jobs when the Council refused to take them back after the strike. Mayor Sir John Timpson KBE requested that, having been sacked, they should return their uniforms, presumably so that the men who had taken their jobs could wear them. (*Portsmouth Times*)

May 7th

1886: Conan Doyle wrote to the *Portsmouth Evening News* opposing any idea of making the proposed North End Recreation Ground freely open to the public, on the grounds that serious sports would be hindered. 'What hope would there be of good cricket upon a pitch which was cut up and scarred by indiscriminate playings? What would be the value of a bicycle track where the rider... [would] be continually on the watch for children or perambulators?' (*The Unknown Conan Doyle: Letters to the Press*, ed. J. Gibson and R. Lancelyn Green, 1986)

———•◆•———

1949: Model Marilyn Cole was born in Portsmouth, making her a Taurus. In 1973, the 'luscious and voluptuous brunette stunner' became the only British model to be Playmate of the Year. Cole has the distinction of being the first ever centrefold to display unrestricted full frontal nudity, and has appeared in several films playing herself. (www.imdb.com)

———•◆•———

1960: Sir Thomas Beecham conducted his last ever concert. Afternoon rehearsals were cut short because he wanted to watch the FA Cup Final at the Queen's Hotel. The evening concert was reported to have 'enthralled' a full house at Portsmouth Guildhall. Beecham died the following year. (*Thomas Beecham* by C. Reid, 1962; *Evening News, Portsmouth*)

May 8th

1853: A letter was published in the press with the heading 'Laziness in the Dockyard', which condemned workers as 'lazy drones', lying around in the cabins of ships that were being fitted out, with similar scenes in the sail lofts and the boat houses. They were, he concluded, 'like beasts in the zoological garden, only waiting to be roused up for feeding time'. The letter was signed, R. Martell, Portsea. The following week, the real Mr Martell wrote to the newspaper stating that the letter was not from him.

In another anonymous letter, a correspondent claimed to have visited Portsmouth Dockyard for an hour, during which 'some sixty or seventy persons came under [his] observation'. Every one of them, he maintained, 'official, or mechanic, appeared to move at the rate of about one and a half miles per hour'. This, he went on, 'is not the usual rate outside the yard, in Queen Street, at the time the men go to dinner'. He watched men sawing, using an adze, boring with an auger and mortising timber, all 'in an idle, slothful way'. Whether these letters were connected with a sawyers' strike at the time, prompted by them having to do 'a certain quantity of work before they were paid for it', is not known. (*Lloyd's Illustrated Newspaper*; *The Times*)

May 9th

1873: What is believed to have been the first co-operative society in Britain was set up in Portsmouth, in 1796, by Dockyard workers who were fed up with being ripped off by local tradesmen. The aim of the early co-operators was to offer an alternative by organising and controlling the production and distribution of goods and services under a system operated by and for the people.

The Portsea Island co-operative was set up by a handful of volunteers in a rented cornershop in Charles Street on this day in 1873. The shop was only open on Friday and Saturday evenings but the white-aproned co-operators did a brisk business. Five years later they moved into purpose-built premises in Besant Road and, by the late 1880s, an impressive department store had been established in Fratton Road with grocery, boots, drapery and bakery departments and stables. (*Co-op: Formation & Early Progress* by J. Mihell, 1970)

❖

1949: The foundation stone of the Nuffield United Services Officers' Club was laid by the Lord Mayor Cllr Miles. Opened two years later by Princess Elizabeth, it was intended to offer officers and their wives leisure and dining facilities and a day nursery. It now houses the University of Portsmouth Medical Surgery and International Office. (City of Portsmouth Records of the Corporation, ed. Gates, Singleton-Gates, Barnett, Blanchard, Windle, Riley)

May 10th

1687: An early example of the ordering of payment of child maintenance took place in a case of 'bastardy'. Lucy King, a widow, gave evidence that Jonathan Godard, a joiner, 'had twice carnal knowledge of her body'. This romantic encounter took place at the Dun Cow at Point. King told the court that since her husband had died over fifteen months previously, she had only had 'carnal knowledge' with Godard. He was ordered to pay 37s immediately and a further 2s a week, payable on Fridays, for as long as the child was 'chargeable to the parish up until the age of eight'. At this age the child, a girl, was to be 'put out as an apprentice', for which Godard was ordered to pay £5. Lucy King was punished by being imprisoned for six weeks. (Borough Sessions Papers, 1653-1688)

May 11th

1753: The expansion of the population of Portsea in the mid-eighteenth century brought with it a need for a church. Worshippers had to walk across fields and dirt tracks to reach St Mary's in the old town.

Once permission had been granted, it was down to the local people to raise the money and to actually build it. They also donated or made most of the fittings. The foundation stone was laid at half past five in the morning of this day. Dockyard shipwrights, three gentlemen, one carpenter, one tallow chandler and a grocer took fifteen months to put it up at a total cost of £2,209. Until 1771, when an organ was installed, services were accompanied by an orchestra. Pew rents paid for the upkeep and costs and ensured that the richest Christians got the best seats, the humble poor at the back straining to hear that it was they who would inherit the earth.

St George's is the oldest church building on Portsea Island that has remained structurally as it was built. (*Churches, Chapels and Places of Worship on Portsea Island* by J. Offord, 1989)

———— • ◆ • ————

1989: On this day the Bridge Shopping Centre in Fratton Road was opened. (*The News*, Portsmouth)

May 12th

1915: A young Dutchman, Haicke Janssen, disembarked at Hull. He immediately registered as an 'alien', as required by the wartime Defence of the Realm Act. He declared that he was a cigar salesman from neutral Holland, with which business continued as normal. Later that month, Janssen travelled to Portsmouth. He visited the main Post Office several times over the next ten days to cable orders to his wholesaler in Rotterdam but the postal Clerk became suspicious as he had ordered 48,000 cigars, a remarkable demand for a town like Portsmouth where, notwithstanding profiteers, the inhabitants were not noted for their high consumption of quality cigars.

The Clerk reported the matter and British Intelligence investigated. It emerged that Janssen's order for 10,000 Cabanas, 4,000 Rothschilds and 3,000 Coronas corresponded with there being ten destroyers, four cruisers and three battleships in Portsmouth Harbour. Janssen was arrested, tried and shot to death on the firing range at the Tower of London on 30 July 1915. (*Keep the Home Fires Burning: The Story of Portsmouth & Gosport in World War I* by J. Sadden, 1990)

———◆———

1982: During the Falklands War, travel writer Paul Theroux travelled to Portsmouth. Scratched on the train door was the message, 'The Argentines are Wankers – Bomb the Barstards [*sic*].' (*The Kingdom by the Sea* by P. Theroux, 2001)

May 13th

... at 4am fired gun and made the signal to weigh, weigh'd and made sail, in company with the Hyaena frigate Supply armed with tender, six transports and three store ships, at 9 fired a gun and made the sign'l for the convoy to make more sail

1787: These words in the logbook of HMS *Sirius* recorded the departure of what became known as the First Fleet. Made up of eleven ships, the fleet was embarking on an eight-month journey for a virtually unknown shore on the other side of the world. As well as the *Sirius*, the fleet included the *Alexander*, the largest ship, which served as an all-male prison; it was reportedly the dirtiest ship and experienced more mutinies than any other ship. The accompanying transports and store ships carried supplies that would last two years. On board were 1,044 people made up of 568 male and 191 female convicts and thirteen children. The official party comprised 206 marines with twenty-six wives, nineteen children and twenty officials. Their arrival in Australia marked the beginning of the British colonisation of Australia, the home of an estimated 300,000 aborigines. (First Fleet Fellowship website)

May 14th

1631: In 1618, the great honour of the Freedom of the Borough of Portsmouth was conferred on Mervyn Touchet. The reason for the honour, which brought considerable political privilege, is not known, but during the previous year he had succeeded his father as Earl of Castlehaven. The inherited fortune augmented a Wiltshire estate he had inherited from his mother.

Thirteen years later, he was beheaded on Tower Hill. He had been found guilty of sodomy, having recruited 'vagabonds and out of work sailors from the ports' to his estate. The specific charges were that he had committed 'an unnatural act' with his page Laurence (aka Florence) FitzPatrick, and that he assisted Giles Broadway in the rape of his second wife, the Countess of Castlehaven. Both Touchet and Broadway were hanged.

The evidence given at the public trial suggested that the aristocratic goings-on within the boundaries of a private estate were far more shocking than those described at Portsmouth when the fleet was in. (*The Trial of Mervyn Touchet* by R. Norton, 2009; *History of Portsmouth* by W. Gates, 1900)

———•✦•———

2001: Portsmouth featured prominently in an episode of popular soap *Eastenders*, the Continental Ferryport and Central Library acting as locations. (www.imdb.com)

May 15th

1701: According to the laws and usages recorded for this day, the Bristol Arms, the Black Bear in Warblington Street and The Fleece 'are very disorderly houses and ought to be Suppressed, for they tend to the debauching age as well as youth'. (Extracts from 'Records in the possession of the Municipal Corporation of the Borough of Portsmouth' by Robert East, 1891)

———— • ✦ • ————

1701: It was resolved that 'the carrying of Gun Powder in open carts through the Streets of this Towne is very dangerous'. (Extracts from 'Records in the possession of the Municipal Corporation of the Borough of Portsmouth' by Robert East, 1891)

———— • ✦ • ————

1865: The first horse-drawn tram began operating, running from the South Western railway station (now Portsmouth and Southsea Station) and Southsea Pier (now Clarence Pier). This enabled passengers to easily transfer to the Isle of Wight steamers. This service is believed to have been the first statutory tramway in the country. A horse-bus service is believed to have run between North End and Southsea as early as 1840. (*Fares Please* by E. Watts, 1987)

May 16th

1842: The Victoria Pier was opened, named after the Queen who was crowned five years earlier. Steamers entering and leaving the harbour picked up and dropped off passengers here, and two waiting rooms were provided nearby. To celebrate the opening, around thirty shareholders of the pier company dined at the George Inn and enjoyed 'dinner and wines of the first quality'. (*Hampshire Advertiser*)

———— • ◆ • ————

1849: A steam tug entered Portsmouth Harbour with a boat in tow. The steamer had attracted the attention of the coastguard when it had left harbour the previous evening without displaying the customary lights. The vessel was challenged by a customs vessel, but put on more power to escape. Several shots were fired after her and other customs boats joined in the chase. Soon the Royal Charter steamer was caught and the crew of thirteen men arrested. A consignment of proof brandy numbering 150 kegs ,containing some 700 gallons, was discovered. (*The Era*)

May 17th

1890: At a quarter past eleven in the morning, fifty-year-old Mr Thomas M'Cheane, Vice Consul for Russia, took a walk along the Southsea Esplanade. He lived in St Thomas's Street and was a well-known man about the town. He engaged in cheerful conversation with several people as he made his way to Southsea.

Mr M'Cheane spent some time looking at a public drinking fountain erected in memory of his deceased brother, Charles. It had been paid for by members of the Royal Portsmouth Corinthian Yacht Club, of which he was the founder. The fountain had been installed six months earlier but was dry, as no water supply had been connected. Mr M'Cheane walked on to Southsea Castle.

A little later, some boys noticed a gap in the railings around the castle moat, the rails having been torn down. They entered the enclosure and found Mr M'Cheane lying dead in the moat, which was dry at the time. Close by, the boys found a revolver with one chamber discharged, and a walking stick.

At the inquest it was established that Mr M'Cheane had had his dog put down two days earlier. A verdict of suicide was returned. (*Hampshire Advertiser*)

May 18th

1814: French painter Louis Garneray, who was captured by the British in 1806 and imprisoned on a prison hulk in Portsmouth Harbour, was released on this day. Unlike many French prisoners who earned money by making scrimshaw, Garneray painted portraits of the guards, selling them for up to a shilling. He came to an arrangement with a Portsea dealer, who thought his seascapes 'not at all bad for a Frenchman', and paid £1 for each of them. ('Art in a Dockyard Town: Portsmouth' by N. Surry, Archives Review Vol. VI, 1982)

———◆◆———

1876: Percy Westerman, children's writer, was born at No. 41 Kensington Terrace, Portsea. Educated at Portsmouth Grammar School, Westerman began to write articles for magazines about sailing but, in 1908, his children's novel, *A Lad of Grit*, was published, the first of over 170 adventure yarns that he published up until his death in 1959. (*Oxford Dictionary of National Biography*)

———◆◆———

1922: The philosopher Gwilym Lane was born. Educated at Portsmouth Grammar School, his studies at Oxford were interrupted by war service with the Special Operations Executive. He is principally known for his ideas on the development of Aristotle. (*Oxford Dictionary of National Biography*)

May 19th

1817: The first steam vessel to operate between Portsmouth and Ryde went into service. The 15hp, 70-ton vessel *Britannia* had originally been designed for the London-Southend service. Consequently, within four weeks of its maiden voyage across the Solent, the service was withdrawn, 'it being ascertained that boats of this description are not calculated for situations liable to heavy seas, accompanied by adverse winds and strong tides'. Local enthusiasm for a cross-Solent passage by steamer appears to have waned until 1825. (*see* April 5th). (*Early Solent Steamers* by F. O'Brien, 1973)

1873: A new tramway to Point from Commercial Road was opened by the Portsmouth Street Tramways Company, linking Portsea with the old town for the first time. The event was celebrated by an event at the Pier Hotel, dominated by civic dignitaries, during which the company manager, Mr White, laid claim to being the 'father of the scheme', and that he thought it would be successful, but that 'it would not be his fault if it were not'. During the evening, Messrs J. Shaw and Frank Pounds 'of Landport railway station' sang 'several songs, comic and sentimental' and fun was had by all. (*Hampshire Telegraph*)

1964: 'Portsmouth's first socialist Lord Mayor', Alderman J.A. Nye was elected unanimously by the City Council. (City of Portsmouth Records of the Corporation ed. Gates, Singleton-Gates, Barnett, Blanchard, Windle, Riley)

May 20th

1937: The Coronation Fleet Review brought King George VI to Portsmouth. It also attracted a young and very gay Quentin Crisp:

> Today a visit to Portsmouth would not be worth the train fare, but in the summer of 1937 the whole town was like a vast carnival with, as its main attraction, a continuous performance of HMS *Pinafore*. As most of the men were in uniform and the girls wore shorts and bras in the street, it seemed that everyone was in fancy dress. This much I saw from the taxi window when I was being driven towards the hotel which the driver had chosen. 'It'll be the best – for *you*,' he said.

The Times on this day carried the headline, 'THE FLEET'S GAY WELCOME'.

Controversy was caused during the Review when retired Lieutenant-Commander Thomas Woodrooffe, employed by the BBC to deliver a radio commentary, had 'a drink' before live transmission. His incoherent commentary on the ceremonial illumination of the fleet at Spithead became famous for the repeated phrase, 'The fleet's lit up' ('lit up' being a euphemism for 'drunk'). (*The Naked Civil Servant* by Q. Crisp, 1977; *The Times*)

———◆———

1212: King John ordered the docks to be enclosed, marking the foundation of Portsmouth Dockyard. (*History of Portsmouth* by W. Gates, 1900)

May 21st

1662: King Charles II married Catherine, Infanta of Portugal, by proxy and without having met her. On this day, a month after the wedding, Charles wrote to Lord Clarendon from Portsmouth:

> I arrived here yesterday about two in the afternoon, and as soon as I had shifted myself, I went to my wife's chamber, who I found in bed, by reason of a little cough, and some inclination to a fever, which was caused, as we physicians say, by having certain things stopped at sea which ought to have carried away these humours. But now all is in their due course, and I believe she will find herself very well in the morning as soon as she wakes.
>
> It was happy for the honour of the nation that I was not put to the consummation of the marriage last night: for I was so sleepy by having slept but two hours in my journey as I was afraid that matters would have gone very sleepily. I can now only give you an account of what I have seen a-bed; which in short, is, her face is not so exact as to be called a beauty, though her eyes are excellent good, and not anything in her face that in the degree can shock me...

(*The Letters, Speeches & Declarations of King Charles II*, ed. A. Bryant, 1935)

May 22nd

1870: A Marmion Road baker, Mr Cox, wrote in his diary: 'Attended St Jude's Church morning and evening, and I record my impression that the practices of this church are becoming more and more ritualistic.'

St Jude's also operated a sort of social apartheid. The lower classes had to enter by a separate entrance and went directly to the gallery. In 1878, a mission hall was erected in Marmion Road for those unfashionable parishioners 'who felt ill at ease among the fashionable worshippers in the Parish Church'. It was also felt that St Jude's services had 'too much music for poorer people'. These attitudes appear to have prevailed well into the twentieth century. In 1920, someone was refused entry for not wearing gloves, though it is not known whether bouncers applied this admittance policy.

Mr Cox took up a pew at St Simon's Church. (*Churches, Chapels & Places of Worship on Portsea Island* by J. Offord, 1989)

May 23rd

1952: Singer, comedienne and actress Dillie Keane, founder member of cabaret trio Fascinating Aida, was born in Southsea. Her father, Dr Francis Keane, who came from Ireland in 1939, ran a general practice in Somers Road South. Her first job was at the King's Theatre, acting as an usherette, working in the box office and as a stagehand. (*Evening Telegraph,* Coventry)

———•◆•———

1913: Founder of the recruitment agency the Brook Street Bureau, Margery Hurst is believed to have been born in Portsmouth. She was the daughter of Samuel Berney, cinema owner. After wartime service in the ATS, Hurst suffered her first nervous breakdown.

In 1946 she founded the Brook Street Bureau of Mayfair, supplying businesses with temporary secretaries. Soon branches were opened outside London and, by 1961, the company provided about one-third of Britain's agency-supplied staff. In the early 1960s, Hurst opened branches in New York and Australia and, by 1965, the company was the largest office employment agency in the world. The company was sold in 1985.

Hurst campaigned for awareness of mental health issues and against discrimination in employment. She died in 1989. (*Oxford Dictionary of National Biography*; *The Times*)

May 24th

1899: The man credited as being the driving force in establishing the School of Science and Art in Pembroke Road (precursor of Portsmouth Polytechnic and University), and with reviving the fortunes of Portsmouth Grammar School, died on this day. Canon Edward Pierce Grant, vicar of St Thomas's, was widely mourned in the town. He sacrificed his prospects of promotion in the Church by his espousal of the Liberal cause. His grandfather, Thomas Grant, had been 'Clerk of the Cheque' in the Dockyard in the early nineteenth century and his uncle, Sir Thomas Grant, invented a machine for condensing salt water into fresh, and a ship's biscuit-making machine, at Clarence Victualling Yard. (*History of Portsmouth* by W. Gates, 1900)

———◆———

1900: Queen Victoria's birthday – her last – was celebrated by 12,000 troops on Southsea Common. A Naval brigade and battery fired a *feu de joie* and gave three cheers for the Queen. (*Illustrated Police News*)

May 25th

1747: Ex-soldier and deserter James Gray enlisted in a marine regiment in Portsmouth and sailed for India, where he was involved in an unsuccessful siege of French fortifications at Pondicherry and received severe injuries in his thighs. After being hospitalised for a year, he eventually returned to Portsmouth, reaching Spithead on this day.

Having been paid off, James Gray revealed that he was, in fact, Hannah Snell, a cloth dyer's daughter from Worcester. She was immediately discharged on the orders of Admiral Hawke.

Snell had borrowed her brother-in-law's clothes and identity at the age of twenty-two and managed to conceal her gender for five years. Her story was told in the press, a ghosted autobiography was written and she toured theatres with an embellished version of events. She also inspired doggerel of which this is part:

> Hannah in briggs [breeches] behaved so well, That none her softer sex could tell, Nor was her policy confounded, When near the mark of nature [genitalia] wounded.

After her celebrity status waned, Snell is reported to have run a pub in Wapping, before marrying twice and ending her days in Bedlam Hospital, the notorious madhouse. (*Female Tars* by S. Stark, 1996)

May 26th

1963: The poet Simon Armitage was born in Huddersfield. He studied geography at Portsmouth Polytechnic in the early 1980s and his time in the city has occasionally featured in his poems. In 1996, the university awarded him an honorary degree. (*Debrett's People of Today 2010*)

1814: The Baltic Wharf, near the Round Tower, was built by a banker, Mr Burridge, so that Baltic trading vessels could unload their cargo. Burridge unsuccessfully speculated on Baltic timber, and on this day, his bank failed, bringing misfortune, misery and ruin to many local people. Baltic Wharf, known by many as 'Burridge's folly', burnt down in 1865. (*Annals of Portsmouth* by W.H. Saunders, 1880)

1827: A Jane Harding of Portsmouth wrote this notice which was published in the *Hampshire Telegraph*:

TO THE PUBLIC. Whereas my husband, Joseph Harding, has thought proper to caution the public against giving me credit on his account, stating as a reason my having eloped from him; I do hereby contradict his assertion of my elopement, and assure him and the public that such is his character that I never did, nor ever will, ask to have credit on his account, being determined to appeal for support to a generous public.

(*Hampshire Telegraph*)

May 27th

1691: Margaret Deane admitted she had led a bad life. She did not 'pray against the sins of uncleanness'. She had committed many sins, but would not say what they were, though she admitted that she did not observe the Sabbath.

At her trial, Margaret Deane said that the man who had fathered her baby daughter had promised to marry her, but abandoned her before the birth and went to sea. She moved from Portsmouth to London and found work as a servant but, without any money, and to 'cover the shame of bastardy', she threw what she said was her stillborn baby down a vault in the 'house of office' or toilet. Her mistress was suspicious, suspected her of murdering her baby and ordered a search. The dead baby's body was found and it was reported to have no wounds or signs of trauma.

On 3 June, Margaret Deane and seven other convicted criminals were transported by three carts to Tyburn and then transferred to one cart, where the nooses were put around their necks. 'After they had prayed for themselves,' the cart was moved away and 'all eight were turned off'. (Old Bailey Proceedings)

May 28th

1974: A Portsmouth orchestra which had become a popular cultural phenomenon performed a concert at the Royal Albert Hall. The Portsmouth Sinfonia had been founded by a group of Gavin Bryar's students at the School of Art in 1970. Players were required to be non-musicians, or unfamiliar with the instrument they were to play. The result was that the classical pieces they played were impressionistic rather than note-perfect. Some modern composers found this intriguing, among them the ex-Roxy Music and ambient musician, Brian Eno, who joined the orchestra and produced their first two albums. (www.oxfordmusiconline.com)

———— •◆• ————

1823: The Portsmouth and Arundel Canal was officially opened, offering the transport of goods from London to the south coast at up to a sixth of the cost of transportation by road. Several barges left Ford near Arundel for Chichester to mark the opening, and a shareholders' celebratory dinner was held in the Swan Inn, followed by another at the George Inn, Portsmouth on the following day.

Barges would enter at Milton Locks from Langstone Harbour and unload near the site of the present (Town) railway station, but, in the event, the service was considered too slow and the extension of the railway to Portsmouth in 1853 superseded the canal. (*Victoria County History of Hampshire: Vol. III*, 1908)

May 29th

1878: The *Hampshire Telegraph* reported this story which perhaps helps explain why convicts, traditionally, were shackled with balls and chains:

> As a gang of convicts were returning from their work at the Portsmouth Dockyard Extension one day last week, three of the gang broke away and ran in the direction of the lake into which they plunged. They swam out some distance until they reached a boat into which they got, and having stripped, proceeded to amuse themselves by taking headers and laughing heartily at the officers who were watching them from the bank. They were surrounded to prevent any possibility of escape and after bathing to their heart's content they swam ashore and surrendered. They were immediately handcuffed and conveyed to separate cells where they are now awaiting the result of their adventure.

The Great Dockyard Extension on which the men were working involved the enclosing of 180 acres of mudland and some of Portsea Island within the Dockyard boundary. (*Hampshire Telegraph*)

May 30th

1866: The landlord of the Heart-in-Hand, James Mitchell, promised a gang of youths a gallon of beer if they 'tin-kettled' a house opposite his pub in Montague Street. Tin-kettling was the beating of tin kettles outside a man's house, the object being to 'make the neighbourhood too hot' for him.

Noah Wareham lived with his wife and seven children in that house. He was teetotal, a wheelwright and a teacher in Southsea Ragged School, a man 'most quiet, inoffensive, his pursuits being very different to those of others who reside in the neighbourhood'.

Mitchell provided the gang with masks and they set about their task with gusto. When Wareham came to his front door, it was reported that a brick hit him. He attempted to put up the shutters of his windows but was set upon. He fetched a walking stick to defend himself, but was pulled to his knees, punched, kicked and beaten on the back of his head with a lump of wood. Mitchell, it was reported, watched the attack from the door of his pub, laughing. On this day, the inquest opened on the death of Noah Wareham. Two months later, Mitchell and the gang were found guilty of manslaughter and imprisoned for between six months and a year with hard labour. (*Hampshire Telegraph*)

May 3-1st

1824: It was reported that a meeting of local inhabitants, chaired by the Mayor, took place in the Beneficial Society's Hall in Portsea to discuss the idea of presenting a petition to Parliament on an issue that had outraged many.

The court martial of a civilian missionary, Revd John Smith, in Demerara, was shocking enough. The sentence of death was what brought people out on this evening to see if there was anything Portsmouth people could do about it.

The charges and evidence against Smith had been vague, but involved 'making the Negroes discontented with intent to excite insurrection and revolt'. Up to 12,000 slaves rebelled against their masters, but some who were called as witnesses testified that Smith had nothing to do with it. The Portsmouth meeting came to a different verdict than that of the court martial. 'Blind prejudice and personal enmity' was behind the charge and sentence. The meeting was held in the knowledge that Smith had died in grim conditions in prison, but was anxious to 'remove the stain' of the sentence of death. The Portsmouth petition was one of 200 received by Parliament, and Smith's death was said to have expedited the abolition of the slave trade. (*Hampshire Telegraph*)

June 1st

1870: The Portsmouth and Gosport School of Science and Art (precursor of the University of Portsmouth) opened in Pembroke Road. This was the first realisation of an educational establishment that was ultimately to become the University of Portsmouth. Practical geometry, artistic anatomy and life drawing, and architectural and mechanical drawing were offered to ladies and gentlemen in separate morning classes' costing a guinea a quarter (£1.05). An evening class was also offered to 'artizans', costing 2s a month (10p). (*Hampshire Telegraph*)

1961: The new Clarence Pier was opened, rebuilt after being destroyed by wartime bombing. The original pier, then called Southsea Pier, was opened exactly 100 years before, on this day in 1861. Also, on this day in 1847, Portsea Pier, known as the Royal Albert Pier, was opened. Portsmouth Harbour railway station now occupies the site. (City of Portsmouth Records of the Corporation, ed. Gates, Singleton-Gates, Barnett, Blanchard, Windle, Riley)

1824: Eight hundred Royal Marine Artillerymen came from Chatham to their new barracks in the Gunwharf. A headquarters was set up in the High Street and additional messes were erected in the garden. There was a brief move to Fort Cumberland before Eastney Barracks was built in the 1860s. (City of Portsmouth Records of the Corporation ed. Gates, Singleton-Gates, Barnett, Blanchard, Windle, Riley)

June 2nd

1227: Henry III was contemplating an attack on France and 'ordered the bailiffs of all the ports of the kingdom to send their properly manned and well-found with arms and provisions to Portsmouth'. In the event, he did not sail, in consequence, it is said, of the advice given him by an astrologer. (*History of Portsmouth* by W. Gates, 1900)

1734: A presentment was made by the Leet Jury ruling that 'the selling of Fruit at the severall Gates and on the Walls or Ramparts within this Burrough by severall persons on the Sabbath day particularly in the Time of Divine Service is a common Nusance and deserves Punishment...'

The punishment for breaching the Sabbath had been a heavy fine in the sixteenth century when the town authorities were zealous promoters of the spiritual welfare of townspeople, and rigorously enforced the Lord's Day. In 1551 they decreed that: 'no bocher, tailor, shomaker neither any other handy craft may kepe open hys shoppe wyndos on the Sabot daye, upon that every man that shall do the contrary shall lose and forfet xiid'. (Extracts from 'Records in the possession of the Municipal Corporation of the Borough of Portsmouth' by Robert East, 1891, City of Portsmouth Records of the Corporation, ed. Gates, Singleton-Gates, Barnett, Blanchard, Windle, Riley)

June 3rd

1803: The first regular daily conveyance of letters to and from Portsmouth was established. Letters were 'sent to and delivered at Halfway Houses, Kingston, Buckland, Fratton, and the neighbourhood early every morning,' and 'receiving houses' were established at 'the Blacksmith's Arms, Halfway Houses and the George Inn at Buckland, to take in letters at one penny each. A messenger called 'every afternoon at four o'clock to convey them to the Post Office at Portsmouth, to be forwarded by the respective mails to all parts of the Kingdom'. (*Portsmouth in the Past* by W. Gates, 1975)

1859: An explosion took place on board the *Eastern Monarch* at Spithead. Barges from Portsmouth rescued the vast majority of those on board and brought them ashore to Point:

> The Quebec Hotel was crammed, the watch house full, and terrified women and screaming children were received into the houses around. Officers and stalwart bronzed soldiers were standing in their shirts, their lower limbs swathed in kilts made of hangings hastily torn down from state rooms or from the saloons. At length military wagons arrived, the women and children were taken to the Garrison Hospital, and the men marched off to the nearest barracks.

(*Annals of Portsmouth* by W.H. Saunders, 1880)

June 4th

1851: A man was remanded in custody for stealing front door mats from several houses in Southsea. (*Hampshire Telegraph*)

———•—•———

1346: King Edward III assembled a fleet of 1,600 ships at Portsmouth and, with his army, set sail for St Helens, en route to Normandy – to stage a major offensive. His army sacked Caen, crossed northern France and won a decisive victory at Crécy. (*History of Portsmouth* by W. Gates, 1900)

———•—•———

1685: A man called Bradley was before the court accused of 'abusing authority', namely calling the Mayor, Richard Ridge, 'a rogue'. Abusing the Mayor was a regular event in Portsmouth reflecting, perhaps, something of the quality of the Mayors or the reluctance of the population to bow to authority.

In 1662 it cost John Allum £20 for saying that he did not 'care a turd for the Mayor or any constable in town' and three weeks later a Sebastian Watts 'mocked at the Mayor'. In 1674, two burgesses were disenfranchised for the same offence. In 1668, William Triggs was convicted by a Grand Jury for 'publishing a libel against the Corporation' and, because he could not pay, was imprisoned. (Borough Sessions Papers, 1653-1688)

June 5th

1763: Melchisedick Meredith appears to have been christened at St Mary's Church. Twenty-two years later, he opened a tailor's business at No. 73 High Street, which was to later become Gieves and Hawkes. Little is known of his early life. He claimed to have come from Wales and to have descended from a family of princes, but was well known for his extravagant storytelling. Melchisedick was churchwarden at St Thomas's in the 1800s and became a prominent Freemason in the town. Old Mel, as he was to become known, was immortalised in his famous grandson's novel, *Evan Harrington*, a satire on snobbery, published in 1861.

George Meredith was born over the High Street shop. He supplemented his vicarious writer's income with a job as a publisher's reader and became influential in the world of letters. He is said to have discovered George Gissing and Thomas Hardy (but rejected George Bernard Shaw and Samuel Butler's *Erewhon*). His friends in the literary world included Robert Louis Stevenson and J.M. Barrie, and in 1892 he succeeded Tennyson as president of The Society of Authors. (*Gieves and Hawkes* by D. Gieve, 1985; *Portsmouth Novelists* by D. Francis, 2006)

June 6th

1894: Electrical engineer and inventor Sebastian Ziani de Ferranti attended the switching-on ceremony of the new Electric Light Works. The station was erected in St Mary's Street on a site previously occupied by the Blue Bell Tavern, the South of England Music Hall and some neighbouring houses. The site was chosen for its proximity to the Camber, allowing the easy import of coal for the boilers and seawater for cooling.

The Mayoress, perched on a specially-erected platform in the engine room, pressed the button. As the wheels began to revolve, 'a murmur of applause broke out and the crowd pressed forward to obtain a good view of the splendid machines'. Ferranti was responsible for inventing the generators which produced an alternating current system, as opposed to the direct current system advocated by Thomas Edison. The electricity for supply 'passed into the street at 2000v but was transformed down to 100v and then supplied to consumers'. One hundred and one arc lamps for street lighting were illuminated in main thoroughfares in Portsmouth, Southsea and Portsea. The crowd applauded a speech saying that it was better that the municipality was running the power station rather than a private company, and that a profit for the town was guaranteed. (*Hampshire Telegraph*)

June 7th

1973: In an interview with *The Times*, the 'cockerel-haired lead singer of the Faces', Rod Stewart, revealed that he once got the sack at Portsmouth.

In 1964, Stewart was recruited to a band called the Hoochie Coochie Men by Long John Baldry after he heard Stewart busking a Muddy Waters song at Twickenham railway station. He was employed as 'second singer' for £33 a week and went on tour.

In October, the band was booked in at the Rendezvous, which had been established in 1960 and was offering 'the best in rhythm and blues'. One night, possibly Saturday, 3 October 1964, Baldry turned up an hour and a half late, and Stewart's 'meagre singing repertoire was exposed to its limits'. Stewart 'called him something' when he eventually arrived and was sacked. Stewart remembered, 'I actually cried when he sacked me.'

In the same month, Stewart had recorded and released the solo single, *Good Morning Little Schoolgirl*, which he performed on the popular television show *Ready Steady Go*, but he had to wait some years before enjoying commercial success. (*Here Come the Sixties* by D. Allen, 2009; *The Times*)

June 8th

1895: Ada White was reported to have been arrested in Queen Street. She appeared before Portsmouth Police Court charged with being a disorderly prostitute. Ada was fourteen years old. The Revd Dolling wrote at the time:

> Quiet as it may seem in the daytime, there are few worse streets at night than Queen Street, Portsea. I am sure there are no courts in the world worse than those that crowd around it. I am sure there are no characters worse than those which infest it … In towns like Portsmouth, nearly all the harm is done by the little public-house… these are really the diseased spots which fester and corrupt – the places where our soldiers and sailors mostly spend their time. And the public house is never by itself. Close to it – perhaps on either side of it – are the houses of shame and evil.

(*Ten Years in a Portsmouth Slum* by R. Dolling, 1896; *Hampshire Telegraph*)

———◆◆———

1956: the Southern Grammar School for Boys on the Eastern Road was opened by the Minister of Education. (City of Portsmouth Records of the Corporation, ed. Gates, Singleton-Gates, Barnett, Blanchard, Windle, Riley)

———◆◆———

1946: A V2 rocket, or doodlebug, was displayed on Southsea Common as part of victory celebrations. (*Evening News, Portsmouth*)

June 9th

1815: A steam vessel entered Portsmouth Harbour for the first time. The *Thames* arrived 'in the most brilliant style', travelling with the aid of wind and tide at the rate of around 13 knots. A court-martial was sitting at the time on board the *Gladiator* frigate, but the novelty of the steam-boat presented an irresistible attraction, and the whole court went aft (except the president).

The *Thames* was 79ft long, weighed 75 tons and had 14hp engines and paddle wheels 9ft (3m) in diameter. When news spread of her arrival from Plymouth, she 'created a greater sensation than at any of the ports she had visited'. Tens of thousands of spectators assembled to gaze at her and the number of vessels that crowded around her was 'so great, that it became necessary to request the Port-Admiral to assign the voyagers a guard'.

Next morning, the Port-Admiral, Sir Edward Thornborough, visited with an entourage of inquisitive top brass and a large number of ladies visited. The morning was spent 'very pleasantly in steaming amongst the fleet, and running over to the Isle of Wight. The Admiral, and all the naval officers, expressed themselves delighted with the *Thames.*' (*The History of Steam Navigation* by J. Kennedy, 2007)

June 10th

2007: Falklands war veterans came from all over the country to attend a twenty-fifth memorial service at Old Portsmouth, held in the shadow of the Square Tower. Veteran David Coomber' who served on HMS *Intrepid*, said, 'Sometimes it can be quite difficult, and especially on days like today it can be emotional because the memories come back more than ever. But it's so important we keep remembering what people did for the country.' (*The News, Portsmouth*)

1899: It was reported that Edward Beeton had been sentenced to three days' hard labour for 'singing for alms' in Marlborough Row. (*Hampshire Telegraph*)

1890: Henry Cull, aged twenty-one, appeared before magistrates charged with having attempted to commit suicide. The young man had been heartbroken after a love affair ended, and had remarkably survived drinking sulphuric acid. He made a solemn promise that he 'would not repeat the act' and was 'given over to the care of his mother'. (*Hampshire Telegraph*)

June 11th

1942: Cyril Garbett was enthroned as ArchBishop of York at York Minster. As a boy, Garbett had attended Portsmouth Grammar School and then studied at Keble College, Oxford. In 1900, he was ordained as a curate at St Mary's Church, where he dedicated himself to visiting the poor of the district for much of his time. In 1909 he became vicar of Portsea, then the Bishop of Southwark and Winchester respectively. He died on New Year's Eve in 1955. (*Cyril Forster Garbett, ArchBishop of York* by C. Smyth, 1959; *The Times*)

1897: Henry Ayers was born in Portsea on 1 May 1821, the youngest son of Elizabeth and William, a shipwright in the Dockyard. He emigrated to South Australia at the age of nineteen and entered the legal profession. Between 1863 and 1872, Sir Henry Ayers was the Premier of South Australia, but is perhaps best known for having a large sandstone rock formation named after him. Though the indigenous people already had a perfectly good name for it, Uluru, the landmark was renamed Ayers Rock. (*Hampshire Telegraph*)

June 12th

1522: It was from this day that the 'mighty chain of iron', designed to span the mouth of Portsmouth Harbour to keep out invaders, probably began to be operational. The previous month, war had been declared with France (and Scotland) and lighters were hired in connection with the chain from this date. Forged at a cost of £40, the chain stretched from Point to Blockhouse and was raised by capstans and supported by lighters. It was observed by John Leland, in around 1540, 'heere is a might[y] chaine of yren to draw from tourre to towre.'

It seems to have encountered problems at a very early stage and by 1664 another chain was made by Edward Silvester of Gosport for £200. This was said to have been replaced by another forged by Henry Cort in Gosport in 1785. It is believed that the last time it was raised was in 1801, amid fears of French invasion.

In the early twentieth century, a boom defence comprising of a number of timber struts secured by steel hawsers, each approximately 30ft long with steel spikes, was in operation. In 1909 it was tested and a specially reinforced torpedo boat broke through the defence with ease. (*Portsmouth: A Century of Change* by J. Sadden, 2009; *History of Portsmouth* by W. Gates, 1900)

June 13th

1877: Ida St Clair, aged eighteen, picked up a poker, twenty-year-old Maria Leggett had a saucepan and nineteen-year-old Julia Smith wielded a long-handled broom. They then proceeded to systematically break sixty panes of glass at the Royal Hospital, having already smashed two dozen plates, five mugs and a water pipe inside. The case, reported on this day, was heard at Portsmouth Police Court, but because of its seriousness was referred on to the Borough Sessions.

Though a civilian hospital, the Royal ran a notorious 'Lock Hospital' under the supervision of the Admiralty in the 1860s and '70s, where prostitutes were imprisoned and forced to be treated for suspected venereal diseases. Such women were seen as solely responsible for the prevalence of sexually transmitted diseases amongst serving men, and therefore detrimental to the nation's fighting forces.

The disturbance was not an isolated instance, with many women incarcerated without committing an offence. Conditions at Portsmouth Lock Hospital were reportedly 'the worst' seen by inspectors, with dirty facilities, inadequate staffing, inefficiency, letters withheld and a regime that was 'too readily disposed to adopt coercive measures to control acts of insubordination'. The women were sentenced to six months' hard labour. (*Prostitution and Victorian Society* by J. Walkowitz, 1982; *Hampshire Telegraph*; *Hampshire Advertiser*)

June 14th

1958: Portsmouth's new Salvation Army Citadel was opened on Lake Road. The original Citadel, which had stood on the same site, was bombed on 10 January 1941. (City of Portsmouth Records of the Corporation, ed. Gates, Singleton-Gates, Barnett, Blanchard, Windle, Riley)

1882: It was reported that Angus McLeod, a private in the Gordon Highlanders, was charged with assaulting Mary Webb of St Mary's Street. Webb said that the soldier 'went home with her' on the previous Tuesday evening but that at two in the morning they quarrelled and McLeod threatened to smash her crockery. He then struck her violently, knocking out three of her teeth.

McLeod claimed that Webb had taken his money and was trying to hit him with a poker when he pushed her. 'Being the worse for drink' she fell in the fireplace and hurt herself. Two references were then given, the first from Inspector Harvey, who said that Webb was 'one of the most abusive women in Portsmouth'. An officer from McLeod's regiment then said that he was 'of good character'. The two male magistrates, one a Captain McCoy, dismissed the case. (*Hampshire Telegraph*)

1747: The first newspaper believed to have been printed in the town, *The Portsmouth & Gosport Gazette*, was published for the first time. (*Annals of Portsmouth* by W.H. Saunders, 1880)

June 15th

1953: The Queen and Duke of Edinburgh reviewed the fleet of 200 ships in the Solent; there would have been more but some ships were still in the Far East serving in the Korean War. The previous day, the Queen had arrived in Portsmouth and travelled through six miles of the city streets which were thronged by flagwavers. They arrived 45 minutes late at the South Railway Jetty and the Dockyard where they were welcomed on board HMS *Surprise*.

A Russian cruiser, the *Sverdlov*, which was taking part in the celebrations, was visited by the Mayor, Mr Miles, together with four former Mayors and Mayoresses. The bulkheads were decorated with portraits of Lenin and Stalin and 'charts illustrating Soviet production achievements'. Stalin had died three months earlier, but it was to be another three years before Khrushchev's repudiation of Stalinism.

Another highlight of the day was a flypast of 300 aircraft of the Fleet Air Arm and the illumination of the fleet. The promenades, beaches and slopes of Portsdown hill were packed to watch firework displays launched from the decks of some of the ships. (*The Times*; City of Portsmouth Records of the Corporation, ed. Gates, Singleton-Gates, Barnett, Blanchard, Windle, Riley)

June 16th

1794: The artist Thomas Rowlandson visited Portsmouth to see the return of the victorious ships taken from the French just over a fortnight earlier on the 'Glorious 1st of June'. This was the first and largest naval encounter in the conflict with France during the French Revolutionary Wars. Lord Howe, with the fleet under his command, tried to stop a French convoy of ships transporting grain from the United States. Seven French ships were lost, with around 7,000 casualties, but the convoy got through. Both sides claimed victory, so the glory was actually shared.

Lord Howe returned with several captured ships and 3,000 POWs. One of them, a mortally wounded seaman, was making his will in one of the sickbays surrounded by grieving shipmates. Thomas Rowlandson commenced a portrait and, despite appeals by his companion, his 'inclination to make a sketch of the dying moment' got the better of him. (*Rowlandson: Watercolours and Drawings* by J. Hayes, 1972)

———•◆•———

1815: There was 'financial panic' in Portsmouth and a run on all the banks. By the following year there was 'great distress in the town' and, as ever, it was those with the least that suffered the most. (*History of Portsmouth* by W. Gates, 1900)

June 17th

1886: The Canoe Lake was opened by the Mayor, having been built by unemployed men from poor areas of the town at a time of high unemployment. It was reported that the lake held 1.5 million gallons of seawater, upon which 'a number of handsome model yachts were launched' during the opening ceremony. (*Hampshire Telegraph*)

———◆•·———

1964: The first regular hovercraft service across the Solent started from Eastney Beach to Ryde. (City of Portsmouth Records of the Corporation, ed. Gates, Singleton-Gates, Barnett, Blanchard, Windle, Riley)

———◆•·———

1766: Cobbler and ragged-school teacher John Pounds was born in St Mary Street, the son of a naval Dockyard sawyer. With little education, Pounds was apprenticed at the age of twelve to a shipwright, but in 1781 he was permanently injured by a fall into a dry dock. Left severely disabled, Pounds took up the more sedentary occupation of shoe-repairing and, from 1800, lived and worked in a small weatherboarded shop in St Mary Street. Between 1818 and 1839, Pounds provided free schooling for an estimated 500 street children. Within a week of his death, High Street printer Charpentier was advertising 'a correct likeness' of the shoemaker 'as seated at his work in the midst of his scholars'. (*Oxford Dictionary of National Biography*; *Hampshire Telegraph*)

June 18th

1850: On the 35th anniversary of the Battle of Waterloo, a grand celebration took place on Clarence Esplanade which attracted an estimated 50,000 spectators, among them Queen Victoria who watched events from the Royal Yacht. The highlight was the unveiling of two statues, representing the naval and military heritage of Portsmouth. The 12ft-high statues of Nelson and the Duke of Wellington were described as 'beautiful' by the *Hampshire Telegraph* and were generously donated by Lord Fitzclarence, the Lieutenant-Governor, who had been instrumental in building the promenade. After the unveiling, troops fired a *feu de joie* and a grand ball was held.

The statues, however, appear to have been unpopular, were 'of questionable taste' and made of inferior material. The faces were blackened with tar by a vandal, or aesthete, and soon afterwards disappeared. Rumour had it that they were pulled down by sailors from a ship at Spithead and given a burial at sea. (*Portsmouth in the Past* by W. Gates, 1975; *Hampshire Telegraph*)

1758: Robert Bowyer, miniaturist and publisher, was born in Portsmouth and baptised on this day. He is best known for an illustrated edition of the Bible and David Hume's *The History of England*. (*Oxford Dictionary of National Biography*)

June 19th

1877: Florence Nightingale appealed for support for Sarah Robinson's Soldiers' Institute in Portsmouth. The Institute, she maintained, helped troops avoid 'on landing ... invitations to bad of all kinds. We may not hope to make saints of them all, but we can make men of them instead of brutes.'

Three years earlier, Sarah Robinson had converted a notorious High Street pub, the Fountain Inn, and provided a place to stay away from the temptations and dangers of prostitutes and 'land sharks', conmen who specialised in relieving seamen of their earnings. Miss Robinson welcomed sailors, marines and soldiers. Troopships were visited and religious books and 'warming but not inebriating coffee' distributed.

In 1879, the Sailors' Welcome, with 220 beds, was opened by Miss Robinson near the Dockyard gates, reflecting the increasing demand. These initiatives were funded by the support and charitable donations from rich patrons, including Florence Nightingale, General Gordon and the Earl of Shaftesbury. Local prostitutes, however, were less keen, reportedly 'snarling and cursing' at Miss Robinson, accusing her of 'taking the bread out of other people's mouths'. An effigy of her was ceremoniously burnt on Southsea Common. (*My Book* by S. Robinson, 1914; *Portsmouth: In Defence of the Realm* by J. Sadden, 2001)

June 20th

1877: A Mr T. Cooper gave a lecture in Lake Road Chapel on 'The Darwinian Theory on the Origin of Man'. In his introduction, Mayor Pink anticipated the gist of what Mr Cooper had come to say, commenting that it was 'extraordinary that any person could suppose that the universe could go on from day to day without a God'.

Mr Cooper did not disappoint the Mayor or the audience. He could not conceive that 'the force of matter could have produced this beautiful world of ours' than he could believe that 'the moon was made of green cheese'. The audience laughed and cried 'hear, hear'. Mr Cooper ended his talk with a long list of rhetorical questions. Did the audience 'ever hear of a monkey making a ship and going around the world? Had they ever dug up any of the metals? Let the meeting imagine a lot of apes attending an iron furnace or working in a coal mine. Had they ever been known to form an alphabet?' The list went on. (*Hampshire Telegraph*)

1856: The foundation stone of Cambridge Barracks was laid (now the Portsmouth Grammar School). (City of Portsmouth Records of the Corporation, ed. Gates, Singleton-Gates, Barnett, Blanchard, Windle, Riley)

June 21st

1949: The Ealing film *Kind Hearts and Coronets*, in which Alec Guinness played eight roles, was released in the UK. Its source novel was written by Roy Horniman, who was born in Southsea in 1872, lived in Cottage Grove and attended Portsmouth Grammar School. (Portsmouth Grammar School Archives; www.imdb.com)

———◆———

1842: The question of whether one can trust one's paymasters came up in the House of Commons. A question was asked about the payment of crews of some of Her Majesty's naval vessels in 'light sovereigns' (containing less gold than they should). Admiral of the Fleet, Sir George Cockburn, who had served as Tory MP for Portsmouth, reassured the House. He had, he announced, investigated the matter and 'the result was that every sovereign had been weighed before it was sent down to Portsmouth'. He found that proprietors of shops were demanding 'an allowance of one shilling in the change of a sovereign'. Cockburn said that these sovereigns were retrieved and found to be of full weight, suggesting that local businesses were fleecing the men. On the other hand, they were perhaps just being cautious because Cockburn did admit, almost incidentally, that some 'light sovereigns' had been paid to men at Plymouth. (*The Times*)

June 22nd

1896: The War Pigeon Service was officially started at Portsmouth Royal Naval Barracks and Devonport, though homing pigeons had been used for some years by naval officers who had been impressed by their effectiveness in delivering messages to shore. A Commander Tufnell of the Signal School and Mr Barrett, an RN gunner with experience of training pigeons, were appointed to take charge of the new service and a Leading Signalman was employed to look after, and presumably muck out, the 200 pigeons. A naval pigeon loft was built on the other side of Portsmouth Harbour at Royal Clarence Yard at a cost of £350, and the annual feeding cost was £150 a year.

In 1904 the stock of birds was increased to 300, and many of the birds set records for overseas flying. At this time, the editor of the *Hampshire Telegraph* expressed astonishment, on more than one occasion, that the French and Germans were permitted to train their carrier pigeons from points along the English coast.

The development of wireless communication led to the demise of the service and the birds were eventually sold and the loft closed in 1908. (*The Royal Naval Barracks* by H. Dannreuther, 1932; *Hampshire Telegraph*)

June 23rd

1873: The Shah of Persia (now Iran) visited Portsmouth and 'astounded all beholders by the brilliance of his entourage and the magnificence of his jewels'. 'Portsea appears to have gone mad', recorded Thelma Merewood in her diary. A Naval Review was arranged in the Shah's honour and Thelma 'went in a steamer to see the fleet, it was a nice breezy day'. In the evening, the Mayor held a banquet and the festivities of the day ended with a ball and fireworks. Three months later, a cruiser was launched from the Dockyard and named the *Shah*. (*Letters from a Portsea Parsonage: Thelma Merewood*, Portsmouth Archives Review Vol. 6)

——— • ◆ • ———

1853: The steam warship *Princess Royal* was launched from the stocks at Portsmouth Dockyard, watched by an estimated 30,000 spectators. *The Times* reported: 'the dogshores were knocked away and the noble fabric glided easily into the water amid the shouts of the multitude and the notes of Rule Britannia and God Save the Queen by the Dockyard battalion band.' The ship had actually been laid down twelve years earlier but was designed by a committee. (*The Times*)

June 24th

1809: A woman was smoking near Lindegren's Wharf at Point where a troop ship was unloading. She struck the bowl of her pipe against the pebbles on the beach and her smouldering tobacco set fire to some loose gunpowder, which exploded a number of cartridges and a cask of powder. 'Arms, legs and portions of human bodies were found on the roofs of the houses in all directions, and the ebb tide carried out of harbour that day a goodly quantity of hats, caps, clothes and portions of mutilated humanity'. The torso of one person was blown over the houses and landed in Bathing House Square, 'where it struck against the Custom Watch house and fell, a most shocking spectacle'.

Remarkably, the woman and child survived, her washing tubs having been blown over them and 'to this she attributes her preservation, which she bewails because she has been the unhappy means of causing the deaths of so many'. (*Annals of Portsmouth* by W.H. Saunders, 1880)

———— • ◆ • ————

1971: The first 'bus lanes' in the city were approved in parts of London Road and Lake Road to reduce the delays caused to buses by increased traffic. (City of Portsmouth Records of the Corporation, ed. Gates, Singleton-Gates, Barnett, Blanchard, Windle, Riley)

June 25th

1913: A man who embodied many contemporary hates and fears, William Clare, was sentenced to five years' penal servitude at the Hampshire Assizes. Not only was this man obviously German, but he had a hunchback and worked both as a pimp and a dentist. But perhaps worst of all, William Clare, whose real name was Wilhelm Klauer, was a spy. Working from a shabby dental surgery in Portsea, Klauer attempted to extract information from his patients, many of whom were naval or Dockyardmen. His wife provided a different service for the men of the port. (*Keep the Home Fires Burning* by J. Sadden, 1990)

1984: Popular radio and television comedian of the 1940s and '50s, Reg Dixon, died at a Portsmouth hospital. (*The Times*)

1868: Herbert Meade, a lieutenant of the gunnery ship HMS *Excellent*, was charging a torpedo and mixing explosives at a rented address in Union Street. Meade's interests in weaponry extended into his private life, and he was being helped by George White, a Dockyard fitter. There was an explosion and both men were killed. (*Illustrated Police News*)

June 26th

1868: Alfred, The Duke of Edinburgh, son of Queen Victoria, was the first English prince to visit Australia, and was received with great enthusiasm, arriving on his ship HMS *Galatea*. While in Sydney, in March 1868, after luncheon, the Prince was walking with the Countess of Belmore and Sir William Manning, when an elderly man came up behind him, and, drawing a revolver, shot him in the back. It is reported that ladies fainted amid loud cries of 'lynch him, lynch him', and the would-be assassin was dragged away by the police, his clothes torn to shreds by the angry crowd.

The bullet entered two inches from the Prince's spine, passed through the muscles of the back, and round by the ribs to the front of the abdomen. However, with the help of six nurses trained by Florence Nightingale, he soon recovered and was able to resume command of his ship and return home. HMS *Galatea* arrived at Portsmouth on this day in 1868 and the Town Council presented an address in which they congratulated him on his 'providential preservation from the atrocious and criminal attempt' on his life.

The attacker, Henry O'Farrell, who had recently been released from a lunatic asylum, was quickly tried, convicted and hanged. (City of Portsmouth Records of the Corporation, ed. Gates, Singleton-Gates, Barnett, Blanchard, Windle, Riley)

June 27th

1893: Private George Mason, aged nineteen, of the 3rd East Surrey Regiment stationed at Fort Widley, was put on a charge by Sergeant James Robinson because he had failed to return a kettle to the cookhouse. He was sentenced to three days' confinement to barracks and an extra two hours' drill a day.

Shortly afterwards, following drill, the company was engaged in shooting practice at the Hilsea rifle range at Port Creek. Mason levelled his rifle at Robinson's back and said to a fellow soldier, 'Here's a good mark.' He then shot him dead. After firing, Mason threw his rifle to the ground and appeared surprised at what he had done. When in custody, Mason was reported as saying 'I shall be either doing a hornpipe in the air one of these days or else get twenty years on account of my youth.'

At his trial at Winchester Assizes, a plea of insanity was made, it being pointed out that Mason's mother, grandmother, aunt and uncle 'were lunatics'. Neither this, nor his youth, saved him from being hanged at Winchester Prison. (*Hampshire Telegraph*; *Hampshire Advertiser*)

1957: Kingston Modern School for Girls was opened. (City of Portsmouth Records of the Corporation, ed. Gates, Singleton-Gates, Barnett, Blanchard, Windle, Riley)

June 28th

1977: Bad weather hit the Queen's Jubilee Fleet Review. Traders had expected 1.5 million visitors to Portsmouth, but only 100,000 turned up. Susan Stowers, who was in charge of a kiosk filled with 2,000 hamburgers, said, 'I have had 20 customers in four hours.' (*The Times*)

1857: Ten thousand people gathered in Hyde Park to see Queen Victoria award a new decoration, named after herself, to its first recipients. She did so without getting off her horse. Among them was Henry Curtis, who was born in Romsey but later moved to Portsmouth. He became a Boatswain's Mate in the Royal Navy.

On 18 June 1855, during the Crimean War, immediately after the assault on Sebastapol, he and two others rescued a wounded soldier under heavy gunfire. Henry Curtis died in 1896 and is buried in Kingston Cemetery. His Victoria Cross was sold in 1999 for £35,000. (*Hampshire Telegraph*)

1958: A 'Bikini Girl Contest' took place on South Parade Pier organised by the Piers, Beach and Publicity Committee. Entrance was restricted to blondes only. Two years later, the Committee decided not to require bikini-clad girls to wear any additional clothing while walking on Southsea promenade. (*Southsea Past* by S. Quail, 2000; *The Times*)

June 29th

1665: Commissioner of the Dockyard, Thomas Middleton, wrote to Samuel Pepys: 'The ropemakers have discharged themselves for want of money, and gone into the country to make hay.' The blockmakers, the joiners and the sawyers all refused to work longer without money. Commissioner Middleton gave short shrift to growing discontent:

> I seized a good cudgel out of the hands of one of the men, and took more pains in the use of it than in any business in the last twelve months; clapped three others in the stocks for some hours and from thence to prison, where they still continue. Has not been troubled since.

('The Administration of the Navy from the Restoration to the Revolution' by J. Tanner, English Historical Review Vol. XII, 1897)

———— • ◆ • ————

1752: The right to hold an annual Free Mart Fair was bought from King Richard I in 1194, and was held on this day up until 1752 (when the Gregorian calendar was adopted) and it was shifted to 10 July. The market was important for the development of the local economy. However, by the early nineteenth century it was upsetting the 'respectable inhabitants of the town' as peep shows, menageries, circuses, theatres and other 'questionable entertainments' took over. After much lobbying, the fair was abolished in 1847. (*History of Portsmouth* by W. Gates, 1900)

June 30th

1794: William Wilberforce, the leader of the movement to abolish the slave trade, wrote a letter to his friend Lord Muncaster briefly describing a visit to Portsmouth, prompted by the ecstatic celebrations at the port following Admiral Howe's victory over the French fleet on 'the Glorious First of June'.

> Would it not have surprised you when the wind had a little cleared away the smoke in which the royal salute had enveloped the skies, to have seen Harry Thornton and C. Grant and your humble servant perched on the poop of the Queen at Spithead. Yet so it was. We thought Portsmouth might be a highly useful as well as interesting spectacle, and accordingly went thither a couple of days and should have stayed longer (I at least) if the Royal family being there had not made the place so very bustling and kept away some persons we principally wished to see. We found matters of lasting reflection.

(*William Wilberforce* by W. Hague, 2007)

July 1st

1868: Passengers on the steamer the *Princess of Wales* left Southsea (Clarence) Pier and were looking forward to a leisurely excursion to the Isle of Wight. Suddenly, when opposite Fort Monckton, they were fired upon, and had to, quite literally, hit the deck.

On this date Lieutenant Colonel Lovell, in charge of artillery at Fort Monckton, wrote a letter to the Secretary of State for War, prompted by a question raised by the Portsmouth MP in the Commons: 'No shot fired that morning passed within 800 yards of a Ryde steamer ... I am at a loss to understand what could have caused a report to this effect.'

Lovell's account was backed up by a Captain in command of the No. 7 Battery, who said that he was 'confident that no shot was fired when any Steamer was within 500 yards of the range.'

Despite these denials, the Secretary of State indicated that there had been a lack of due care and attention and that the matter would be looked into. (Parliamentary Debates; *Hampshire Telegraph*)

July 2nd

1940: Two local fascists were jailed and another cleared at the Central Criminal Court. Mrs Marie Ingram of Marmion Road, who had been born in Germany and was married to a sergeant in the RAF, was found guilty of conspiring to assist an enemy by 'endeavouring to persuade a corporal in the Royal Tank Corps to communicate information useful to an enemy'. Ingram's husband was to later claim 'constructive desertion', which was reported under the headline: 'Preferred Fuehrer to Husband.'

William Swift of Copythorn Road was found guilty of attempting to acquire arms and ammunition through the Local Defence Volunteers or Home Guard, 'in order to support enemy invaders', and also of endeavouring to spread disaffection. They received ten and fourteen year sentences respectively. Perhaps surprisingly, a third man who was charged, a local leader of the British Union of Fascists and former tram and bus driver Archibald Watts, was found not guilty of any involvement. (*The Times*)

July 3rd

1760: A bolt of lightning struck the main stores in Portsmouth Dockyard. The stores, containing tar, oil, turpentine and hemp, were totally destroyed. (*Chronicles of Portsmouth* by H. and J. Slight, 1828)

———— •◆• ————

1865: Arthur Mackley, actor and director of films of the silent era, was born in Portsmouth. Mackley appeared in over 150 films, the vast majority of them westerns, with titles like *The Prospector*, *The Daughter of the Sheriff* and *Every Man Has His Price*. In 1912 alone, he appeared in forty-six films, many of which he also directed. Over sixty titles are attributed to him as a director, and three as a writer.

Mackley joined the Essaney company shortly after its formation and was responsible for 'fillers', which did not feature the studio's best-known stars but sometimes made use of real cowboys. Production was tight, with the aim to make 'one western a week', though the actual filming in Los Angeles sometimes only took one day. In a review of *The Prospector*, Mackley was commended for his use of 'a variety of camera positions in both the interior and exterior spaces to give the film a far more elaborate visual style than might be expected'. Mackley died in Los Angeles in 1926. (*Oxford Dictionary of National Biography*; www.filmpreservation.org)

July 4th

1863: George Ford, a boy of unknown age, was charged with scrumping apples from the orchard at the rear of Colonel Tate's house in Grove Road, Southsea. The Court heard that George had been confronted by PC Stevens at 6.30 in the morning in Osborne Road, and was asked what he had hidden under his coat, to which George replied, 'Nothing.'

Under questioning the boy said he lived in Green Row and 'had himself to keep'. Asked by the Bench how he made a living, he replied, 'I go with an ash cart and by what few bones I get I gets my living.' The Bench 'were inclined to deal leniently with the prisoner' and sent him to prison for seven days with hard labour. (*Hampshire Telegraph*)

1968: A crowd of 200,000 people gathered on the seafront and lined the streets of Portsmouth and Southsea to welcome round the world yachtsman Alec Rose at the end of his 28,500 -mile journey. He stepped ashore at 12.33 p.m. and hugged and kissed his wife Dorothy, with whom he ran a greengrocer at No. 38 Osborne Road. During the epic journey he faced a succession of gales, nearly lost a mast in the Antarctic, and was rendered unconscious by fumes when repairing a leaking exhaust. (*Daily Mirror*)

July 5th

1940: In May, Germany had begun its successful invasion of France, the Netherlands and Belgium. On this day it was reported that all beaches along the Hampshire coast were closed to the public, prompted by the imminent danger of enemy invasion. The Luftwaffe carried out incursions and it was realised that the 'phoney war' was over.

There was great activity at Southsea 'denuding the seafront of its civilian interests and tourist trappings. The stores of seaside shops, kiosks and teahouses were removed – sweets, cigarettes, books, beer, minerals, toys, souvenirs, amusement arcade machines and fittings'. The piers, funfair, Rock Gardens, Canoe Lake, miniature golf course and Southsea Common were closed, though some of these measures were relaxed a month later as the moral-boosting spirit of 'business as usual' was encouraged. (City of Portsmouth Records of the Corporation, ed. Gates, Singleton-Gates, Barnett, Blanchard, Windle, Riley; *Evening News, Portsmouth*)

———◆———

1253: In the Patent Rolls, reference was made to a small hospital for lepers that was situated at the eastern end of St Michael's Road. On this day, protection was granted for ten years to 'the Master and brethren of the Hospital of St Mary Magdalene without Portsmouth'. (City of Portsmouth Records of the Corporation ed. Gates, Singleton-Gates, Barnett, Blanchard, Windle, Riley)

July 6th

1886: Southsea GP and aspiring author Dr Arthur Conan Doyle was a regular correspondent on issues of the day, as revealed in the Portsmouth *Evening New*s. A letter expressing opposition to Home Rule in Ireland appeared, in spite of Doyle's support of Liberal opinions on other matters. 'An Irish Parliament would not conduce to the strength or prosperity of [the Empire]', he maintained. (*The Unknown Conan Doyle: letters to the Press*, ed. J. Gibson and R. Lancelyn Green, 1986)

———◆•———

1933: New immigrants Angelo Maria Verecchia and his son Augusto (Tony) opened their famous Guildhall Square ice-cream shop. During the war, Angelo's wife Gemma ran the business while he worked as an interpreter for the RAF. The parlour became the 'in' place to meet, and stars performing at the Guildhall, including singer Dusty Springfield, were among its customers. Another shop was opened in London Road, North End, and the company's ice cream vans were a familiar sight around the city for many years. (*Portsmouth in Archive Photographs* by J. Sadden, 1997; *Evening News*, Portsmouth)

July 7th

1992: Portsmouth Polytechnic was renamed the University of Portsmouth. At the inauguration ceremony held at the Guildhall, a rich property developer, Lord Palumbo, was installed as Chancellor. A Service of Dedication was held at St Thomas's Cathedral and a ball held in Ravelin Park. In the late 1960s, thirty Polytechnics had been set up by the Labour Government to ensure that there was some democratic accountability in the running of higher education (unlike in the universities), and to cope with the burgeoning demand for full-time and sandwich courses.

Locally, in 1969, it was a natural progression for Portsmouth College of Technology to become Portsmouth Polytechnic, and this was a significant step in establishing the city as a major centre of higher education. Between 1966 and 1974, the number of students increased from around 1,700 to 4,300. The expansion continued and' in the late 1980s, Portsmouth was considered one of the largest and best-performing polytechnics in the UK, and was a vibrant part of the local economy. The Complete University Guide 2010 ranks the University of Portsmouth at 89 out of 122. Notable alumni include television presenters Ben Fogle and Kate Edmonson, novelist Shirley Conran, poet Simon Armitage, artist Grayson Perry, comic book artist Frazer Irving, politicians David Chidgey and Ron Davies, and television reporter Rizwan Khan. (*The Times*)

July 8th

1953: The aircraft carrier *Glory* arrived at Portsmouth after sailing 167,500 miles in two and a half years. The ship's company was granted additional leave for their arduous service during the Korean War in which twenty-one of their fellow crewmen lost their lives. (*The Times*)

1892: The poet and author Richard Aldington was born in Portsmouth, the son of a solicitor. He is best known for the novel *Death of a Hero*, published in 1929, his First World War poetry and his biographies. He was ostracised following the publication of his biography of T.E. Lawrence (Lawrence of Arabia) which questioned his sexuality and the veracity of his account of his exploits. (www.imdb.com)

1903: The bronze statue of Queen Victoria was erected in the Guildhall Square, paid for by public subscription. In the 1970s, the statue was relocated to a site directly in front of the Guildhall when the area was enclosed by the Civic Offices. (City of Portsmouth Records of the Corporation, ed. Gates, Singleton-Gates, Barnett, Blanchard, Windle, Riley)

1889: A gang of urchins picked on a homeless man in Stamshaw, dancing around him and calling him 'Jack the Ripper'. The terrified man was eventually rescued by the police and taken to the workhouse. (*Evening News, Portsmouth*)

July 9th

1888: Norman Holbrook was born in Southsea. He was educated at Portsmouth Grammar School. By the time of the outbreak of the First World War, he was Lieutenant-Commander of *B11*, an old and obsolete submarine.

On 13 December 1914, *B11* entered the Dardanelles and, against the current, dived under five rows of mines and torpedoed the Turkish battleship *Mesudiye*. *B11* was attacked but kept submerged for nine hours. In recognition of his bravery, Holbrook became the first submariner to be awarded the Victoria Cross and his was the first naval VC gazetted in the war. (*The Times*)

———— • ◆ • ————

1945: A month before VJ Day, Portsmouth's first pre-fab bungalow was opened by the Lady Mayoress, Mrs Allaway. It was one of fifty-three erected at Northern Parade following a decision by the Council to erect a minimum of 1,400 to start to address the problems of replacing properties lost in the blitz. (City of Portsmouth Records of the Corporation, ed. Gates, Singleton-Gates, Barnett, Blanchard, Windle, Riley; *Yesterday*)

———— • ◆ • ————

1908: The politician Ian Mikardo, the son of a Jewish refugee who escaped from the oppression in Tsarist Russia, was born in Portsmouth. An obituary suggests he had 'that rarest of qualities among professional politicians – integrity'. (*Oxford Dictionary of National Biography*; *The Independent*)

July 10th

1794: Austrian composer and musician Joseph Haydn arrived. It is not known how long he stayed. He was drawn to Portsmouth to view the French vessels that Lord Howe had captured and towed back to Portsmouth Harbour and, while in town, made notes of what he observed.

I inspected the fortifications there, which are in good repair, especially the fortress opposite in Gosport ... I went aboard the French ship-of-the-line called *Le Just*; it has 80 cannon; the English, or rather Lord Howe, captured it. The 18 cannon in the harbour fortress are 36-pounders. The ship is terribly shot to pieces. The great mast, which is 10 feet 5 inches in circumference, was cut off at the very bottom and lay stretched on the ground. A single cannon-ball which passed through the captain's room killed 14 sailors...

The Dockyard, or the place where ships are built, is of enormous size, and has a great many splendid buildings. But I couldn't go there, because I was a foreigner.

(*Portsmouth as Others Have Seen it: 1790-1900* by M. Hoad, 1973)

July 11th

1934: The leader of the British Union of Fascists, Sir Oswald Mosley, outlined what his party stood for, at a Portsmouth Rally. Mosley's extreme right wing ideas were enthusiastically supported by the *Daily Mail* but the previous month, at a large rally at Olympia, black-shirted fascists had brutally beaten up people who disagreed, resulting in bad publicity. At the Portsmouth rally, Mosley announced: 'A new national idea which admitted of no compromise. A new political and economic programme and a new system of government and a new attitude to life.' That 'new attitude to life' was brought home to the people of Portsmouth exactly six years later to the day. (*The Times*)

———— ◆ ————

1940: On a fine summer's evening, twelve Heinkel bombers escorted by twelve Messerschmitt fighters approached Portsmouth. The radar station at Ventnor detected them and Hurricanes crews at Tangmere were alerted. As a result of the encounter, two Heinkels collided and fell into the sea, but the remainder proceeded to attack the city. On this, the first air raid of the war, nineteen people were killed and twenty-six seriously injured. The Rudmore gas holder, the Blue Anchor pub, several houses and part of Drayton School were destroyed. (City of Portsmouth Records of the Corporation, ed. Gates, Singleton-Gates, Barnett, Blanchard, Windle, Riley)

July 12th

1811: Tryce Okey, a seaman of His Majesty's ship *Cyane*, having been accused of neglecting to properly clean a cannon, was ordered to strip in front of the crew to receive a flogging. He refused and his clothes were cut from him but, as he was about to be tied up, he made a dash to jump overboard. Captain Collier stepped out to prevent his escape. At the subsequent court martial at Portsmouth, Okey was charged with striking Captain Collier. Rear Admiral Hargood had no hesitation in sentencing him to death.

Four months later the notorious yellow flag was hoisted above Portsmouth Harbour, telling the inhabitants that a seaman was to be run up the yard-arm. It was the practice to hang a weight from the victim's feet to prevent him from kicking as he was strangled to death.

At 11 a.m., Okey was led up to the deck of the *Royal William* accompanied by the chaplain, his path lined by marines. The sentence was read out by the Captain in charge of the execution. Then he pulled a letter from his pocket from the Prince Regent who, having received an appeal from Captain Collier, agreed to commute the sentence to transportation for life. (*Caledonian Mercury*; *Hampshire Telegraph*)

July 13th

1377: In the fourteenth century, the French frequently attacked Portsmouth. One such attack took place when the town was burnt but the French were 'driven back with great slaughter'. (*History of Portsmouth* by W. Gates, 1900)

1933: A letter appeared in the *Evening News* defending the Portsea mudlarks, claiming that many had gone on to be valued members of the services. The behaviour of adult sunbathers at Southsea, the writer maintained, was far worse. (*Evening News, Portsmouth*)

1801: A letter appeared in the *Portsmouth Telegraph* drawing readers' attention to the 'truly whimsical, if not ridiculous' philosophy and practices of the Gentoo (Hindu) people of the East Indies. In view of the high price of meat, the writer suggests that the bizarre Gentoo practice of 'living entirely upon fruit and vegetables' be considered. The editor jokingly cut short the letter because of 'our attachment to the Landed Interests of the Country'. The consequences would be 'the turning of butchers into skeletons, the farmers into scarecrows … and landholders into will-o'-the-wisps, seeking over hill, dale, wood and lawn for their former incomes'. (*Portsmouth Telegraph* [later *Hampshire Telegraph*])

July 14th

1966: Sarah Robinson House, a twenty-one-storey block of flats, was opened for viewing in Queen Street. It was named after the Christian lady who, in 1874, founded the Soldiers' Institute in the High Street and devoted her life to the comfort and care of servicemen (*see* June 19th). (*Portsmouth: in Defence of the Realm* by J. Sadden, 2001; City of Portsmouth Records of the Corporation, ed. Gates, Singleton-Gates, Barnett, Blanchard, Windle, Riley)

———◆———

1749: The *Chesterfield*, a man-o'-war, was stationed off the African coast when growing unrest over prize money provoked a mutiny led by Lieutenant Samuel Couchman. Together with a fellow lieutenant, John Morgan, and some of the crew, they managed to seize the ship and carry her to sea while the captain was on shore. Some of the crew fought back and the ship was retaken from the mutineers thirty hours later. The Chesterfield was eventually brought to Portsmouth and a court martial held. On this day, Couchman and Morgan were shot to death. Six crewmen were hanged. (*Annals of Portsmouth* by W.H. Saunders, 1880)

———◆———

1829: Henry Bird, chess player, was born at Portsea. He wrote extensively on the game and gave his name to Bird's Opening and Bird's Defence. (*Oxford Dictionary of National Biography*)

July 15th

1919: The first three Portsmouth policewomen were appointed, selected from fifty applicants. They were issued with wide-brimmed helmets and tall lace-up boots. However, when the force was reduced in strength from 308 to 290 in 1922, the women constables were asked to resign. (*A History of the Police of Portsmouth* by J. Cramer, 1964)

———•◆•———

1666: This was a plague year. In this letter from Thomas Middleton, Navy commissioner at the Dockyard to Samuel Pepys, Secretary at the Admiralty, Middleton speaks of the situation in Portsmouth:

> The Dockyard continues in good health but the town very bad... The graves are left so shallow that they are commonly covered with crows and ravens, except when the grave digger is at work. Has told the Mayor of this, but he refuses to interfere. It is like the rest of his actions.

Earlier that year, Thomas Middleton had reported that the plague was not spreading in the town, and that a visiting physician judged that 'the air of Portsmouth is naturally so pernicious to man, that the man whose body is able to be supported in this air is plague free, and that no contagious distemper is apt to seize on him'. (Extracts from 'Records in the possession of the Municipal Corporation of the Borough of Portsmouth' by Robert East, 1891)

July 16th

1804: The French planned to invade Britain. On this day 'the wind being favourable and the atmosphere light and clear, the action between the British Squadron with the French gunboats at Havre was distinctly heard at Portsmouth'. (*History of Portsmouth* by W. Gates, 1900)

2001: Portsmouth MP Syd Rapson, who stated that he was 'Old Labour', vowed that he would not blindly back 'New Labour' and that he would be a 'thorn in its side'. In the event, he is reported to have had a low profile around Parliament, rarely contributed to debates and was totally loyal to the Blair project. Rapson also hit the headlines in 2001 when, along with other politicians and celebrities, he was duped into making a bizarre appearance on the controversial spoof television series, *Brass Eye*. (*The News*, Portsmouth)

1967: Alec Rose set off in a 36ft ketch, the *Lively Lady*, which he had bought four years earlier for £250. An attempt to sail around the world the previous year ended when his boat was hit by a freighter in the Channel. Rose shunned sponsorship and paid for everything himself on a very small budget. He considered the voyage a private affair, designed to satisfy his own ambition and provide a chance to visit his son's family in Melbourne (*see* July 4th). (*Oxford Dictionary of National Biography*)

July 17th

1913: The Great Suffragist March from Portsmouth to London set off from the Town Hall Square. One campaigner for the vote, Harriet Blessley, kept a diary, in which she describes how 'the band played a march to suit masculine strides' and that she had a hard job to keep up. While there was 'a cheer or two', a tomato was thrown which hit her hat. When the procession reached Cosham, the inhabitants were 'excited and displeased', shouting, 'Go home and mend your stockings' and 'You'll drop dead before you reach London'.

The first militant act locally in support of women's suffrage was actually carried out by a man – Blessley's brother Frederick was charged with smashing a pane of glass worth 12*s* (60p) at the Town Hall. When asked by the bench to explain his actions, he said, 'The warfare and militancy that women are going in for is very largely a question of breaking windows. It is rather a piffling, idiotic way of going about it, I admit.' (Votes for Women: the Women's Fight in Portsmouth by S. Peacock, 1983)

———•◆•———

1937: The Savoy Cinema (later the ABC) opened on the corner of Fitzherbert Street. (*The Savoy* by M. Rodgers, 1987)

July 18th

1842: A star attraction at the Free Mart Fair, held in the High street, was announced. Mr Wombwell's Royal National Menagerie was not, as the billing suggested, a collection of untamed kings, queens and princes, but 'an extraordinary and beautiful group of performing lions, tigers and leopards'. The biggest draw, though, was 'an immense moving castle in which is conveyed the enormous Siamese Elephant'. Mr Wombwell, however, had some difficulty getting the elephant to the fair because it was 'of too ponderous a size to pass through the gates of Portsmouth'. (*Hampshire Telegraph*)

1933: Mike Barnard, who has the distinction of having played both for Pompey (1953-59) and for Hampshire Cricket Club (1952-66), was born in Portsmouth. His sporting talent was nurtured at Portsmouth Grammar School. (*Mike Barnard: Good at Games* by D. Allen, 2010)

1871: John MacTavish, shipwright and educationalist, was born in Scotland. In 1906 he moved to Portsmouth to work in the Dockyard and soon became the first Labour member of Portsmouth City Council. His opposition to the First World War in 1914 cost him his seat. He became chief of the national Workers' Education Association after delivering an electrifying speech: 'I claim for my class all the best that Oxford has to give.' (*Oxford Dictionary of National Biography*)

July 19th

1749: Second-Lieutenant Baker Phillips was aboard the ship Anglesey when there was engagement with a French privateer. Anglesey's Captain and Master were killed, sixty crewmen lay dead or badly wounded and the ship was taking on water. Phillips decided the situation was hopeless and surrendered. At the court martial, mercy was recommended but ignored. On this date Phillips was 'shot by a platoon of musketeers on the forecastle' of the *Princess Royal* at Spithead. (*The Naval Heritage of Portsmouth* by J. Winton, 1989)

———— • ◆ • ————

1545: The French fleet appeared at Spithead and the *Mary Rose* sank. This record of the disaster was written in 1587:

> ...the navie of the Englishmen made out, and purposed to sette on the Frenchmen, but in setting forward through so much follie, one of the Kynges shippes called the *Mary Rose*, was drowned in the middest of the haven by reason that she was over laden with ordinance, and had the portes lette open, whiche were very lowe, and the greate artillerie unbreeched, so that when the ship could tourne, the water entred, and suddainely shee sunke.

(*The Holinshed texts*, 1587)

———— • ◆ • ————

1972: The television presenter Amanda Lamb, most famous for Channel 4's *A Place in the Sun* and the Scottish Widows advertisements, was born. (*The News*, Portsmouth)

July 20th

1895: Samuel Steward was a flagman for the Corporation steamroller. It was his job to walk ahead of the steam roller, warning of its approach. One summer's day in 1895, maintenance work was being carried out in Marylebone Road when two small girls suddenly ran out in front of the rollers. Steward pushed them off the road to the safety of the pavement. At the same time, a nearby horse, which was drawing a watercart, was alarmed, distracting Steward. He was drawn under the rollers and crushed to death.

At the inquest, reported on this day, it was established that, according to regulations, the flagman should have been twenty yards in front of the steamroller. It was also clear that the driver was not aware of this regulation, or that of the maximum speed. The coroner recommended that workmen should be made aware of the regulations and that a guard be fitted in front of the rollers. (*Hampshire Telegraph*)

———•◆•———

1934: The Co-op department store in Fratton Road burnt down, bringing national criticism, the fire having not been stopped from spreading because of 'the insane desire of the Corporation to economise at the expense of the fire brigade' resulting in 'criminal undermanning'. (*Go to Blazes* by P. Smith, 1986)

July 21st

1866: Denis Flood, a soldier of the garrison, was charged with 'wilfully and wantonly knocking at the door of Mr Henry Moncreaff at the upmarket address of No. 9 Wish Lane, Southsea (now Elm Grove). At about 1.45 in the morning, Mr Moncreaff was awoken by a loud knocking. Upon opening his window and asking the soldier what he wanted, he received the reply: 'Mary Jane'. Moncreaff told Flood that no such woman lived there.

The defendant explained that he 'kept company' with a young woman who told him to call at No. 9 Wish Lane. The Clerk suggested that Flood might want to call Mary Jane as a witness, but, clearly embarrassed, he declined. It emerged that he had called at the same address a fortnight earlier at four o'clock in the morning, asking for her. Flood was fined 10*s* and costs, or seven days' imprisonment.

Mr Moncreaff worked as the Inspector of Weights and Measures for Portsmouth, a post requiring a sense of balance and proportion. (*Hampshire Telegraph*)

July 22nd

1731: John Davis was one of eight young men ordered for execution at Newgate. Born in Portsmouth, Davis and an accomplice enjoyed a career of several years as highwaymen in the London area. Davis was indicted for assaulting a man on the King's Highway near Islington and stealing his coat, waistcoat, breeches, hat, wig, sword and ninepence and a halfpenny. He was also convicted of murdering Thomas Tickford, who, Davis maintained, had been stabbed by his partner.

Just before his execution, Davis was asked how many robberies he had committed. He replied that he did not keep a tally, but:

> they were very numerous, he having had no Way of Living for some Years past, but by Thieving or Robbing in the Streets and Highway. His Conscience often checq'd him, and when his Friends told him, what would be the End of his loose idle Life, he made Vows of an Amendment, but never had the Virtue or Grace to perform them.

One robbery that Davis confessed to had been attributed to a Francis Hackabout, who appears to have been wrongly hanged for the offence. (Account of the Ordinary of Newgate, 1731)

———— • ◆ • ————

1953: Rock musician Brian Howe, former lead singer of Bad Company, was born in Portsmouth. (www.brianhowe.com)

July 23rd

1899: A rainstorm 'of unparalleled magnitude' lasted an hour, dropping 347 million gallons of water on the Borough of Portsmouth. Everywhere, streets were flooded; Old Portsmouth and Southsea Common were completely under water, Commercial Road was 'like a river' and boys were swimming in Stanhope Road. 'The air was so charged with electricity that several fire alarms were set going, the lightning was most terrifying, and several houses were struck and damaged'. It was also reported that, at the Town Hall, the water broke through the roof and fell 'in tons' all over the building causing great damage. Remarkably, no one was reported to have been injured as a result of the deluge and its aftermath. The extraordinary event prompted the *Evening News* to publish a special edition that evening. (*Hampshire Advertiser*; City of Portsmouth Records of the Corporation, ed. Gates, Singleton-Gates, Barnett, Blanchard, Windle, Riley)

———— • • ————

1948: The deputy leader of the Conservative Party and future Prime Minister, Anthony Eden, visited the King's Theatre in Southsea to award prizes at Portsmouth Grammar School's annual Speech Day. (*The Portmuthian*)

July 24th

1935: Portsmouth's open air swimming pool at Hilsea Lido was opened by Lord Mayor Frank Privett. The pool took nine months to build and boasted a 10m-high diving tower, 'the only one in Hampshire'. The Lido complex included a café with dance floor, a paddling pool, facilities for sunbathing, changing facilities for 768 adults and 189 children, and room for 1,000 spectators. Floodlighting was installed for night bathing and a public address system enabling 'gramophone recordings to be radiated'. (*The News*, Portsmouth)

1833: Sir Francis Wogan Festing, after whom Festing Road and Festing Grove are named, was born in Somerset. Festing was a highly decorated Royal Marine Artillery Officer and hero of the third Anglo-Ashanti war, amongst others.

In April 1886 he took part in the Easter Volunteer Review, commanding 1,000 men of the garrison to 'dispute the possession of Portsdown Hill'. After 'an interesting fight' of nearly two hours, the Volunteers were beaten. Five months later, Festing was made Colonel-Commandant of the Royal Marine Artillery, but died a few weeks later. His funeral procession travelled through a mile of local streets lined with local people before the burial with full military honours at Highland Cemetery. (*Oxford Dictionary of National Biography*; *Hampshire Telegraph*)

July 25th

1808: Mr Belam, a chemist and druggist trading in the High Street, offered a cure for a 'dreadful evil, which contaminates our enjoyments'. The cure boasted none of the 'inconvenience and dangers of mercury'. Mr Belam was offering 'vegetable syrup' which was guaranteed to clear things up. (*Hampshire Telegraph*)

———◆———

1866: It was reported that labourers William Harris and George Williams were up before the Police Court for 'conveying a quantity of night soil through Middle Street at twenty minutes to twelve at night'. The defendants, it was explained by the Clerk, would be entitled to remove the soil after midnight, but not twenty minutes earlier. Harris and Williams, in their defence, explained that they had worked in the town for several years and had never been complained of before. The Clerk replied jubilantly, 'Ah, this is under a new law.' The defendants were fined 6s each. (*Hampshire Telegraph*)

July 26th

1879: South Parade Pier was formally opened, the last main girder being laid, probably not personally, by Her Serene Highness Princess Edward of Saxe-Weimar. The pier was not finished for another six weeks, when it offered visitors 'commanding marine views of unrivalled beauty'. The pier was partially destroyed by fire in July 1904 and rebuilt on a grander scale. (*Evening News, Portsmouth*)

———— • ◆ • ————

1926: The Municipal Golf Course at Great Salterns was opened, following conversion from marshland and swamp. Previously, the only golf course available in Portsmouth was the 6-acre miniature course at East Southsea, which had been designed by the golf professional James Braid. (*Charpentier's Guide to Portsmouth & Southsea*, *c.* 1924; City of Portsmouth Records of the Corporation, ed. Gates, Singleton-Gates, Barnett, Blanchard, Windle, Riley)

———— • ◆ • ————

1861: After the Government had commandeered Portsdown Hill for military use, the Portsdown Fair was held for what was intended to be the last time. Local people were unhappy about this and, the following year, in defiance of the Act of Parliament, resuscitated it in Cosham Park; 7,000 people attended. It was alleged that 'the scenes witnessed were not creditable, and there was much drunkenness'. (City of Portsmouth Records of the Corporation, ed. Gates, Singleton-Gates, Barnett, Blanchard, Windle, Riley)

July 27th

1914: One week before the outbreak of the First World War, Lieutenant-Commander Cecil Talbot, Commanding Officer of the submarine *E6*, was in Portsmouth Harbour. He wrote in his diary:

> Summer leave was to have started in the evening, but in the afternoon it was cancelled owing to the strained international situation. I tried to get torpedoes and warheads into the boats, but no one in authority seemed to think matters were serious. Went ashore at 4.

(*The War at Sea 1914-18* by J. Thompson, 1999)

Dr Conan Doyle wrote to the *County Times* from his Southsea surgery defending the practice of compulsory vaccination against smallpox, prompted by a letter of opposition by a Colonel Wintle. The doctor's defence was summed up in the question, 'Would it be immoral to give Colonel Wintle a push in order to save him from being run over by a locomotive?' (*The Unknown Conan Doyle: letters to the Press*, ed. J. Gibson and R. Lancelyn Green, 1986)

———◆———

1963: The last trolleybus returned to Eastney Depot on the 17/18 route. A wreath was hung over the offside driving mirror commemorating twenty-nine years of trolleybus operation. (*Fares Please* by E. Watts, 1987)

July 28th

1887: The American artist James McNeill Whistler completed a series of sketches which included one of local children on the beach, and ships in the Solent taking part in the Golden Jubilee Review. (*A Portsmouth Canvas: the Art of the City and the Sea* by N. Surry, 2008)

1864: It was revealed that a plainclothes policeman had been assigned to patrol the street to eradicate the 'begging nuisance'. A persistent offender, Mary Bird, appeared on this day and was sentenced to twenty-one days' imprisonment with hard labour for 'soliciting alms' in St Thomas's Street. Her attempts to gain sympathy from the magistrates were, according to the report, 'extremely ludicrous'.

The police operation had also netted two other unfortunates. One, who 'behaved in an impudent manner' to the magistrates, was sentenced to seven days' imprisonment, while 'a miserable looking man', a 'tramping cripple', who was charged with begging in Commercial Road, promised to get out of town, thereby managing to avoid punishment. (*Hampshire Telegraph*)

1970: The Council's application for exemption on the legal requirement to 'provide adequate accommodation for gipsies' was granted. (City of Portsmouth Records of the Corporation, ed. Gates, Singleton-Gates, Barnett, Blanchard, Windle, Riley)

July 29th

1900: John Lucas, a gunner in the locally based Royal Artillery, together with his friends Driver Hill and Gunner Clark, went for a bathe in Hilsea moat. At the subsequent coroner's court, it was surmised that Lucas had walked into the water and disappeared without a sound, his friends being oblivious to his disappearance. Seven men who tried to retrieve his body had difficulty extricating themselves from mud that came up to their middles. A verdict of accidental death was returned on this, the last of many drownings to have occurred with tragic regularity throughout the nineteenth century.

In 1895, a seventy-nine-year-old inmate of the workhouse was found drowned there. His son insisted he had been in his right senses, but had been housed in the 'imbecile ward' of the workhouse. The son was disbelieved and a verdict of suicide while of 'unsound mind' was returned. In 1894, George Berry, said to be 'addicted to drink' and 'in the habit of backing horses', and who was heavily in debt, was found with pawn tickets in his pockets and one halfpenny coin. (*Hampshire Telegraph*)

July 30th

1883: Gladys White was born in North End. Her father, Mr A.W. White, a prominent local businessman, named Gladys Avenue after his new-born daughter. She was destined, however, to make a name for herself. After training as a surgery nurse, she volunteered for service during the First World War and was sent to France. She recorded her experiences in her diary:

December 1914: Very busy admitting each night, all bad cases. This week has been awful, it's not surgery but butchery.

January 1915: First experience of an air-raid, bombing increased and shelling was heavy. It's still pouring with rain – those poor souls in the trenches.

September 1916: A horrid week of amputations ... barges keep coming with the badly wounded – difficult to keep pace.

May 1918: It's awfully trying, getting to know RAF boys and then getting them smashed up ... You feel each time you say goodbye to one that you will probably not see him again. It's a dreadful life for such young boys.

('Gladys Avenue recalls First War heroine' by C. Salter, *Hampshire Magazine, 1980*)

July 31st

1869: Thomas Hague, a private in the 1st West Riding Regiment (33rd Regiment) was described as 'a good soldier'. He had served in India and was 'the first man wounded' by lance-wielding Abyssinians at the storming of Magdala. The British soldiers had just been issued with new breech-loading rifles that fired ten rounds a minute, resulting in a massacre of 700 of the enemy against two British dead. As his fortress was being seized, the Abyssinian Emperor shot himself.

A year later, while stationed at Cambridge Barracks (now part of Portsmouth Grammar School), Hague fell in love with Rose Rickman. Unfortunately, she was a prostitute who worked in a brothel at the unlikely address of Nobbs Lane. Rickman was also courting a Lance-Corporal George Green of the same regiment. Hague had been seeing her for several months and was smitten. He accused her of being unfaithful and tried to dissuade her from seeing others. But, while Rickman was with Green, Hague shot himself in the head and bled to death. At the inquest, the 'good soldier' was also described as being 'a peculiarly sensitive man'. The jury returned a verdict of 'suicide whilst in a state of temporary insanity'. (*Hampshire Telegraph*)

August 1st

1868: A coroner's inquest took place on two prisoners who had died within a day of each other while imprisoned in the Convict Prison at Portsea. William Kerrigan and William Brooks had been perfectly fit when they started their sentences two and four years earlier, but their health appears to have been broken by the prison regime. (*Hampshire Telegraph*)

———•◆•———

1861: HMS *Warrior*, the fastest and most heavily-armed and armoured warship the world had ever seen, was commissioned. She was designed by Portsea-born naval architect and engineer, Thomas Lloyd, with Isaac Watts.

Born in 1803, Lloyd was educated at Portsmouth Grammar School. He served his apprenticeship as a shipwright and worked at Portsmouth Dockyard, taking charge of Marc Brunel's blockmaking machinery before moving to the Woolwich steam factory, becoming the Navy's chief engineer in 1842. This period spanned the Navy's industrial revolution, seeing the introduction of steam fighting ships, iron hulls, and the screw propeller. (*Oxford Dictionary of National Biography*)

———•◆•———

1946: The actor David Calder was born in Portsmouth. His television credits include *Widows*, *Star Cops*, *Bramwell*, *Between the Lines*, *Spooks*, *Waking the Dead* and *Midsomer Murders*. (www.imdb.com)

August 2nd

1823: William Cobbett, the radical journalist and farmer, visited the area, he reflected:

> It is impossible that there can be, anywhere, a better corn country than this (on the south side of Portsdown Hill) … Portsdown Hill is very much in the shape of an oblong tin cover to a dish … I observed that it was a rule that if no wheat were cut under Portsdown Hill on the hill fair-day, 26 July, the harvest must be generally backward … I came on to Wimmering…and there I saw, at a good distance from me, five men reaping in a field of wheat of about 40 acres … Here the first sheaf is cut that is cut in England: that the reader may depend upon …

The only mention made of Portsmouth is that it was a good source of manure. (*Rural Rides* by W. Cobbett, 1936)

———•◆•———

1842: At the Portsmouth Regatta, huge crowds cheered a team of four women rowers from Plymouth who took on a team of local male rowers. The course ran from Point, up harbour, around the *Royal George* yacht, then back to Point. The women won 'to the astonishment and delight of all', and it was remarked upon that one of the women was the mother of ten children. (*The Era*)

August 3rd

2000: A mob went on the rampage in Paulsgrove, hurling stones and bottles at a house, following the naming of a paedophile by the *News of the World*. Cars outside the house were attacked and one was overturned and set on fire. A police sergeant had his nose broken and local council rent offices were also attacked. More than fifty police officers, ambulance crews and the fire service were involved.

Two further riots took place over the next few days, leading to more violence and damage. Police with riot shields used CS spray to restore order. Nationally, at least four innocent men were reported to have been 'named and shamed' by the *News of the World*.

In his diary, author and playwright Alan Bennett wrote of the events:

Appalling scenes on the Portsmouth housing estate which is conducting a witch hunt against suspected paedophiles and the nation is treated to the spectacle of a tattooed mother with a fag dangling from lips with a baby in her arms proclaiming how concerned she is for her kiddies.

(*Untold Stories* by A. Bennett, 2006; *Daily Mail*; *Daily Mirror*; *The Guardian*)

August 4th

1800: John Reilly Beard, the radical and militant Unitarian minister and educationalist, was born on this day in Charlotte Row, Landport in 1800. He argued increasingly that most of the ills of society flowed from a lack of education, and published a number of popular educational journals and dictionaries which made his name widely known. (*Oxford Dictionary of National Biography*)

———◆———

1960: HMS *Vanguard* – the biggest warship in operation at the time – was being towed out of Portsmouth Harbour for a Scottish breaker's yard when she ran aground at Portsmouth Point. Her great bows towered over the Still & West pub and other buildings in Old Portsmouth. She was eventually pulled off by five Dockyard tugs and exited the harbour to the cheers of crowds that had amassed on the seafront. Scenes for the film *Sink the Bismarck* were filmed on board the ship when she had been part of the reserve fleet, moored in the upper reaches of Portsmouth Harbour. (*The Times*)

———◆———

1973: Cumberland House opened its door to excited visitors keen to peer at 'a small quantity of moon dust' which had been collected by the Apollo astronauts and 'presented to the Nation by President Nixon'. (Portsmouth City Museum programme, 1973)

August 5th

1872: On this, the first ever official summer Bank Holiday, fêtes were held in a meadow in North End and in the People's Park, which 'would have been successful but for the weather'. (*Hampshire Telegraph*)

———— • ◆ • ————

1899: A review of the fleet was held in Portsmouth in honour of the new German Emperor and King of Prussia, Wilhelm II. Proceedings had to be postponed for a day because of a gale. A tiny part of the press coverage mentioned the deaths of two seamen: a British sailor fell overboard HMS *Aurora* and a German sailor fell to the deck from the rigging of the ship the *Kaiser*. (*Pall Mall Gazette*; *Hampshire Telegraph*)

———— • ◆ • ————

1896: What is believed to be the first film to be shown in Portsmouth was screened at Victoria Hall (on the site of the University's Mercantile House). The show included *The Prince of Wales' Horse Winning the Derby*. (*The Cinemas of Portsmouth* by J. Barker, R. Brown, W. Greer, 2009)

———— • ◆ • ————

1776: There was a gunpowder explosion on board the *Marlborough* in Portsmouth Harbour in which twelve men, three women and three children were killed. A gunner was found guilty of carelessness and sentenced to one year's imprisonment. (*History of Portsmouth* by W. Gates, 1900)

August 6th

1940: Cecil Fletcher loosened the rear door of a parachute mine. It had been retrieved from a field in Kent and delivered to HMS *Vernon* Mining Department (now the site of Gunwharf Quays):

> The suction of the rubber jointing-band between it and the main body yielded a bit. A sudden whirring sound. A blinding flash. A roar. Then blank. Hodges and Forest looked up quickly to see the roof blown out of the mining-shed. [Commander Sayer's] window shook. He thought it was a bomb in the city. Lieutenant Hight was with him. Both looked out of the windows. A sailor rushed in. 'There's been an explosion, sir.' An ambulance moved across to the shed. [Commander Sayer] and Hight ran over.
>
> An incredible sight. Blackened men, brutally burned, were being helped out by the south door … The shed was a shambles … The sky gaping through the roof. Glass – and blood. A contorted figure flung into a corner. A sailor collecting charred remains … putting them on a trolley. A leg. Mr [Reginald] Cook, commissioned gunner, was dying before their eyes. No one could save him. Little was left of Fletcher.

(*Service Most Silent* by J. Turner, 1955)

August 7th

1947: 'Laurel and Hardy are coming!' The *Portsmouth Evening News* headline welcomed the 'firm favourites of the film-going public who had made no fewer than 169 pictures during the last 20 years'. Stan and Ollie were the guest stars in a week-long stint at the King's Theatre in 1947, presented by theatrical impresario Bernard Delfont.

The comedy duo had arrived at Southampton Docks on the *Queen Elizabeth* and quickly began a gruelling tour, playing up to thirteen shows a week. Suffering from ill-health, their declining years were spent making three tours of Britain playing out sketches for their adoring public. Appearing alongside them on the bill at Southsea was a dog act and a trick unicyclist. (*Evening News, Portsmouth*)

1842: The eighty-nine-year-old landlord of the Three Pigeons Tavern near Union Gate, Mr Thomas Williams, was reported to have walked 5 miles to the annual Portsdown Fair for the eightieth consecutive time. He was said to be in good health 'with a rose-like bloom on his aged cheek'. Mr Williams was the oldest licensed victualler in the Borough and had been landlord of the Three Pigeons since 1798. (*Hampshire Telegraph*)

August 8th

1914: Max Greenbaum, a naturalised Russian who ran a bakery at No. 73 Arundel Street, found that his shop was surrounded by a crowd of hostile people. His window was broken and a local woman, Maria White, was subsequently charged with criminal damage. At the Police Court, Mr Greenbaum explained that things had been quiet since the attack by the mob, who had assumed he was a German spy, and he had no wish to press the charge. (*Hampshire Telegraph*)

———— • ◆ • ————

1874: The Mayor read the Riot Act and sent troops armed with live ammunition to disperse between 3-4,000 people from Southsea Common. They had gathered there in defence of the right of free access to the Common for ordinary people, and for the right of access along Southsea beach. These rights were threatened by the commercial interests of the Pier Company.

In a confrontation that lasted four days, many people were badly beaten by police. Staves were issued by the police to their supporters and passers-by and bystanders were attacked with equal brutality as those who were trying to keep the Common open. Fortunately, no shots were fired and the demonstrators achieved their aims. (*The Battle of Southsea* by J. Field, 1981)

August 9th

1890: The new Portsmouth Town Hall was opened amid much civic celebration and ceremony by the Prince of Wales, four years after the foundation stone had been laid. When the foundations were being dug, out a decapitated skeleton with the head lying beside it was found alongside some other human bones. As the small roots of ancient trees were found entwined around them, it was concluded that they had been interred many years earlier.

The Town Hall cost £137,098 and two lives to build. In July 1888, Thomas Vesey, aged nineteen, a bricklayer's labourer, had been one of three men supplying bricks to a bricklayer on a platform with no railings. He was passing a keystone to an arch when he overbalanced and plunged to his death. The jury recorded a verdict of 'accidental death' and that there was 'no negligence attaching to anyone'.

In September of the same year, William Loughlin, aged thirty, also a bricklayer's labourer, was working on a platform when a block of Portland stone weighing a quarter of a ton fell through it. The jury recorded a verdict of 'accidental death' but helpfully pointed out that 'considering the nature of the work carried out at such a height ... every possible care should be taken in future'. (*Hampshire Telegraph*)

August 10th

1848: A promenade was opened at Southsea during the Royal Portsmouth Regatta, which was attended by Queen Victoria. It was named 'Clarence Esplanade' after Lord Frederick Fitzclarence who was instrumental in getting it built, though the work was carried out by anonymous convicts. (City of Portsmouth Records of the Corporation, ed. Gates, Singleton-Gates, Barnett, Blanchard, Windle, Riley)

———•◆•———

1962: Singer-songwriter Julia Fordham was born prematurely in the front room of the family home in Portsmouth. (www.juliafordham.com)

———•◆•———

1840: Following a campaign by the Royal Society for the Prevention of Cruelty to Animals, a bye-law was enacted banning 'the use of dogs to draw or assist in drawing carts' in the borough. (*Hampshire Telegraph*)

———•◆•———

1865: Jane Austen's brother Admiral Sir Francis Austen died at Portsdown Lodge. He attended the Royal Naval Academy in Portsmouth at the age of twelve, and had an illustrious naval career. He was believed to be the model for William Price in *Mansfield Park*. (*Hampshire Telegraph*; *Oxford Dictionary of National Biography*)

August 11th

1954: 'Joe' David Jackson, musician and singer-songwriter, was born in Burton-on-Trent, but moved to Portsmouth at the age of one. He grew up in Paulsgrove and learned to play the violin but then persuaded his father to install a piano in their cramped council home. He attended the City of Portsmouth Boys' School but the family moved to Bridgemary when he was fifteen.

He won a scholarship to the Royal Academy of Music, travelling to London to study. Jackson acquired the name Joe at around this time due to a resemblance to the *Joe 90* puppet character. Locally, he played in the band Edward Bear, which changed its name to Arms and Legs. Disillusioned with the band's lack of success, Jackson did cabaret, including piano at the Playboy Club at Southsea. His first ever gig as the frontman took place at the Cumberland Tavern with a new band. Jackson recorded some demos at Telecoms recording studio in London Road, North End, and took it around the record companies. Rejected by Virgin, Stiff and United Artists, he was finally signed to A&M. The album was *Look sharp!* and his first hit *Is she really going out with him?* charted on both sides of the Atlantic. (*Twenty Missed Beats* by A. Rollinson, 1996)

August 12th

1712: Jonas Hanway was born in Portsmouth, the second of Thomas Hanway's four children, who was the Navy's agent victualler in Portsmouth. At the age of sixteen, Jonas was sent to London and apprenticed as a merchant in Lisbon before accepting a partnership in St Petersburg. He inherited a fortune and began a career of philanthropy, co-founding the Marine Society and the Magdalen and Foundling Hospitals. He also took up many other diverse causes, including the paving and lighting of streets, the plight of boy chimney sweeps, opposing the naturalisation of Jews and 'entertaining reformed prostitutes in his home'. Having 'impaired his fortune by his liberality', he was appointed a Navy victualling commissioner, which involved supervision of the bakery and mills, and led to a campaign to improve the quality of bread and diet.

In 1766 his campaign to protect workhouse and parish children led to an act being passed that required parishes to remove infants from London to the care of rural nurses, saving an estimated 1,500 lives a year. For many, however, Hanway will be remembered for being the first person in England to use an umbrella. (*Oxford Dictionary of National Biography*; *History of Portsmouth* by W. Gates, 1900)

August 13th

1946: H.G. Wells died, but his autobiography reveals that when he was a draper's apprentice (working at Southsea Drapery Emporium in King's Road between 1881 and 1883, he was so unhappy that he entertained thoughts of ending his life:

> Among other things, during that dismal two years, I had thought out some very fundamental problems of conduct. I had really weighed the possibilities of the life before me, and when I used suicide as a threat to shake my mother's opposition to my liberation, it was after a considerable amount of meditation along the Southsea sea front and Portsmouth Hard. I did not think suicide an honourable resort, but it seemed to me a lesser evil than acquiescence. The cool embrace of swift-running, black deep water on a warm summer night couldn't be as bad as crib [job] hunting or wandering about the streets with the last of one's courage gone ... Why should I torture myself to earn a living, any old living? If the living isn't good enough, why live? Not perhaps with that much virility did I think at the time, but in that fashion, I was beginning to think.

(*Experiment in Autobiography* by H.G. Wells, 1969)

August 14th

1958: It was reported that a husband jumped up on the stage at the Miss Southsea beauty competition, held in front of an audience of 1,700 at South Parade Pier, and took his wife out of the line-up. He later explained that he withdrew her because he felt jealous. (*Evening News, Portsmouth*)

———•◆•———

1836: Writer and historian Sir Walter Besant was born at No. 3 St George's Square, Portsea, the fifth child of William Besant, a local wine merchant, and his wife, Sarah Ediss. Like Dickens, Besant attempted to draw attention to the plight of the poor, though Besant's novels have not endured. He also wrote popular histories of London, was a champion for writers' rights and was knighted for his charitable works. He died in London in 1901, shortly after completing an introduction to William Gates' *History of Portsmouth*. (*Oxford Dictionary of National Biography*)

———•◆•———

1939: Sid Greeman began his career as a barber in Somers Road. By the 1960s, 'Sid's' was established at the junction of Locksway Road and Milton Road, where a short back and sides with obligatory Brylcreem cost 1*s* and 6*d*. Sid's career lasted over fifty years. (*The News, Portsmouth*)

August 15th

1823: The last crossroad burial took place by the Air Balloon pub at the junction with Kingston Crescent. It was the custom to refuse a Christian burial to those who had committed suicide and bury them at crossroads. (*The Portsmouth That Has Passed* by W. Gates, 1987)

1900: Portsmouth Town Council passed a bye-law prohibiting street betting. (*Hampshire Telegraph*)

1967: Following torrential rain, two aeroplanes crashed at Portsmouth Airport. After their undercarriages failed, the first slithered across the wet grass runway on its belly into a grass bank, while the other slid across the Eastern Road. Miraculously, no one was killed in the accidents.

Channel Airways re-routed their services to Eastleigh (now Southampton) Airport, and Portsmouth Airport slowly declined, officially closing on 31 December 1973. The last person to use the airport as a passenger was the leader of the Labour Party, Harold Wilson, who arrived by helicopter on a visit to the city on 16 February 1974 to be met by popular local MP Frank Judd in the run-up to the first of two General Elections that year. The Conservatives crashed on both occasions. (*Portsmouth Airport* by A. Triggs, 2002; City of Portsmouth Records of the Corporation, ed. Gates, Singleton-Gates, Barnett, Blanchard, Windle, Riley)

August 16th

1824: The Duke of Wellington, the hero of the Battle of Waterloo, arrived in Portsmouth on what he hoped would be an incognito visit. He proceeded to the Dockyard to admire the innovative block machinery. However, when he visited HMS *Victory* in Portsmouth Harbour he was recognised and given a 19-gun salute which very effectively blew his cover. This was repeated from the platform battery when he landed. He finished the day by surveying the lines of the garrison, during which a Royal Marine Artillery sentry ordered him off the parapet. (*The Morning Post, Annals of Portsmouth* by W.H. Saunders, 1880)

———— ◆ ————

1882: Dr Arthur Conan Doyle's brother, Innes, a pupil at Portsmouth Grammar School, wrote to their mother reporting on the doctor's progress at his Southsea surgery. 'The patients are crowding in. We have made three bob this week. We have vaxenated [*sic*] a baby and got hold of a man with consumtion... [*sic*]' Among the first patients was an epileptic grocer. Doyle made what he called 'a ghoulish compact, by which a fit to him meant bacon and butter to me, while a spell of health for him sent me back to dry bread and savelovs.' (*Arthur Conan Doyle: A Life in Letters*, ed. J. Lellenberg et al., 2008)

August 17th

1840: A 'wonderful player possessing flexibility of wrist and velocity as well as grasp of finger, perfectly marvellous ... the new star in the musical world' was billed to appear at the Green Row Rooms at a Grand Evening Concert to commence at 8 p.m.

Hungarian composer and piano virtuoso Franz Liszt began a south coast tour in the town, organised by a French entrepreneur and cellist, Louis Lavenu. The concert was marketed to 'the Nobility and Gentry' of the town, who could afford the six shilling ticket price, though a family of four could be admitted for the discount price of a guinea. The tour schedule was evidently tight, with a morning concert performance due at Ryde Town Hall the following day. (*Music in Portsmouth 1789-1842* by F. Warren and I. Cockman, 1988; *Hampshire Telegraph*)

———— • ◆ • ————

1934: The vicar of St Matthew's, Bruce Cornford, wrote: 'On Friday evening we listened, on the wireless, to the frenzied talk of Adolph Hitler at Hamburg, which lasted over an hour and a half. HOT AIR!'

St Matthew's Church in Fawcett Road was destroyed by the Luftwaffe six years later. (*The Gadfly* [St Matthew's parish magazine])

August 18th

1940: John 'Nine Guns' Coghlan was one of 110 old boys of Portsmouth Grammar School to have died in the Second World War. As a Hurricane pilot during the Battle of Britain, Coghlan shot down six enemy aircraft before being awarded the Distinguished Flying Cross. During one dogfight, his machine guns ran out of ammunition and he pulled out his Smith & Wesson pistol (carried in case of capture) and emptied it, firing out of his cockpit at the enemy. Henceforth he was known as 'Nine Gun' Coghlan.

Coghlan was selected for a clandestine mission to drop a French agent in Boulogne, but disappeared on the night of 17 August 1940. There are two versions of how he met his death. In September, a pilot's body was washed up on a French beach and it was assumed by some that he had been shot down over the Channel. The other version suggests that Coghlan and his passenger were captured and shot. (*Old Boys of PGS who died in the Second World War*, Porstmouth Grammar School, 2002; www.acesofww2.com)

———◆———

1875: The Royal Yacht tender *Alberta*, with Queen Victoria aboard, ran down a schooner in the Solent, cutting it in two and killing three people. The Queen was unscathed. (*Pall Mall Gazette*)

August 19th

1893: Ten boys between the ages of seven and sixteen were reported to have appeared in Portsmouth Police Court before the magistrate, Sir William King, having been summoned for 'larking' in the mud for coppers off the Common Hard. In doing so, they 'caused an obstruction on the pontoon where a large number of people were assembled' and also, 'in consequence of the odour created by the continual stirring-up of the mud some people could hardly live in the neighbourhood'. Two of the mudlarks were fined 5s and the rest cautioned. Sir William King suggested that the police should summon some of the people throwing money, if they did not move on when requested. (*Hampshire Telegraph*)

———— • ◆ • ————

1729: The Mayor and Justices of the Peace decided that, 'no persons living out of the Juresdiccon of this Burrough shall sitt in the market here to Sell Cabbages Coleworts Turneps Carrots or any other Garden Stuff except on Tuesdays Thursdays and Saturdays on payne of being prosecuted for the same.'(Extracts from 'Records in the possession of the Municipal Corporation of the Borough of Portsmouth' by Robert East, 1891)

August 20th

1936: Two employees of Airspeed Ltd climbed into a courier plane at Portsmouth Airport and took off. The pilot, Joseph Smith, had never flown before. As the plane lifted its right wing, it hit a tree on the banks of the old ramparts at the northern end of the airfield. The plane crashed, throwing the men out of the cockpit. The machine was wrecked. Both men were taken to Portsmouth Hospital. Mr N.S. Norway, the managing director of Airspeed (also known as author Nevil Shute), described their flight in the aircraft, valued at £3,400, as 'foolhardy'.

Smith was charged with stealing the aircraft which, he said, he intended to sell to Spanish forces in the civil war that had broken out a few weeks earlier. They also believed they could earn £150 each to work as air mechanics in Spain. Smith was sentenced to four months' imprisonment, but shortly afterwards his accomplice, Arthur Gargett, died in hospital, and Smith was tried again, this time for manslaughter. He received another eight months.

It was stated at the first trial that this was the first ever charge of stealing an aeroplane in the country. (*The Times*)

August 21st

1846: Well-to-do Portsmouth people paid a shilling to see fourteen-year-old Charles Stratton. The lad was appearing at the Green Row Rooms, though a publicity poster refers to him being 'exhibited'.

Freak shows were acceptable entertainment and generated huge profits for entrepreneurs and showmen. Phineas T. Barnum immediately spotted the potential of Charles Stratton. Born of normal size and good health, he grew normally until he was 18 months old, 'when nature put a veto upon his further upward progress'. He was 25 inches (63cm) high and weighed 15lbs (7 kilos). Not content with stripping him of his dignity, Barnum also renamed him 'General Tom Thumb'. (*Yesterday*)

———•◆•———

1895: A public meeting held in Hughes' Store in Queen Street condemned the Council's 'continued indifference ...apathy and culpable neglect' in not carrying out slum improvements in Portsea. Three years later, a prominent councillor was reported to have described Portsea as a 'God-forsaken hole that ought to be burnt'. Countering accusations that the people were a 'drunken lot', a member of the Portsea Improvement Association argued that 'if the ArchBishop of Canterbury himself lived in such a place probably he would take to drink'. (*Hampshire Telegraph*)

August 22nd

1868: A correspondent in the *Hampshire Times* complained that the inhabitants of Milton, east of the Artillery Arms on the old canal, had suddenly been 'cut off from the postal delivery, after having enjoyed that accommodation for fourteen years'. The writer pointed out that there was a thriving fishing community there with at least twenty-eight houses, a pub and a landing place that was busy all the year round. The writer said that the Postmaster General had not replied to a letter they had addressed to him, and the Portsmouth postmaster had said that delivering to that area was not profitable. (*Hampshire Telegraph*)

———— • ————

1961: Raoul Jaime Orzabal de la Quintana was born in Portsmouth of a French father of Basque descent and an English mother. Two weeks later he was renamed Roland and, after moving to Bath, co-founded a band named after a book by Arthur Janov called *Tears for Fears*. Roland Orzabel was the main songwriter and vocalist, and amongst the group's hits was the song, *Mad World*. (*The Faber Companion to 20th Century Popular Music*, 2001)

August 23rd

1628: Many seamen and their families at Portsmouth were starving, having not been paid for months. Ill-advised military expeditions which proved costly in British soldiers' lives did not help the mood of the town. With the streets full of disaffected soldiers and seamen, the Duke of Buckingham, who had led the campaigns, was in danger.

The Duke had attained his position through being intimate with King James and was one of the most successful courtiers in history, continuing in favour under King Charles I. He was, however, less successful at war.

In Portsmouth in 1628, Buckingham's coach was surrounded by 300 sailors demanding their back pay. One bold sailor tried to drag Buckingham out of his coach, but was arrested. The situation calmed down, and the man was released. However, Buckingham later had the man rearrested, and when the crowd attempted to get him released, Buckingham and his men, on horseback with their swords drawn, drove them down the street to Point Gate, murdering some of them.

On 22 August, the bold sailor was hanged on a gibbet between Portsmouth and Southsea Castle. The following day a soldier, John Felton, stabbed Buckingham in the Greyhound pub in the High Street, and became a hero in many people's eyes. (*The Naval Heritage of Portsmouth* by J. Winton, 1989; *Oxford Dictionary of National Biography*)

August 24th

1782: Between 20,000 and 100,000 people gathered on the Common, many of them having walked great distances to be there. They had come to watch David Tyrie, who had been convicted of high treason, be hanged, decapitated and disembowelled.

Unfortunately, when Tyrie arrived from Winchester Prison, it was realised that nobody had thought to bring a rope. With great presence of mind, the executioner acquired some from a lugger that was moored offshore. This gave Tyrie some extra time to read from his Bible.

The *Hampshire Chronicle* reported that Tyrie was hanged for twenty-two minutes, his head severed from his body, his heart taken out and burnt, his genitals cut off and his body quartered. It is assumed that the executioner remembered to bring a knife. The same account reported that after the body parts were buried on the beach, some sailors dug up the coffin and cut the body into 1,000 pieces to distribute as souvenirs. Another account stated that 'such was the singular avarice of many who were near the body, that happy was he who could procure a finger or some relick [*sic*] of the criminal'. (*Death on the Common at Portsmouth* by J. Cramer, 1986)

August 25th

1975: 'This country must be the worst in the affluent western world for looking after its kids,' argued Roger Daltrey, lead singer of The Who, in *The Times* on this day. 'When I was on location in Portsmouth with *Tommy* there was a huge council estate with one little youth club for what seemed like ten thousand kids. Is it surprising that they walk around the streets breaking windows?'

The previous summer, the ageing *enfant terrible* film director Ken Russell had filmed The Who's rock opera *Tommy* in the Portsmouth area, infamously burning down South Parade Pier in the process. On that day, 11 June 1974, as the flames spread, Mr Russell said: 'We shall probably have to find another set.' (*The Times*)

———— • ◆ • ————

1803: Betsy Fremantle, the wife of a naval officer, went sightseeing. After a day's viewing of French prisoners of war at Portchester and on a harbour hulk, her party returned to Portsea. She recorded in her diary: 'Walking home poor Justine received such a hard pinch from a sailor that passed us, that she was quite frightened.' (*A Portsmouth Canvas: the Art of the City and the Sea* by N. Surry, 2008)

August 26th

1892: John Walker drove the fastest milkcart seen in Southsea for some time. Walker, a milkman of East Street, appeared before magistrates charged with 'furious driving' in Blackfriars Road. Inspector Moss identified the defendant as the driver of a four-wheeled milk van. He was 'holding the reins loosely and the horse was going at stretch gallop' in a road where there were children around. Walker said that the horse ran away with him, but he was disbelieved and fined 10s. (*Hampshire Telegraph*)

1902: The first submarines of the Royal Navy arrived in Portsmouth Harbour from the Barrow-in-Furness shipyard of Vickers. They were named *Holland I* and *Holland II* after their American designer John Patrick Holland and were viewed with some suspicion, there being concerns that they might blow up. Some admirals were not keen on them for other reasons, saying they were 'underhand, unfair and damned un-English'.

In 1905, the Admiralty took over Fort Blockhouse and established the Royal Navy's first Submarine Boat Station. The first Holland subs were unreliable and, in 1903, an attempt to sail around the Isle of Wight on the surface resulted in four of the new vessels breaking down. (*British Submarines in the Great War* by E. Gray, 2000)

August 27th

1842: The *Hampshire Telegraph* reported a number of complaints from residents appalled at the sight of nude bathing in the Mill Dam and at the Hard. (*Hampshire Telegraph*)

———•◆•———

1996: The discovery of the drug Viagra was reported for the first time in a British newspaper. It was discovered by Dr Ian Osterloh, a former pupil of Portsmouth Grammar School. (*The Guardian*)

———•◆•———

1958: Lieutenant David Franklin RN, aged twenty-nine, died at Haslar Hospital. The Admiralty announced that 'there was no cause to connect the death with his service in the Pacific'. The police stated that there was 'no question of an inquest'. However, the coroner disagreed and at the inquest he heard how Franklin served on HMS *Warrior* during the hydrogen bomb tests in the Christmas Islands in 1957 and was suffering from a blood disease, aplastic anaemia, which was associated with exposure to radiation. Bone and blood samples were sent to the Harwell Atomic Research Station. In 1954, reassurance was given that all ranks attended short instruction in 'personal protection against atomic attack' at HMS *Phoenix* at Tipnor, Portsmouth. (*The Times*)

August 28th

1931: A murder was committed that almost resulted in an innocent Portsmouth man being hanged.

William Kell, a nineteen-year-old photographer, had a date with fifteen-year-old Madge Cleife, who was a member of the Band of Hope and girl guides. Despite her tender age she looked much older. They had been going out for five months, mostly to the pictures or for walks around town. On this evening they walked, arm in arm, to Copnor and parted at the White Stone Bridge over the railway line at around 9.45 p.m. They had a tiff after Madge said she was going to meet someone else. William went straight home.

The following day some boys were playing on the Great Salterns golf course when they found a dead body. Madge had been raped and strangled. Kell was immediately suspected by the police, but, when it came to court, was fortunate to have been assiduously defended. When he was cleared, the judge complimented Kell's lawyer for defending his client when he was receiving 'small remuneration' for a 'Poor Prisoner case'. Following the acquittal, *The Times* newspaper apologised for misreporting and inventing some of the evidence which they admitted was 'quite without foundation'. (*The Times*)

August 29th

1782: HMS *Royal George*, one of the most famous ships in the Navy, was at Spithead being careened (listed to port) to enable minor repairs to be made. According to a witness, a carpenter called James Ingram, a sloop carrying rum came alongside at about nine in the morning and started unloading. Water lapped over the gun ports which Ingram pointed out to the officer of the watch, who gave him 'a very short answer'. The problem worsened and Ingram spoke again to the officer, who replied, 'Damme, sir, if you can manage the ship better than I can, you had better take command.' Then a sudden breeze forced her further over, water poured in and the ship rolled on to her side and sank in an instant. She took with her around 1,200 people, about 230 of whom managed to escape from the ship. Up to 300 women and sixty children who were visiting the ship were amongst those who died. Bodies resurfaced, thirty or forty at a time, for several days afterwards. Portsmouth watermen tied ropes around their ankles and towed them ashore. (*The Naval Heritage of Portsmouth* by J. Winton, 1989)

———•◆•———

1956: The Victoria Barracks was vacated by the Navy and closed. (City of Portsmouth Records of the Corporation, ed. Gates, Singleton-Gates, Barnett, Blanchard, Windle, Riley)

August 30th

1818: A row galley beached near Fort Cumberland. The eleven men got out, looked around to ensure their activity was unobserved, and proceeded to unload the cargo. However, the activity was observed by an officer at the fort, who watched until they had finished and began to transport their cargo up the road. The officer then sallied forth and the smugglers fled, leaving him in possession of 1,132 yards of French silk, nineteen Angola shawls, 132 pairs of Angola gloves, eighty-six pairs of silk stockings, forty-two snuff boxes, 672 pairs of kid gloves, 225 yards of cambric or chambray, sixteen silk sashes and one fur petticoat.

According to Mr Moncreaff, the Borough Inspector of Weights and Measures, smuggling was rife at this time and local tradesmen were willing recipients of goods which they then sold on. Farm labourers were employed to help, and coastguards were sometimes bribed to turn a blind eye. On one occasion it was reported that smugglers buried a customs officer up to his neck in the shingle on the beach after it was discovered he was honest. (*History of Portsmouth* by W. Gates, 1900)

August 31st

1966: Two new pubs were officially opened in the Tricorn. The Casbah and the Golden Bell served their first pints, crowds having been attracted by a themed publicity stunt. A large camel and young ladies dressed in harem costume paraded around the Charlotte Street area, causing surprise and ribald comments amongst the shoppers there. 'The camel,' joked the *Evening News* weakly, 'was the only one present not offered a drink [and] went off with the hump.' He was hired from Robert's Circus, which was visiting Southsea at the time.

The Golden Bell replaced the Charlotte Street local which had been demolished the previous year. Its customers became known as 'the Bell boys' and gained a bad reputation at a time when skinheads and violence gave the dark Tricorn spaces a certain edginess. The Tricorn Club, which became Granny's then Basins, attracted emerging and top acts, including Marc Bolan, Slade, Mud, Sweet, Status Quo, Mary Wells, Edwin Starr and Vinegar Joe as well as regular local bands Smiling Hard, The Image, Heaven and Hector. Slade's unique stomping sound and loud vocals prompted a police complaint that the band could be heard as far away as The Hard. (*The Tricorn: The Life and Death of a 60s Icon* by C. Clark and R. Cook, 2009; *Evening News, Portsmouth*)

September 1st

1899: Entrepreneur Mr A.W. White trialled a new motor tram intended for the new Cosham to Horndean service. Unfortunately, a stone in the tramlines caused it to derail and crash into his garden wall at North End, causing considerable damage and minor injury to passengers. (*Hampshire Telegraph*)

1835: John Crossley, a marine, and William Upton, an Army corporal, had a few drinks in the Royal Swan pub. Upton asked Crossley back to Southsea Castle where his regiment was based. The following morning, Upton's body was found on the Common with a 6-inch bayonet wound in his chest. Crossley admitted stabbing him but, strangely, the case was dropped 'as none of the witnesses could prove the name of the deceased'. (*Trewman's Exeter Flying Post*)

1969: Bob Dylan cut short his planned stay on the Isle of Wight after appearing at the second IOW festival and boarded a chartered hovercraft bound for Portsmouth. (*The Times*)

1800: A 'tumultuous meeting' of local people took place in St George's Square, prompted by anger over the high price of bread. Many windows were reported to have been broken. (*Annals of Portsmouth* by W.H. Saunders, 1880)

September 2nd

1642: Parliamentarian forces at Gosport began opening fire across the harbour, their shot hitting Town Mount (now the site of the Portsmouth Grammar Upper Junior School). (*Portsmouth* by A. Temple Patterson, 1976)

———— •◆• ————

1803: Convicts were put to work as free labour on many major works in Portsmouth throughout the nineteenth century, including the building of the promenade, barracks, Dockyard walls and basins, the formation of Whale Island and the levelling of Southsea Common. On this day, Betsy Fremantle, a naval officer's wife, visited Southsea Castle and then travelled on to Fort Cumberland where convicts were at work. She recorded in her diary: '...it is a melancholy sight to see many wretches at work with heavy chains to their feet. And I was much shocked to discover among them numbers of quite young lads fourteen or fifteen years of age.' (*A Portsmouth Canvas: The Art of the City and the Sea* by N. Surry, 2008)

———— •◆• ————

1834: The civil engineer and architect Thomas Telford died. In 1784 he took on the first important position of his career, working on the Dockyard Commissioner's house and chapel. While at Portsmouth he widened his knowledge by observing harbour and dock work under construction. (*Oxford Dictionary of National Biography*)

September 3rd

1859: Albert Cotterell, a well-known waterman and Point character, was born. For many years, Albert lived rent-free in a house on the beach at Point. Several rent collectors used to knock on his door demanding money, but always went away empty-handed. 'Tell me,' he asked them, 'who is the landlord and I will gladly pay the rent.' Albert was aware that when the original owner died the title deeds were lost, and no proof of ownership could be established. The house, undermined by the sea, was eventually demolished. (*Evening News, Portsmouth*)

———•◆•———

1921: Cab Kaye, musician, singer and entertainer, was born in London. The family moved to Portsmouth shortly afterwards when his father, Ghanian pianist Caleb Jonas Quaye, was killed in a railway accident. Kaye attended St John's primary school and, briefly, Hilsea Secondary School.

At the age of fifteen he joined Billy Cotton's band and went on to become a leading singer on the British jazz scene from the late 1930s until the 1960s, performing with many famous jazz names. One of his best-known discs was a collaboration with Humphrey Lyttelton, but Kaye had a strong sense of cultural nationalism and often worked with fellow black Britons. He died in Amsterdam in 2000. (*The Times*; *Oxford Dictionary of National Biography*)

September 4th

1827: A letter appeared in the *Hampshire Telegraph* drawing attention to the plight of 'those miserable little beings', the 'climbing boys' who cleaned chimneys. The writer referred to the diseases caused through the inhalation of soot, and the fatalities that often occurred. He urged the inhabitants of Portsmouth who had 'a high character for active benevolence and public spirit' to employ machines to do the work. Thirteen years later legislation was passed prohibiting the use of children in chimney sweeping.

In 1870, workhouse guardians briefly considered employing inmates to clean their chimneys, but rejected the idea when the Governor described a workhouse where inmates 'put the brushes in the fire and, when they were drunk, beat the sticks about each other's heads'. The contract was awarded to local sweep James Boulter who, far from employing young boys, was aided by a seventy-two-year-old labourer who later died while lifting a heavy sack of soot. (*Hampshire Telegraph*)

———•◆•———

1930: Legendary pilot Amy Johnson landed her biplane at Alexandra Park and was greeted by a cheering crowd. Earlier in the year she had made a solo journey from England to Australia. Johnson was driven to the Guildhall for a civic reception. (*The News, Portsmouth*)

September 5th

1993: Arms buyers from seventy countries attended a Government naval and military equipment exhibition at Portsmouth and Aldershot. When questioned by the *Guardian* about the ethics of selling arms to Saddam Hussein's regime in Iraq, Sir Alan Thomas, head of the Ministry of Defence export services said, 'I feel embarrassed our press is constantly shouting down good news.' (*The Guardian*)

———— • ◆ • ————

1967: Portsmouth City Council formally approved plans for the development of a comprehensive education system. Selection had been largely discredited amongst professional educationalists, with the appreciation that it was inherently unfair and that the eleven-plus created too much anxiety for children. A correspondent in the *Portsmouth News* argued that the examination was weighted against 'the working class child, the nervous, the handicapped, the child of the unemployed, bereaved or widowed parent and the child of a large family'. The News Chief Correspondent agreed and several feature articles called for an end to it. Some traditionalists, however, argued that grammar schools had been a means of social mobility for a few working-class children. (*Portsmouth's Schools 1750-1975* by P. Galliver, 2011; City of Portsmouth Records of the Corporation, ed. Gates, Singleton-Gates, Barnett, Blanchard, Windle, Riley)

September 6th

1919: Admiral Lord Charles Beresford was one of the most talked-about personalities of his generation: colourful, idiosyncratic, maverick, brave, high-spirited, an enthusiastic sportsman, rich and of noble birth. To many he was John Bull personified and was often seen with his pet bulldog. Educated at Stubbington House, near Fareham, his distinguished naval career was marred by spats with Jackie Fisher over naval reforms. Upon retirement he became MP for Portsmouth between 1910 and 1916. He died on this day. (*Oxford Dictionary of National Biography*)

———◆———

1913: PC Francis Cross was on duty in Great Southsea Street when he noticed a woman dragging a small child along the pavement. He walked with them to their home in Little Southsea Street, a respectable area, where he established that both mother and daughter were drunk. The child, aged four, had lost the use of her legs and her eyes were glassy. The Chairman of the magistrates told Helena Lewis that 'it was a sad thing to see a young mother like her in such a position', advised her to give up drink and was bound over in the sum of £5 to be of good behaviour for three months. (*Evening News, Portsmouth*)

September 7th

1938: The former Empire Cinema in Stamshaw Road, built in 1911 as the North End Cinema, was reopened as the Forum, spelled out in a new neon sign, 'with a colossal two feature programme, Will Hay in *Oh, Mr Porter* and Glenn Morris in *Tarzan's Revenge*.

The new, lavish interior boasted 'tangerine' as 'the predominant hue' and, at a time when mass smoking could obscure the view of the screen, a state-of-the-art Plenum ventilation plant ensured that stale air was extracted to be replaced by filtered fresh air. (*Evening News, Portsmouth*)

1838: Johann Strauss, the elder, the Austrian composer famous for his waltzes, played a concert at the Theatre Royal in the High Street. Surprisingly, he did not draw a full house but 'the precision and perfect harmony which distinguish this band, the numerous variations given on each theme of each dance, the curious and cheerful changes of sound produced by the introduction of little brass bells ... rendered their music the most stirring and enlivening accompaniment that has ever been heard'. Strauss returned again at the end of the month and played at the Beneficial Hall on 29 September, which was 'brilliantly attended'. (*Music in Portsmouth* by F. Warren and I. Cockman, 1998)

September 8th

1925: In 1921 Peg Marks was appearing at the King's Theatre in a show entitled *Have a Dip!* She met Bill Sellers one day in the local Lyon's Corner House café where he was playing, I'm Forever Blowing Bubbles, on the piano. They were married in London two years later.

Back again on tour in Southsea in 1925, Peg was heavily pregnant. She gave birth immediately after a show, having been rushed back to a flat above a shop on the corner of Castle Street. On this day, Dr Little of Southsea delivered a baby boy who was to be christened Richard Henry.

Richard was soon called Peter after his elder stillborn brother. Described as an 'outrageously spoiled child', Peter was unusually close to his mother. He attended a Roman Catholic School in Highgate and was an unruly pupil at Miss Whitney's School of Dancing in Green Road, Southsea. The rest of his life was marred by psychological problems and a succession of failed relationships, but his professional life as a comic and character actor had many highlights, including the innovative radio show, *The Goon Show*, and the films *The Ladykillers* (in which he acted with his idol Alec Guinness), *I'm All Right Jack*, *The Pink Panther* films and *Being There*. He died in 1980. (*Peter Sellers: The Mask behind the Mask* by P. Evans, 1980; *Oxford Dictionary of National Biography*)

September 9th

1855: Houston Stewart Chamberlain was born in the heart of Thomas Ellis Owen's fashionable Southsea. The third son of a Rear-Admiral, the adolescent was sent to the Continent for 'finishing' where his appointed tutor, an Otto Kuntze, did a good job instilling Prussian ideals. As a young man Chamberlain stayed in Germany, pursuing an obsession with Wagner which resulted in Chamberlain divorcing his half-Jewish wife and marrying Wagner's only daughter, Eva.

In 1899, after publishing several minor works on music and drama, Chamberlain produced a major historical study, *The Foundations of the Nineteenth Century*. In it, Chamberlain sought to demonstrate that Jews were a negative influence on civilisation and that the Aryan peoples were inherently superior to all. As a result, Chamberlain became friends with the Kaiser. Later he joined the Nazi Party and was admired by Hitler, who attended his funeral in 1927. (*Keep the Home Fires Burning* by J. Sadden, 1990; *Hampshire Telegraph*)

1908: A pig walked into a bar in Portsea. The animal made itself at home in the saloon bar of Tottersell's Hotel and refused to leave. Without a wolf in sight, he was eventually driven from the bar by men with sticks. (*Evening News, Portsmouth*)

September 10th

1832: The great violinist Paganini gave two concerts in Portsmouth on this day, a morning concert in Green Row Rooms and an evening concert at the theatre in the High Street (on the site of what is now Portsmouth Grammar School). Both were well-attended and, according to the *Hampshire Chronicle*, were 'rapturously encored, in the most condescending manner, and was greeted with long incessant cheers'. (*Hampshire Chronicle*)

———— • ◆ • ————

1956: By way of contrast, Portsmouth has another musical claim to fame. On this day, at approximately 7.45 p.m., a new six-piece British band, Tony Crombie and his Rockets, took to the stage at the Theatre Royal. A jazz and dance band drummer from London, Crombie was seeking to exploit the new Rock 'n' Roll genre which had taken off in the States. The Rockets was one of the first British bands to release a Rock 'n' Roll record and, according to music historian Dave Allen, was the first to tour. Citing Pete Frame, the band gigged at Portsmouth before any other venue, suggesting that on this night, Portsmouth 'had an important role in the birth of British Rock 'n' Roll'. (*Here Come the Sixties* by D. Allen, 2009)

September 11th

1800: A letter written by French prisoners of war incarcerated in Portchester Castle was forwarded by Commissioners of the Transport Service to ministers of Government. It read:

> It cannot be necessary to lay before you a minute picture of the state of nakedness to which we are reduced; a state the more deplorable, as our debilitated bodies are more susceptible of the severity of the season, and the want of repose. The many sufferings we endure from the total want of clothing, and other necessaries of this kind, are already so well known to you, that there can be no difficulty in your interceding in our favour…

Conditions at Portchester were, indeed, grim and overcrowded, with up to 8,000 prisoners incarcerated at any one time. The press maintained that French prisoners were kept in better conditions than English prisoners, and that 'their lot was aggravated by their own vices'. It was reported that they gambled for food, bedding and clothing, and that it was not unusual for prisoners to go around completely naked as a result. The high death rate through neglect or suicide was, it was suggested, of their own making. (*The Morning Post*; *History of Portsmouth* by W. Gates, 1900)

September 12th

1903: The *Portsmouth Times* reported that:

A highly respectable citizen of Portsmouth was discovered recently in Brighton, rakishly attired in a greasy suit of rough serge overalls and a top hat. He had not run away from home, and he was perfectly sober. He had become possessed of a motor car.

(*Portsmouth Times*)

———— ◆ ————

1792: The trial started at Portsmouth of the most celebrated mutineers in naval history, ten members of the crew of the *Bounty*. They were accused of having forced Captain Bligh and eighteen others into a boat and setting them adrift. The mutineers then settled in Tahiti and the Pitcairn Islands, attracted by the lifestyle. Those who had been found in Tahiti were repatriated, though four died en route. The remaining ten were put on trial. Captain Bligh survived to give evidence and three men, John Millward, Thomas Ellison and Thomas Burkitt, who were alleged to have played a more active role in the mutiny, were convicted and hanged aboard HMS *Brunswick* in Portsmouth Harbour on 29 October 1792. (*The Bounty: A True Account of a Famous Mutiny* by A. McKee, 1962)

September 13th

1966: The decision was taken by the Governors to close one of Portsmouth's most famous schools, Chivers Independent Grammar School for Boys. In the inter-war years, Chivers was considered by some to be on a par with Portsmouth Grammar School. Founded in 1881 by William Chivers in Abingdon Road, by 1904 it had relocated to Esplanade House in Cottage Grove until the bombing of 1941 forced another move. It set up at St Bartholomew's Hall until the site was sold for residential development.

In 1959, following the death of the headmaster Mr Ashton-Caine, the school found more temporary premises at Buckland Congregational Church Hall in Queen's Road until space at St Mary's Institute was secured, where it was hoped the school would rekindle its former glories. But, by the time of the Governors' decision, the school roll had fallen to nineteen boys and continuation was not considered viable. (*Saving Chivers School* by R. Gouge ; Hampshire Magazine, *Evening News, Portsmouth*)

———— • ◆ • ————

1920: Miss E.H. Kelly CBE, Portsmouth's first woman Justice of the Peace, took her seat on the Bench. (*The Times*)

September 14th

1825: Tens of thousands of people from all over the country gathered to watch HMS *Princess Charlotte* being launched from the Dockyard. Unfortunately, the launch caused a massive surge of water which swept away a bridge:

> Immediately a dreadful crash was heard and a scream from the persons precipitated into the water; at the same instant a tremendous rush of water issued into the dock ... a stupendous wave, bearing on its surface many of the struggling sufferers, mingled with large fragments of broken timber, all of which was dashed with inconceivable fury against the farther end of the dock... carrying in the tremendous conflict the bodies of the sufferers, large pieces of timber, cloaks, hats and clothes of the unfortunate victims...

Sixteen people drowned, most of them children. (*Chronicles of Portsmouth* by H. & J. Slight, 1828; *Hampshire Telegraph*)

———◆———

1805: Nelson left the George Hotel in the High Street and embarked from Portsmouth for the last time. The wind died and *Victory* could not sail until the next day. (*The Naval Heritage of Portsmouth* by J. Winton, 1994)

———◆———

1931: Crowds at Southsea watched the British team set a new world speed record – 379mph – and win the Schneider Trophy. (*The Portsmouth Region*, ed. B. Stapleton and J. Thomas, 1988)

September 15th

1921: A public auction took place in the Hall, Pain & Goldsmith sale room in Commercial Road. Up for grabs were Portchester Farm – 242 acres – and Paulsgrove Farm – 293 acres – situated 'adjacent to Portsmouth Harbour on the main road to Fareham, only a mile from Cosham railway station'. Included in the sale were all farm buildings, eight cottages, 'the celebrated Paulsgrove chalkpit' and 'a private quay on the Harbour'. (*The Times*)

1805: Benjamin Silliman, an American traveller, spent his first full day in the town. He wrote his impressions:

> The streets of Portsmouth are dirty, and the town presents little that is pleasing or interesting beyond the various means of war, of which it is little else than a great magazine ... As I walked about the streets, I met, every where, crowds of military men, both of the army and Navy, by whom Portsmouth is said to be almost exclusively supported – At the inn where I dined I saw a great number of young midshipmen ; some of them were tender boys who seemed more fit subjects for maternal care than for war and bloodshed; it is from such beginnings, however, that Blakes and Nelsons are formed...

(*A Journal of Travels in England, Holland and Scotland* by B. Silliman, 1820)

September 16th

1914: Thirty-seven wounded soldiers, including fourteen German wounded prisoners, arrived at Fratton railway station from Southampton Docks and were transported to the Girls' Secondary School in (now Priory School) Fawcett Road, which had been converted to a military hospital. They were reported to look 'a bit rough, and none the better for want of a shave'. There was disappointment amongst the crowd that gathered outside that the Germans wore 'peaked caps, not the spiked helmet which one usually associates with German soldiers'. (*Hampshire Telegraph*)

———◆———

1709: Two women travelled to Portsmouth and entered a goldsmith's shop. After some negotiation, they were given twenty shillings for two silver spoons. Neither of the women had been born with silver spoons; one of them, Ann Harris, had stolen them, along with a watch and some money, from a chest of drawers in her master's house in Southwark. After being convicted of theft at the Old Bailey, Harris expressed the wish that she had 'done more good and less evil'. Along with other convicted criminals, she was taken to Tyburn in a cart, a noose put around her neck, and the cart pulled away. (Old Bailey proceedings)

September 17th

1854: Matilda Lodge and a friend were chatted up by a Lieutenant Knight, a Royal Marine, while waiting for the floating bridge back to Gosport. They went to the Fortitude pub at Point and were then invited to his ship in the Harbour. A waterman rowed them to a hulk attached to HMS *Dauntless*.

The next morning, Matilda was taken to Portsmouth Hard by a waterman. She was missing her stays, the sleeves and hooks of her dress were torn, and her bosom was exposed. Her arms from her shoulders to her wrists were black with bruises, she had a black eye, a bruised chin and bruises extending from her lower ribs up to her shoulder blades and on her thighs and knees. She was taken home to Gosport where she died as the result of a ruptured bladder.

Lieutenant Knight maintained that she had been drunk and had fallen off a chair or a bed. The local magistrates could not find enough evidence to send him for trial on a manslaughter charge. A court martial on HMS *Victory* found him guilty of bringing two 'improper women' on board and giving them drink, and for not wearing proper uniform, for which he was demoted. (*Reynold's Newspaper*; *Hampshire Telegraph*)

September 18th

1740: Admiral George Anson sailed from Portsmouth with six man-o'-war and two victuallers on a voyage around the world, during which his mission was to disrupt or capture Spanish interests in the Pacific. Unfortunately, the only troops made available for the mission were 500 sick and wounded soldiers who had been hospitalised. But when word reached them of the long voyage, 'all those who had limbs and strength to walk out of Portsmouth, deserted, leaving behind only as such were literally invalids, most of them being sixty and some of them upwards of seventy'.

The remaining 259 men were brought on board, many on stretchers. This military force was bolstered by newly-recruited marines, many of whom had never used a gun before.

Anson returned four years later with only one ship, the *Centurion*. It is said that his first act on landing was to fall upon his knees on Southsea and thank God for his deliverance. Of the 1854 original crew members who set off from Portsmouth, only 188 survived. (*A Voyage Round the World 1740-1744* by G. Anson and R. Walker, 1974)

September 19th

1901: The first electric tram to carry passengers in Portsmouth was due to run, but because of the funeral of the US President, Mr William McKinley, the maiden trip was delayed by five days. (*Fares Please* by E. Watts, 1987)

1770: The forcible impressments of seamen, described as 'un-English, arbitrary and despotic', was a colourful feature of life in Portsmouth at the turn of the nineteenth century. Merchant seamen were especially valued because they 'knew the ropes'. Press warrants from the Admiralty were sent to Portsmouth and the following morning press gangs boarded merchant vessels in the harbour and 'stripped them of all hands they thought useful' before word spread. Without the element of surprise, press gangs were ineffectual, as able-bodied men either went into hiding or armed themselves. The pressed men were secured in a tender and the gang went ashore and picked up 'many good sailors' off the streets and from the public houses. The pressed 'good sailors' were, perhaps not surprisingly, said to be those most likely to mutiny. (*History of Portsmouth* by W. Gates, 1900; *Annals of Portsmouth* by W.H. Saunders, 1880)

September 20th

1963: A new rhythm and blues band from London appeared at the Savoy ballroom. Three months earlier they had released their first single, a cover of Chuck Berry's, *Come On*, which the band disliked and their label did not promote. However, the band's agent sent fan-club members out to music shops, polled by the charts, to buy copies and managed to get it to number twenty-one in the charts. On the back of this they were signed on an autumn tour which brought them to Southsea. This tour was considered important in the development of the band.

The Rolling Stones appeared with the Vigilantes and a ticket cost 5s. Eleven days after their local appearance, their second single, a cover of Lennon and McCartney's, *I Wanna be Your Man*, was released and reached number twelve in the chart. The following year the band returned, playing two gigs at the Guildhall on 16 February, ten days after the rebellious icons had recorded a jingle for a Kellogs Rice Krispies television advertisement. (*Here Come the Sixties* by D. Allen, 2009)

September 21st

1945: The playwright, author and diarist Simon Gary started at Portsmouth Grammar School. The son of a Hayling Island doctor, the family moved away two years later. In a forty-five-year writing career, Gray published five novels and forty original plays, adaptations and screenplays. Among his last books were diaries, The *Smoking Diaries* trilogy and *Coda,* reflecting wittily on his everyday observations, decline and imminent death. (www.simongray.org.uk)

* * *

1801: In the evening, beacons were lit announcing that a French invading flotilla had been sighted. Thousands of inhabitants were quickly sworn in as volunteers to repel the invaders. The defenders waited until daylight, prepared to defend their town and country, but the news was then imparted that it had been a ruse to test the loyalty of the people and the military preparedness of the garrison. (*Annals of Portsmouth* by W.H. Saunders, 1880)

* * *

1880: A local RSPCA meeting at Portland Hall reported a total of eighty-six local convictions that year for cruelty to animals, the vast majority related to working animals while they were in an unfit state. The Revd Dr Kennedy-Moore said that 'cruelty to animals tended to degrade and brutalise our feelings towards each other'. (*Hampshire Telegraph*)

September 22nd

1866: Letters from indignant Dockyard workers were published in the local press responding to 'a dastardly, ungentlemanly, scandalous and libellous' attack on Dockyardmen, which claimed that every ship was 'plundered of everything loose and portable' and that storerooms were raided and 'spirits abstracted'. A long-serving employee said that the only time he had been aware of the theft of spirits was when a sentry charged with looking after a store was found to be stealing it. To brand thousands of men in this way was 'false and unwarrantable', 'a more respectable, honest, sober and industrious body of operatives will not be found the country over'. (*Hampshire Telegraph*)

1918: The Coliseum Music Hall in Edinburgh Road advertised a revue entitled 'All Black', comprising '25 coloured performers' and a full chorus of 'Creole Beauties'. (*Evening News, Portsmouth*)

1939: Newly-appointed First Sea Lord, Winston Churchill, visited HMS *Vernon* (on the site of Gunwharf Quays), which was responsible for mine disposal and developing mine countermeasures during the war. (*HMS Vernon* by E. Webb, 1956)

September 23rd

1803: The *Naval Chronicle* reported that, at eight o'clock in the evening:

> A very hot press took place in Portsmouth, Portsea and Gosport, in the Harbour, and most places in the neighbourhood; no protestations were listened to, and a vast number of persons of various descriptions were sent on board the different ships in this port, most of whom were this morning liberated, being master tradesmen, apprentices, and such persons; very few were detained in comparison with the number taken on board. On the whole it is not supposed the service has acquired 50 serviceable men.

On 7 March of the same year, pressgangs made up of 600 seamen 'indiscriminately took out every man on board the colliers' and 'picked up many useful hands' at Point and locked them in the Guard House on the Grand Parade. The following day, a record 500 men were rounded up in Gosport. (*Naval Chronicle*)

September 24th

1917: Captain Morrison-Scott of the Royal Marine Artillery wrote a letter to Jane Heaton of No. 83 Adair Road, Eastney:

It is with the greatest sorrow that I write to tell you that your husband Sergt Heaton was killed today by enemy shell fire at the battery position while fighting the Hun. He did not suffer, for he received a fragment of shell through the brain. Poor, poor dear fellow – we all – officers and men alike – regarded him with affection and high esteem. He is for me personally the greast loss sustained.

I should not tell you, but I do so to show you how highly he was held in esteem – Sgt Heaton was recommended just a few days before for the Military Medal and it will almost certainly be granted. This of course is no consolation, but I know you will like to know that his courage, cheerfulness and soldierly qualities were fully appreciated by his officers and comrades generally. God bless him and you dear Mrs. Heaton.

P.S. There were unfortunately five other fatal casualties at the same time and they have all been buried together in the military cemetery.

(*From Trench and Turret* by S. Holloway, 2006)

September 25th

1916: Commander Heinrich Mathy and his crew climbed into the gondola of Zeppelin *L31* and weighed off, heading for England. His main target was London, but he concluded that an attack on the heavily-defended capital would be difficult because of the clear weather. Instead, he decided, they would bomb the Dockyard at Portsmouth where, as Mathy pointed out to his crew, 'nobody has ever visited and it is sure to be very interesting'.

Mathy attacked from the south. One of his crew members recorded, 'Dozens of searchlight clusters find us and fix on us. An unearthly concert is unleashed, conducted by Satan himself,' probably referring to anti-aircraft fire from Point Battery and Whale Island as *L31* came over the harbour. A heavy bomb load of 8,125lbs was dropped and Mathy, blinded by the searchlight, reported that 'all bombs had fallen on the city and Dockyard'.

However, the bombs appear to have fallen harmlessly into the harbour. Six days later, *L31* was attacked by fighter pilot, Second-Lieutenant W. J. Tempest over Potters Bar and the crew were burned alive. Mathy chose to leap to his death from the plunging inferno and his body was found embedded in a field. (*Keep the Home Fires Burning* by J. Sadden, 1990)

September 26th

1931: At sunset, the evening gun was fired for the last time from the eastern end of the fortifications. (City of Portsmouth Records of the Corporation, ed. Gates, Singleton-Gates, Barnett, Blanchard, Windle, Riley)

1989: Work began on the Cascades Shopping Centre in the summer of 1987 and was opened on this day two years later. The development covered the area once occupied by Meadow Street, Moore's Square, Little Charlotte Street, Waterloo Place, Ridge Street, a large part of Spring Street and Stoke Street. Spring Street linked Edinburgh Road with Charlotte Street. Meadow Street, which linked Commercial Road with Charlotte Street, became the site for the main entrance to the Cascades.

In the 1880s, Meadow Street boasted a pawnbroker, two butcher's, two clothier's, a grocer, fishmonger, printer, confectioner and beer house. Between the wars, Moore's Square housed a slaughterhouse, a china riveter and Fogaty's pickle manufacturers. (*Kelly's Directory 1937-38*; *Chamberlain's Directory 1887-88*)

September 27th

1943: Maureen Bolster, a Wren Stoker based in Portsmouth, wrote this letter to her boyfriend, Eric Wells:

There are seven of us on the course – only 25 have ever done it. We are ERA Wrens – Engine Room Artificers. Doesn't it sound gorgeous? The course lasts a month. It's the very same as the men's, the leading stokers. We run around looking too terribly boats' crews with glamorous white lanyards draped around our necks and over our fronts. We have classroom instruction for two weeks. Our instructor is a delightful, dignified bald-headed little chief petty officer with rows of medals.

It's a very concentrated course indeed. Today we wrestled with the intricacies of four-stroke and two-stroke engines, pistons, valves, cylinders, camshafts, cranks, water pumping and all sorts of other things which, dearest; I didn't really understand a word about.

But, by the following week, Maureen was writing:

I'm quite an engineer and, would you believe, I find pumps most interesting. I dote on the little fuel pump with anti-dribble valve on the diesel compression engine. It's awfully ingenious, isn't it? We've spent the morning having a film show – demonstrating diesels. Pictures of bathing belles and pin-up girls appeared every so often to keep the sailors awake...

(*Entertaining Eric* by M. Wells, 1989)

September 28th

1811: Water for the population of Portsmouth was traditionally obtained from wells in the Elm Grove area and Lion Gate Road, and was described as 'abundant and pure'. It was distributed by horse-drawn carts laden with large barrels and cost a penny for three buckets. By 1811, two reservoirs and a pumping station had been built at Farlington Marshes and pipes laid to supply water to affluent areas of town. On 24 September, inhabitants flocked out to the fortifications in great expectation, ready to witness a torrent of sparkling spring Farlington water gushing into the moat. In the event, the pipes were leaky and a trickle of rusty red water appeared. After four days of hasty repairs, on this day in 1811, the supply was officially opened. The water was still red, but ran clear after a week. The supply to Portsea was started on 6 October. (*History of the Portsmouth & Gosport Water Supply* by D. Halton Thomson, 1957)

———•◆•———

1918: An American baseball match took place at North End Recreation Ground, attracting many spectators including US servicemen who were based in the town. (*Evening News, Portsmouth*)

———•◆•———

1923: The Schneider Trophy seaplane race took place over the Solent for the first time on this day. (www.hydroretro.net)

September 29th

1916: The *Evening News* carried an advertisement offering insurance against Zeppelin attacks. (*Evening News, Portsmouth*)

———◆———

1882: John Knibb, a labourer of Oxford Road, Southsea, was summoned for assaulting Owen Overington, a gardener, in the Royal Albert public house in Albert Road. Overington claimed that Knibb had punched him in the face. Knibb, however, claimed that Overington kept a brothel and that he hit him because his daughter had been encouraged to go and work for him. The magistrates dismissed the case and suggested that police might want to investigate the house in question. (*Hampshire Telegraph*)

———◆———

1531: Thomas Carpenter, who is believed to have been the first Mayor of Portsmouth, took office. He is said to have built the first Town Hall in the middle of the High Street at his own expense. (*Annals of Portsmouth* by W.H. Saunders, 1880)

September 30th

1896: The Mayor of Portsmouth was snubbed by the Russian royal family. Tsar Nicholas and Tsarina Alexandra had been staying at Balmoral and were on their way to France to help cement the Franco-Russian alliance. It was known that they were scheduled to arrive at Portsmouth Dockyard, by train, on the evening of 4 October before leaving on the Royal Yacht for Cherbourg the following morning. The Mayor, John Young, asked through his deputy if he could present an address on their arrival at the Dockyard. The reply explained upon arrival, 'they would then require a rest and as they would sleep on board the *Pole Star* so as to leave early Monday morning, it would not be desirable to present their Majesties with an address'. (*Hampshire Telegraph*)

———— • • ————

1879: The Borough Lunatic Asylum was opened at Milton. Until 1862, 'Portsmouth lunatics' had been sent to Knowle and later Fisherton. A lavish banquet was held by the Mayor to celebrate, attracting criticism from the local press that it was inappropriate. Initially covering 75 acres, though later extended, it eventually became a self-sufficient community with a farm, chapel, laundry, bakery and workshops for patients to practice crafts and trades. (*The Hospitals of Portsmouth: Past and Present* by M. Gange, 1987)

October 1st

1923: The torpedo school HMS *Vernon* took over the Gunwharf site. HMS *Vernon* was the idea of Jacky Fisher, who recognised the potential of the torpedo as he did of virtually every other innovation of the era. *Vernon* was commissioned in 1876 and Fisher was put in charge.

It was made up of a group of old wooden hulks centred on HMS *Vernon*, the instructional ship, afloat on Fountain Lake close to the Dockyard. The hulk *Ariadne* provided accommodation, while *Actaeon* served as a workshop. Other ships were added, including the *Donegal*, *Marlborough* and *Warrior*. Between 1885 and 1889 a massive torpedo range was constructed by the joining together of Great and Little Horsea Island using thousands of tons of chalk from Paulsgrove chalk pit. By 1895, *Vernon* was moved to Portchester Creek, where she remained until her transfer ashore. (*Portsmouth: In Defence of the Realm* by J. Sadden, 2001)

2008: Copnor Road fire station was closed, despite local opposition prompted by fears that lives would be lost as a result. It was opened on 29 April 1957, replacing the Hilsea Fire Station and the brigade headquarters in Craneswater Park. (City of Portsmouth Records of the Corporation, ed. Gates, Singleton-Gates, Barnett, Blanchard, Windle, Riley)

October 2nd

1906: King Edward, nicknamed 'The Peacemaker', launched the battleship *Dreadnought* from the stocks at Portsmouth Dockyard. An impertinent bottle of Australian wine bounced back off the stern causing embarrassment, but otherwise 'the most important naval event leading up to the First World War' went smoothly.

The *Dreadnought* heralded a revolution in naval design and gave its name to a whole new type of battleship. The name was well chosen. The firepower of a Dreadnought was such that it could shell a coastal town without being in sight of it, a potential that was awesome by Edwardian standards. The ship was designed by Sir Philip Watts, who was born in Deptford but brought up in Portsmouth. He came from a long line of master shipwrights, his great grandfather having helped build HMS *Victory*. (*Keep the Home Fires Burning* by J. Sadden, 1990; *Oxford Dictionary of National Biography*)

1876: Train passengers wishing to travel to the Isle of Wight would alight at the Town (Portsmouth and Southsea) Station and have to catch a tram to Clarence Pier to catch a steam launch. With the opening of the upper -level platform passengers on this day, could travel on to the new Harbour railway station and go straight onto a ferry. (City of Portsmouth Records of the Corporation ,ed. Gates, Singleton-Gates, Barnett, Blanchard, Windle, Riley)

October 3rd

1735: Elizabeth Marsh was christened at St Thomas's Church, having been conceived in Jamaica, possibly of slave descent. Her father, Milbourne Marsh, was a ship's carpenter, who rose to a higher status, so much so that Elizabeth described herself as 'the daughter of a gentleman'. Milbourne's brother George rose from a humble Navy Clerkship to occupy the position once held by Samuel Pepys.

At various times Elizabeth Marsh lived in London, Gibraltar, and Menorca, and visited the Cape of Africa and Rio de Janeiro. She enjoyed a scandalous eighteen-month tour of eastern and southern India accompanied by a dashing, unmarried British officer. She endured many ordeals in her full and turbulent life, including being captured by Barbary pirates at the age of twenty, being imprisoned in a Moroccan harem, and suffering a mastectomy without anaesthetic in Calcutta. She was also involved in land speculation in Florida and in international smuggling. Her one and only published book, a travel memoir entitled *The Female Captive* was the first on Morocco by an Englishwoman.

Elizabeth Marsh 'travelled further and more dangerously by sea and in four continents than any female contemporary for whom records survive'. (*The Ordeal of Elizabeth Marsh* by L. Colley, 2008)

October 4th

1823: Gas was used for the first time in the streets of Old Portsmouth. Six months earlier, tenders had been invited by the 'Commissioners for Lighting, Paving and Watching the Town' for illuminating Portsmouth with gas and providing 80-100 cast-iron pillars and lamps. Applicants were required to specify the rate for lighting a 'Batswing Burner' from 'dusk till daylight' for from nine months to a year, and for providing lamps and pillars for ten years.

After installation, the Commissioners found themselves with 200 obsolete oil lampposts on their hands and offered them for sale in the *Hampshire Telegraph*. The newspaper congratulated residents on the improvement to their town, but regret was expressed about a rumour that:

> The elegant gas column which has been erected in St George's Square in 1821, and which is so highly ornamental to that part of the Town, is about to be removed to the Parade for want of sufficient contributions from the inhabitants of that part of Portsea to bear the expense of lighting it

Later, a petition was signed by 137 residents of Landport urging the provision of gas lighting there, but they had to wait until 1825 before their demands were met. (*Hampshire Telegraph*)

October 5th

1753: John Wesley wrote in his diary:

> After preaching at six [at Newport], I left this humane, loving people, rode to Cowes, and crossed over to Portsmouth. Here I found another kind of people, who had disputed themselves out of the power, and well nigh the form of religion. However, I laboured (and not altogether in vain) to soften and compose their jarring spirits, both this evening and next day.

Wesley made a total of twenty-two personal visits to Portsmouth between 1753 and 1790.

(*The Reverend J. Wesley's Journal, Methodism in Portsmouth 1750-1932* by W. Cooper, 1973)

———•◆•———

1822: *The Times* published a letter from a Portsmouth resident on the subject of the new Marriage Act, which was intended to prevent 'clandestine marriages', especially those of young people under twenty-one years old without parental permission, or bigamous marriages:

> As a proof of the estimation the new Marriage Act is held in this place, there has not been one mechanic, tradesman or independent person married [in Portsmouth] since its passing [5 weeks earlier]. The only persons that have consented to undergo its fiery ordeal are three sailors, two soldiers and two marines.

(*The Times*)

October 6th

1936: José Levy, theatre manager and playwright, died. Born in Portsmouth in 1894 and educated at Portsmouth Grammar School, he attempted to import the *Grand Guignol* aesthetic to British theatre audiences. Sybil Thorndike took part in the productions, but after two years the new genre was curtailed due to strict censorship.

In 1936, Levy was awarded the *Légion d'honneur* for his promotion of French theatre. (*The Times*)

———•◆•———

1860: Arthur Gregory was reported to be up before the magistrates charged with 'furious driving' at Portsea. A police constable had witnessed the defendant hurtling along Butcher Street in a horse-drawn cart, whipping the horse. The 'manner of [Gregory's] driving tended to endanger the lives of passengers, as he was going about ten miles an hour'. Gregory pleaded guilty, saying in his defence, 'This here hoss was brought to me by a dealer for sale; it was what ye call a 'jibbing hoss'. He was a very bad tempered animal, and her would go very fast or her would not go at all.' Gregory was fined £1 with 9s costs. (*Hampshire Telegraph*)

October 7th

1959: 'One can drive through miles of streets [in Portsmouth] without ever seeing a poster in a window or a sticker on a car,' lamented a correspondent on the eve of the General Election of 1959. Two years earlier, Harold Macmillan had made his assertion that Britons 'had never had it so good', but few people seemed to share his belief, at least, not out loud.

> Only the abysmal record of the football club can be relied on to provoke heated speculations, and any candidate who could promise a few more goals would be welcome indeed.
>
> The undemonstrative campaign has been surprising considering that Portsmouth has a slightly higher percentage of unemployment than the national average, that wages in the town are low and that the prosperity of the Dockyard, which employs 23,000 people, is largely dependent on the future strength of the Navy.

The apathy, it was suggested, might be down to the fact that 'Portsmouth is a rather insular community', that 'dockies are long accustomed to low pay' and that 'naval tradition tends to subdue electioneering'.

The following day, four Conservative MPs were elected in the four Portsmouth seats. (*The Times*)

———◆———

1932: The Northern Secondary School in Mayfield Road was opened. (City of Portsmouth Records of the Corporation ,ed. Gates, Singleton-Gates, Barnett, Blanchard, Windle, Riley)

October 8th

1914: Albert Clarke, aged ten, appeared before the Portsmouth Police Court charged with stealing a bottle of sauce, valued at 10*d* from Messrs Pink and Sons Ltd of No. 110 Commercial Road. An assistant spotted the bottle was missing after the boy had been asked if there were any cracked eggs he could have. On being told he could not have any, he left, the assistant followed him and found the sauce in his bag. Clarke, 'whose character was not a good one', tried unsuccessfully to blame two other boys, but was ordered to receive three strokes of the birch. (*Hampshire Telegraph*)

1765: The night sky was broken by an incredible sight of:

> ... a wonderful celestial phenomenon reaching its climax over Portsmouth. It was evidently a meteor of extraordinary proportions. In London it was observed as a globe of ruddy fire as large as the full moon a little after rising; at Chichester it was about the size of a man's head, and the light it diffused was almost as brilliant as sunlight; by the time it reached Portsmouth the light had paled and when over the town the meteor burst with a noise surpassing the loudest peal of thunder.

(*History of Portsmouth* by W. Gates, 1900)

October 9th

1845: Two farms of 310 acres at Milton and Eastney were auctioned by Crook, Son & Diaper at the George Hotel in High Street, Portsmouth. The farms had belonged to Lady Henderson Durham and covered the area east of what is now Winter Road and south of what is now Locksway Road. The farms boasted spacious barns, numerous stabling, piggeries, cattle houses and waggon sheds. Eastney Farm covered 146 acres of 'remarkably rich land' and was available as one lot as 'a fine investment', while the Milton estate was divided into twenty-seven lots which varied in size from three to fifteen acres. The land fetched more than £100 an acre, a large amount for arable land. (*Hampshire Telegraph*; *Yesterday*)

———— • ◆ • ————

1822: 'A large and commodious' Baptist chapel was opened in Lake Lane to cope with increased demand. The former chapel next door remained in use for the Sunday School to teach about 700 poor local children. Despite their poverty, these children raised £15 a year 'to support a native school in India which is called the Lake Lane School'. (*Baptist Magazine*)

October 10th

1921: Charles Edmund Dumaresq Clavell was born in Sydney, the son of Capt. Richard Clavell RN, and Eileen Ross. His parents returned to Britain when he was nine months old and the family settled in Portsmouth. Educated at Portsmouth Grammar School between 1935 and 1940, he was known to his friends (including Alan Bristow, the future helicopter entrepreneur) as Jimmy. He took an active part in school life and sports. However, the outbreak of the Second World War prevented him from attending university and he joined the Royal Artillery.

In 1941 he was sent to Singapore and was captured later that year by the Japanese and imprisoned for four years in the notorious Changi camp where only one in fifteen survived their internment. He later claimed that Changi was his university, triggering a lifelong fascination with the East.

On 26 February 1949, he married April José Stride, a dancer and actress from Southsea. The couple emigrated to the United States where James Clavell became an internationally bestselling author. Most of his novels were filmed, including *King Rat*, *Shogun* and *Noble House*. He also worked in the film industry, directing *To Sir With Love* and writing the screenplay for *The Great Escape*. (*Oxford Dictionary of National Biography*; Portsmouth Grammar School Archive)

October 11th

1930: Roy Horniman died at the age of sixty-two. According to his *Times* obituary, 'fiction and the stage were his chief occupations', though he was also active in the protection of animals. He was born in Southsea and educated at Portsmouth Grammar School. In his twenties he went on the stage but became interested in writing and theatre management.

His most famous work *Israel Rank* was the subversive and 'morally toxic' source novel for one of Ealing Studio's best films, *King Hearts and Coronets*, which was made in 1949, and starred Dennis Price and Alec Guinness. (*The Times*)

———— • ♦ • ————

1982: The *Mary Rose*, flagship of King Henry VIII, was raised to the surface after 437 years at the bottom of the Solent. One piece of ordnance recovered from the ship had the makers' inscription, 'Robert and John Owyn, Brethryn, borne in the cyte of London, the sonnes of Inglish, made thys bastard AD 1537' (*The Times*)

———— • ♦ • ————

1947: Olympic hurdler Alan Pascoe was born in Portsmouth. He was educated at Southern Grammar School. (*Debrett's People of Today 2010*)

———— • ♦ • ————

1898: Portsea Parish Institute was opened (*see* January 30th). (City of Portsmouth Records of the Corporation, ed. Gates, Singleton-Gates, Barnett, Blanchard, Windle, Riley)

October 12th

1971: The Secretary of State refused permission to demolish the Theatre Royal for a year, in expectation that it would be listed and preserved. It was made a Grade II listed building but the Council still wanted to demolish it.

The theatre was built in 1884 by C.J. Phipps and redesigned in 1900 by Frank Matcham, the greatest British theatre builder of the era. Under the management of John Waters Boughton, it became 'the major theatre in the south of England' and is now considered by experts to be 'one of the finest Victorian theatres surviving in the land'. (*The Theatres of Portsmouth* by J. Offord, 1986; City of Portsmouth Records of the Corporation, ed. Gates, Singleton-Gates, Barnett, Blanchard, Windle, Riley)

1883: 'A curious marriage' took place at Portsea. 'The contracting parties and the bridal party were mutes'. (*Leicester Chronicle*)

1971: Portsmouth City Council was informed that 450 trees in the city were affected by Dutch Elm Disease. The Ladies' Mile was lined with fine elm trees until Dutch Elm Disease and the Great Storm of 1987 ravaged them. (City of Portsmouth Records of the Corporation, ed. Gates, Singleton-Gates, Barnett, Blanchard, Windle, Riley)

October 13th

1755: The Beneficial School or 'Old Benny' in Kent Street opened its doors. A lucky few of the poor children of Portsea were educated there for nearly 200 years. The ground floor was designed as a large classroom, the upper floor as a meeting place for the Beneficial Society. This was a pioneering 'mutual aid' society whereby members paid a shilling a month so that they could 'support each other in affliction', but also provided schooling for some boys, nominated by members, who were chosen by lottery. (*The Portsmouth Beneficial School* by L. Gatt, 1986)

---◆---

1888: It was reported that two Dockyard policemen visited 'a house of ill-repute' in Southampton Row (off Queen Street), on business. They found a sailor who was absent without leave, arrested him and were about to take him back to the Dockyard when they were 'set upon by several roughs of the neighbourhood'. According to a correspondent, the men assaulted the policemen and enabled the sailor to escape. Subsequently, no action was taken against the culprits. The *Hampshire Telegraph*, describing them as 'brothel bullies', argued that the police should be better supported in their 'arduous and disagreeable duties'. (*Hampshire Telegraph*)

October 14th

1799: The *Portsmouth Telegraph*, or *Mottley's Naval and Military Journal,* was published for the first time. The newspaper changed its title twice more, before the name *Hampshire Telegraph and Sussex Chronicle* was adopted in July 1803.

In 1801, the population of Portsmouth was 33,000. This grew to nearly 195,000 by 1901. The newspaper provided a chronicle of events for the busy naval port of Portsmouth throughout the century. (19th Century British Newspapers, http://newspapers.bl.uk/blcs/)

———— • ◆ • ————

1736: Elizabeth Smith was found guilty of stealing an apron from Elizabeth Knight and sentenced to be taken from the jail:

> to the publick whipping post in the Market Place ... and to be stript from the middle upwards and then fixt to the said whipping post and there receive Twenty Lashes with a Cat of Nine Tails from the hands of the Comon Beadle on her naked back and till the same be Bloody and then return to the said Gaol and there remain until her fees are paid.

At this time, floggings also took place on Southsea Common, at the Dockyard Gate or while being led through the town on a cart. A fee of sixpence was paid to the beadle or constable for each person flogged. (Extracts from 'Records in the possession of the Municipal Corporation of the Borough of Portsmouth' by Robert East, 1891)

October 15th

1666: Five weeks after the Great Fire of London, it was enacted 'that every person having his chimney on fire in the daytime should pay 10s for the first offence; if at night 20s'. (*Annals of Portsmouth* by W.H. Saunders, 1880)

———◆◆———

1795: Sir Thomas Tassell Grant, an inventor, was baptised at St Mary's Church. In 1812 he joined the Admiralty and in 1828 won promotion to storekeeper at the Royal Clarence Victualling Yard. It was here he began his career as an inventor. In 1829 he devised machinery for making ship's biscuits; this was installed in the victualling yard three years later. In 1834 he invented a desalination plant which distilled fresh water at sea; this was adopted by the naval authorities and was described by *The Times* as 'the greatest benefit ever conferred on the sailor, materially advancing the sanitary and moral condition of the Navy'. Other innovations were a steam kitchen, a new naval fuel and improved types of lifebuoys and paddle wheels. (*Oxford Dictionary of National Biography*; *The Times*)

———◆◆———

1924: The Royal Naval War Memorial on Southsea Common was unveiled by the Duke of York. The number of men listed on the memorial at that time was 9,279. (City of Portsmouth Records of the Corporation, ed. Gates, Singleton-Gates, Barnett, Blanchard, Windle, Riley)

October 16th

1987: For PC Steve Woodward, based at Southsea Police Station, the previous evening had been the 'usual collection of calls, nothing unusual…' Then, in the early hours of this day in 1987, the fiercest winds recorded for over 250 years hit the area. Steve and a colleague witnessed the storm at its height, rescuing people and helping where they could:

> A large tree had fallen from Milton Park and was now blocking the road. I informed Charlie-one. I reversed back into Goldsmith Avenue and headed east down to the White House pub, where I turned left into Milton Road. I saw that another tree had fallen across the road, but there appeared to be a gap big enough to get through on the offside pavement. I was just about to move forward when Dave screamed out 'Shit, look at that'.
>
> He pointed towards a large oak tree positioned on the edge of Milton Park. It was visibly shaking at its base. Then, like a Saturn 5 rocket, it took off, slowly being pulled from the ground, taking the footpath and attached fencing with it. After it left the ground it seemed to be tossed around like a matchstick before being flung into the park. 'Sod this, I'm off.' I slammed the car into reverse and got far enough away from the trees as quickly as possible.

(*Kilo Sierra Five One: Policing Portsmouth in the 1980s* by S. Woodward, 2010)

October 17th

1943: An enemy aircraft flew over the city and machine-gunned the Southsea district in a random attack. Slight damage to one house was reported, but there were no casualties. (City of Portsmouth Records of the Corporation, ed. Gates, Singleton-Gates, Barnett, Blanchard, Windle, Riley)

———— • ◆ • ————

1888: Gunner John Roberts, one of the first men awarded the Victoria Cross, died at Southsea. During the Crimean War, Roberts and two others landed on a heavily-defended beach but managed to destroy enemy equipment and ammunition dumps. Roberts is buried in Highland Cemetery. (*Hampshire Telegraph*)

———— • ◆ • ————

1817: Ben Terry, the son of publican Benjamin Terry, was baptised at St Thomas's Church. As a boy, Ben helped out making props, playing in the house band and learning the trade of acting at the Portsmouth Theatre in the High Street.

In 1838 he married Sarah Ballard, the daughter of a local Wesleyan minister. Sarah came to share Ben's passion for the theatre, and they left the town to seek their fortune as actors. They had eleven children. Alice Ellen was born in 1847 and, as Ellen Terry, became the most famous actress of the last quarter of the nineteenth century. The dynasty continued with Sir John Gielgud, who was her nephew. (*A Pride of Terrys* by M. Steen, 1962)

October 18th

2005: The Spinnaker Tower was opened, following years of delays and spiralling costs. With a height of 170 metres it is the tallest accessible structure in the UK outside of London. In a profile of Portsmouth, the *Guardian* reported that 'a certain chippy provincialism still haunts the place, starting with the council. Culture has been ignored for decades. The Spinnaker Tower – some call it an icon, those with eyes in their head call it a carbuncle. It doesn't know how beautiful its geography makes it.' (*The Guardian*)

1890: A mass demonstration of Dockyard workers took place on this Saturday, calling for a reduction of the working day to eight hours, six days a week, so that unemployed workers could have jobs. About 3,000 men, accompanied by a brass band and six policemen, marched via the Terraces to Southsea Common. On arrival, two carts were pushed together to form a platform from which the famous Socialist, Tom Mann, addressed the crowd. Mann argued that there was 'something rotten' in a system that created a situation where 700,000 men were unemployed while others in work slaved for fourteen to sixteen hours a day. (*Hampshire Telegraph*)

October 19th

1915: Fernando Buschman, a Frenchman of Brazilian descent, played his violin through the night into this new day in 1915. When the guard came for him at a few minutes before seven in the morning, he kissed his beloved violin saying, 'Goodbye, I shall not need you anymore.'

Having arrived in London on 14 April claiming to be a commercial traveller in the food business, Buschman settled into the Piccadilly Hotel. On 23 April he caught the 9 a.m. train from Waterloo Station, claiming to a friend that he was visiting food merchants on the south coast. When he returned he said he had been to Portsmouth. While there he had incriminated himself as a naval spy by taking notes of his observations.

Very early on the morning of 5 June 1915, Buschman was arrested at his lodgings by Inspector George Riley of Scotland Yard. When he was questioned, Buschman stated that he had, indeed, been asked to find out information for the German Secret Service, but had refused.

Fernando Buschman's courtmartial took place on 29-30 September 1915, at Middlesex Guildhall. He pleaded 'not guilty' and presented evidence on his own behalf, but was sentenced to death by shooting. He refused a blindfold. (*Keep the Home Fires Burning* by J. Sadden, 1990)

October 20th

1707: The local court called on Thomas Appleford to cease melting tallow in his outhouse 'for it caused such a nauseous stink that it is very prejudiciall and hurtfull to the neighbours inhabiteing the houses adjacent.'

The cleanliness and smell of the old town was a constant concern as these extracts from the early eighteenth century illustrate:

...the Dung laying just without the Land Port Gate, and at the end of Leek Lane, is a great Nusance. We present as a very intolerable nusance the noisome stench arising from the Filth of the Hogs kept by Sir Thomas Ridge at his Brewhouse near Cold-arbour.

We present John Cobb and John Valeur for ... casting Ordure on the Poynt Beach and carrying the same in such laky and unsound Carriages as to skatter the same in passing the Streets...

the Emptying of the Boghouse in James' Court in this Burrough into a hole there lately dug not sufficient to containe the excrements put into it whereby it run over and was washed downe the gutter of ... Warblington Street ... is a common nusance.

(Extracts from 'Records in the possession of the Municipal Corporation of the Borough of Portsmouth' by Robert East, 1891)

October 21st

1957: A service was held at Milton Cemetery when the remains of up to 2,000 people were re-interred after being exhumed from land that had formerly been St Mary's graveyard at Highbury Street. The land was needed for the extension of the power station. (City of Portsmouth Records of the Corporation, ed. Gates, Singleton-Gates, Barnett, Blanchard, Windle, Riley)

———◆◆———

1869: William Robert Bellenie was born in Walworth Surrey, of Italian ancestry. As an adult, he changed his name to Walker. He joined the Navy and trained as a diver at HMS *Vernon* in Portsmouth Harbour, later working for a private company. He was in demand to deal with flooded mines and working on shipwrecks. In 1905 he became famous for his work in helping to underpin Winchester Cathedral, where the high water table – only 10ft below the surface – required an expert diver with stamina who could work in dangerous conditions. (*Oxford Dictionary of National Biography*)

———◆◆———

1833: Israel Harding was born in Portsmouth. Educated at the Royal Victoria School, Bath Square, Harding trained as a naval gunner at HMS *Excellent*. In 1882, his ship was hit by a live shell at Alexandria, Egypt, which he picked up and put it in a tub of water, saving many lives. He was awarded the Victoria Cross for his bravery. (*The Times*)

October 22nd

1915: The vicar of Portsea, Cyril Garbett, wrote a letter to members of his parish about the German war atrocities that filled the press at the time. Uppermost in people's minds at the time was the execution of Edith Clavell, a British nurse who had been shot by a firing squad ten days earlier for helping 200 Allied soldiers escape from Belgium.

Acknowledging that there was:

> …among us, a burning hot indignation and anger at the cold-blooded atrocities committed by our enemies', Garbett argued that 'we must not let anger or panic carry us away in demanding reprisals of a like nature upon the Germans. Many are asking that our airmen should be ordered to bombard defenceless towns in Germany. But the killing of German women and children would not restore to life those who have been [killed] … we would dishonour our cause if we used these weapons of reprisal. Reprisal would lead to reprisal, and the Germans would always be able to out-bid us in a competition of frightfulness.

(*Portsea Parish Church Magazine*)

———◆———

1955: The Lord Mayor laid the foundation stone of the Church of St Michael and All Saints, which was built to serve the new estate of Paulsgrove. (*The Times*)

October 23rd

1905: On the centenary of the Battle of Trafalgar, John Masefield walked down to Point and set sail into Portsmouth Harbour. Masefield was probably most famous for his poem *Sea Fever,* which begins: 'I must go down to the seas again, to the lonely sea and the sky, And all I ask is a tall ship and a star to steer her by...'

After passing *Victory*, 'gay with flags', he 'came to an old coal hulk, a decayed ship of the line, which ... now awaited the breakers.' He was shocked to see the old ship:

> ...once so stately, now so lonely and ruinous. Her sides were broken about and her ports gone and they had nailed canvas on parts of her where the poor seams gaped most. She had once been a splendid vessel, with a glorious carved stern and colours at her peak. Now she was all falling apart, a thing infinitely melancholy ... I confess I had not expected more of Portsmouth. The town is peopled by those who express their patriotism in their lives.

(*The Guardian*)

———•◆•———

1942: General de Gaulle visited Portsmouth and thanked the Lord Mayor for the city's hospitality and wartime support for French sailors. (City of Portsmouth Records of the Corporation, ed. Gates, Singleton-Gates, Barnett, Blanchard, Windle, Riley)

October 24th

1818: Thomas Huntingford, a seventy-one-year-old Dockyard shipwright, was found covered in blood in bed in his lodgings in Orange Street, Portsea. A doctor was called but on arrival pronounced the man dead, and declared that he had died from a burst blood vessel. Just before leaving, he asked that a handkerchief that was wrapped around Huntingford's head be removed, and four deep wounds were found.

Sarah, his sixty-one-year-old wife, claimed that two intruders had murdered him, a story maintained throughout her trial and imprisonment before her public execution at Gallows Hill, Winchester on 8 March 1819. According to a contemporary account:

> When brought out of the gaol, she stepped on the sledge with firmness, and did not appear otherwise at the place of execution, even when the fatal cart was removed, and she was launched into eternity. She was drawn to the place of execution on a hurdle, and her body delivered to the surgeon of the gaol to be dissected and anatomised. It is conjectured, that nearly 10,000 persons were assembled to witness the awful ceremony. All the other capital convicts were reprieved before the Judges left the city.

(*Salisbury & Winchester Journal; The Times*)

October 25th

1856: The following advertisement appeared in the *Hampshire Telegraph*:

> WANTED, a SITUATION as indoor SERVANT by a Black Man, aged 22 years, who understands his business, has been accustomed to the charge of a horse and carriage, can produce good testimonials, and is permitted to refer to his late master, whom he has just left, and others of respectability.
> Apply to Mr Hunt, Scripture Reader, Somers Town, Southsea.

(*Hampshire Telegraph*)

———◆———

1809: There was general rejoicing in Portsmouth on the Jubilee of George III. The day started with the ringing of church bells and fifty guns being discharged from the Platform Battery. Between 5–6,000 poor inhabitants 'were regaled, at their own houses, with beef, strong beer and bread'. Debtors were released from the Borough Jail and Poorhouse inmates were 'regaled with roast beef, plum puddings and strong beer'.
(*Hampshire Telegraph*)

———◆———

1977: *The Times* asked the question, 'Is there a connection between the skateboard craze in Portsmouth and the disappearance of wheels from trolleys in the city's supermarkets?' (*The Times*)

October 26th

1704: The Leet or Grand Jury stated that:

> the anointing of Ratts with Turpentine and putting fire to them is of Dangerous consequence especially in this Towne where there are Magazeens of Powder, and tends to the setting the dwelling houses of the Inhabitants on fire.

(Extracts from 'Records in the possession of the Municipal Corporation of the Borough of Portsmouth' by Robert East, 1891)

———•◆•———

1885: The Provincial Tramway Co. found itself being prosecuted at Portsmouth Police Court for operating an overcrowded horse-tram. Town Council regulations limited the capacity of a one-horse tram to eighteen persons so that the horse was not overworked.

However, PC Moss and PC Coles spotted a poor horse struggling to pull the No. 6 tram from Hilsea, laden with forty-eight passengers, not including the driver and conductor. The conductor explained that there had been a football match at Hilsea and that the players had piled on. 'Young fellows who play football would be rather awkward people to push off a car?' asked the Clerk of the Court sympathetically. 'They would, sir,' replied the young conductor. The Court was told that the manager of the tram company, Mr White, had been 'called away to London' and the case went undefended. A fine of £1 was imposed. (*Hampshire Telegraph*)

October 27th

1894: The foundation stone of St Agatha's Church in Conway Street was laid. Father Robert Radclyffe Dolling arrived in the town in 1885 and became one of the most famous priests of the Victorian era. The area had one pub for every 155 inhabitants, nineteen slaughter houses and numerous brothels; Dolling conceived of building 'the most splendid church in the most squalid part of Portsea'. Exactly a year later, St Agatha's was consecrated.

Father Dolling was a High Anglican and Christian Socialist and it was these attributes that shaped and guided his ministry. Earlier in 1894, Dolling had 'brought a hornet's nest around his ears' by describing Portsmouth as a 'sink of iniquity'. Stung by this criticism, the Mayor, Abraham Emanuel, rushed to condemn Dolling, accusing him of only having been in the town 'five minutes'– actually nine years –said his description was 'wanton', 'wicked', 'a slander' and 'a lie'. It is 'without a shadow of foundation in fact' he maintained to his audience of members of the Northsea Cycling Club at a meeting in the Dairyman's Arms in Stamshaw. (*Churches, Chapels and Places of Worship on Portsea Island* by J. Offord, 1989 ; *Hampshire Telegraph*; City of Portsmouth Records of the Corporation ed. Gates, Singleton-Gates, Barnett, Blanchard, Windle, Riley)

October 28th

1905: Sir Harry Broadhurst was born in Frimley. He joined Portsmouth Grammar School in 1915 and left in 1922 to become an articled pupil to a surveyor. Meanwhile, he served in the Hampshire Territorial Army and was seconded to the RAF on appointment to a short service commission.

Known as 'Broady', he earned his reputation as a fighter leader early in the Second World War, at squadron, group, and station level, personifying the fighting spirit of the RAF. Awarded the Distinguished Flying Cross (DFC) in 1940, he served with the British Expeditionary Force air component in France, then successively commanded Coltishall, Wittering, and Hornchurch stations during the Battle of Britain. He often piloted a Spitfire with squadrons under his command, and his final kill claims were a total of thirteen destroyed, seven probables and ten damaged.

Broadhurst took command of the Desert Air Force in 1943, becoming the youngest Air Vice-Marshall in the RAF. After serving with distinction in support of the Eighth Army, Broadhurst was posted back to the UK to participate in planning for Operation Overlord, the D-Day landings in Normandy. In the post-war years Broadhurst, held high commands. He died in Chichester in 1995. (*Oxford Dictionary of National Biography*)

October 29th

1871: Revd Charles Kingsley, author of *The Water Babies*, preached two sermons at a packed St Jude's Church in Southsea. In the morning, Kingsley drew attention to the plight of 13,000 local people who lived in 'misery and squalor' and employers 'left them alone, caring only for the money they could make out of them'. It was, he maintained to his wealthy congregation, the duty of the rich to be charitable. The plate was passed around and £62 was collected. In the evening sermon, Kingsley explained that feeling self-satisfied about being charitable was not enough. One had also to be humane and to actually care. This time, he only raised £35.

In 1863, Kingsley delivered a lecture to the boys of Wellington College, suggesting that school holidays were not a good thing, likening them to:

> ...Jack when he is paid off at Portsmouth. He is suddenly free from the discipline of ship-board. He has plenty of money ... to have a lark, and makes a fool of himself til his money is spent; and then he is very poor, and sick, and seedy, and cross and disgusted with himself and longs to get a fresh ship and go to work again...

(*Letters and Memories* by C. Kingsley, 1879; *Hampshire Telegraph*)

October 30th

1895: The 'Status and Sphere of Women' was considered by the Portsmouth Literary and Scientific Society at a meeting held in the Mayor's Banqueting Hall. The President, Mr T. Bramsdon, said that:

> ...a physically finer race of young women was growing up in England than ever before, a circumstance largely due to them joining in outdoor sport and exercises, tennis, boating, cricket, swimming, hunting and even football, while the 'new woman' on her bicycle was taking the roads by storm.

This observation prompted laughter from the floor. Bramsdon contended that 'women were intellectually inferior to men, were more emotional and that, in their case, instinct had not been replaced by reason to the extent that it had in the male sex'. There was no recorded dissent amongst the exclusively male audience. (*Hampshire Telegraph*)

———•◆•———

1895: The foundation stone was laid of a new Congregational Church on the corner of Stanhope Road and Edinburgh Road on land that had been vacated by the War Office. Opened the following year, it was the successor to the old King Street Chapel which had been closed three years earlier. The church was demolished in 1972. (*Churches, Chapels and Places of Worship on Portsea Island* by J. Offord, 1989)

October 31st

1808: The first state lottery was chartered by Queen Elizabeth I in 1566 and took place in 1569; its aim was to provide money for the defences of Portsmouth and other ports. Each ticket holder won a prize, and the total value of the prizes equalled the money raised, so it provided an interest free loan. Prizes were in the form of silver plate, jewellery and tapestries. The lottery was promoted by scrolls posted throughout the country showing sketches of the prizes.

Lotteries continued into the nineteenth century, by which time it was organised through brokers. Details of a new state lottery were announced on this day in 1808 in the *Hampshire Telegraph*. Tickets were available from W. Woodward, the town's licensed lottery agent, at The Hard, Portsea. There were 20,000 tickets with one winner in every four, and prizes ranged from £15 to £20,000. Most people were unable to afford the cost of a ticket, and so shares in tickets were sold.

By the 1820s, the idea had fallen out of favour, one of the concerns being the morality of speculators fleecing the poor who were desperate to improve their lot. (*Hampshire Telegraph*; *History of Portsmouth* by W. Gates, 1900)

November 1st

1892: Ferdinand Green Foster entered public life, being elected councillor for All Saints Ward. He had built up a successful business as a pharmacist. In 1907, he became Mayor for the first time and, as a widower, installed his daughter Doris, aged five and a half years, as Mayoress.

Foster became an Alderman in 1911, was Mayor again in 1922 and Lord Mayor in 1931. His most noteworthy achievements were in education, and he opened the Municipal College in 1908. He served as the first chair of the Higher Education committee and was also chair of the Education Committee. Secondary education facilities were expanded under his chairmanship and he was instrumental in the establishment of the Training College for teachers against considerable opposition, a contribution later recognised in the naming of Foster Hall at the Teachers' Training College at Milton in 1938.

He set up the Naval Disasters Fund, following the accidental sinking of two ships in April 1908, HMS *Tiger* – where thirty-five lives were lost – and HMS *Gladiator* – where thirty lives were lost. This fund was so successful it continued to help the families of men killed in later accidents. (*A Record of Public Service*: Alderman F.G. Foster, 1939; City of Portsmouth Records of the Corporation, ed. Gates, Singleton-Gates, Barnett, Blanchard, Windle, Riley)

November 2nd

1813: It was reported that 'a majestic lion and two beautiful Arabian horses' had arrived in Portsmouth, a present from the Emperor of Morocco to the Prince Regent. (*Hull Packet*)

———◆———

1891: The Empire Theatre in Edinburgh Road was opened, offering music hall or variety acts. The band of the 1st Yorkshire Regiment from local barracks 'tested the acoustic properties of the auditorium'. A full house of 800 seated and 300 standing enjoyed a varied bill which included acrobats, dancers, a comedian, a banjo player, songs, comedy sketches and 'living marionettes'.

In 1913, the theatre was renovated and renamed the Coliseum. Marie Lloyd topped the bill at the gala reopening and patrons were greeted by 'daintily attired waiting maids'. Pantomines were a popular draw in the 1930s and, post war, the theatre flourished under its original name until the mid-1950s when television became popular. The last performance took place on 30 August 1958 and the premises was sold and demolished to make way for a supermarket. (*Theatres of Portsmouth* by J. Offord, 1986; *The Era*)

November 3rd

1791: William Cobbett landed at Portsmouth from New Brunswick and applied for a discharge from the Army. He had become disillusioned with the treatment of ordinary soldiers and the attitude of the officer class. From his experience as a sergeant major, and familiarity with regimental accounts, he knew that corruption was rife and decided to leave the Army to expose it. The quartermaster was keeping provisions for himself and four officers were selling their men's rations of food and firewood for profit. The only evidence of fraud he had was the regimental accounts and so Cobbett made copies of all the relevant entries, stamping them with the regimental seal in the presence of a faithful witness, Corporal Bestland. He put the incriminating papers in a box and entrusted them to a custom-house officer, who hid them in his house at Portsmouth.

When he exposed the corruption, the authorities put obstacles in the way of a prosecution and Cobbett learned of an attempt to discredit him with an accusation that he had proposed a Jacobin anti-royal toast. Cobbett decided to abandon the court martial and fled to France. This was Cobbett's first confrontation with the establishment. (*The Life and Adventures of William Cobbett* by R. Ingrams, 2006)

November 4th

1864: A respectable-looking woman applied to the Portsea Island Workhouse for a wet nurse for a lady in London. The woman said she had been sent by Sir John Creamer's wife. The matron recommended the last inmate who had given birth, Hannah Turton. A new life in London at £15 a year was offered and the matron recommended it, saying it was 'a very good opening for her'. In due course, Turton and her baby were put on a train and sent third class to Waterloo, where she was to be met and transported by carriage to Peckham House. Meanwhile, the respectable-looking woman disappeared with Turton's baby.

Sixteen days later, the police interviewed Mary Flucks, aged twenty-seven, at a house in Cowes, who maintained that the baby she was looking after was her own, a story backed up by her mother who claimed to have delivered it. It emerged at trial that Flucks had recently miscarried. She was sentenced to six months' imprisonment with hard labour, and her mother was imprisoned for three months. (*Hampshire Telegraph*)

—◆—

1908: Five De La Salle brothers opened the first St John's College at No. 27 South Parade. (*History of the Parish and Church of St Swithun's* by P. Tansey, 1984)

November 5th

1906: A stokers' mutiny at the Royal Naval Barracks in Queen Street ended. It was provoked the previous day by a command ordering men to go 'on the knee', which was perceived as insulting and demeaning. A year earlier, the offending officer had given the order 'On your knee you dog' to a stoker, but had been forced to apologise for his conduct. On this occasion the men mutinied, supported by many local people. *The Times* reported that 'the crowd outside, picking up stones, broke a number of windows in the officers' quarters'. Stoker Moody, who was picked out to be made an example of, argued that there 'was no order in the drill book or any written authority' for the command. He was sentenced to five years' detention, reduced to three on appeal. (*The Times*)

———— • ◆ • ————

1977: The Tatler Cinema (previously the Rex, later the Classic) in Fratton Road offered a new attraction to boost wilting audiences, 'live exotic striptease' plus 'two new uncensored films'. This was every Monday, for members only, while non-members could enjoy 'the best in film entertainment for adults only'. In the first weeks they showed *Emmanuelle*, which brought a taste of exotic Bangkok to the heart of Fratton. The cinema closed in 1983, reopening later as a snooker hall before demolition. (*Portsmouth & District Post*)

November 6th

1947: The children's author Michelle Magorian was born in Southsea, the daughter of William Magorian and Gladys Evans of Victoria Road North. As a child she spent her spare time at the King's Theatre and her ambition was to go on the stage, for which she later trained. However, she found success with her writing, and is probably best known for her 1981 novel, *Goodnight Mister Tom*, which was televised in 1998, and starred John Thaw, and *Just Henry*, which won the Costa Children's Book Award in 2008. (*Who's Who 2010*; *Financial Times*)

———— ◆ ————

1914: A sergeant attached to the temporary First World War hospital in Fawcett Road (now Priory School) was reported to have been approached by a well-to-do lady, who said to him, 'Oh, would you please give these cigarettes to the wounded soldiers?' While the sergeant was expecting to receive a few packets, the lady extracted from her handbag, with a flourish, two Woodbines. (*Hampshire Telegraph*)

———— ◆ ————

1903: Following a suggestion that HMS *Victory* be taken from Portsmouth Harbour and embedded in concrete on Southsea Common, the *Portsmouth Times* gave its view. The idea was 'too ludicrous for comment by anyone who has the least pretence to common sense'. (*Portsmouth Times*)

November 7th

1864: The first detachment marched into the new Royal Marine Artillery Barracks at Eastney. The RMA had first come to the Portsmouth area in 1817 and were initially stationed at Fort Cumberland, relocated to Fort Monckton, then established in barracks in the Gunwharf in 1824. A headquarters was also set up in the High Street and additional messrooms were erected in the garden. There was another brief sojourn at Fort Cumberland before Eastney Barracks was purpose-built, being completed after two years. Fort Cumberland was retained for gunnery instruction, artillery drill and bridge and trestle building. (*Portsmouth: In Defence of the Realm* by J. Sadden, 2001)

———◆———

1854: The first interment in Highland Road Cemetery took place. The Victoria Cross was instituted two years later at the end of the Crimean War and subsequently, seven soldiers who had been awarded the VC for individual acts of bravery were buried there.

A former England and Pompey player, a veteran of the Battle of Waterloo, German POWs from the First World War, Royal Flying Corps veterans, two of Charles Dickens' paramours, an Austrian Count and an American Civil War veteran also share the space. (*Highland Cemetery: A Guide* by Portsmouth City Council)

November 8th

1904: Complaints of 'foul emanations' were common in St Thomas's Church (now Portsmouth Cathedral). For centuries it had been the custom to inter the bodies of the favoured, great and good beneath the church floor, rather than in the graveyard where ordinary mortals were consigned. For worshippers, dressed in their Sunday best and praising God, the smell was becoming intolerable.

A new vicar of Portsmouth, the Revd Daniel C. Darnell, was appointed in 1899, and very soon became aware of the problem. He initiated a complete restoration of the church and the floor was pulled up. Examination revealed that the soil beneath was mainly composed of decayed coffins and human remains and the Revd Darnell, who rolled his sleeves up to help out, contracted typhoid from which he died.

The church was officially re-opened, 'safe and sanitary', by the Bishop of Winchester on this day. Mrs Darnell paid for a memorial for her late husband in the form of black and white flooring for part of the church. (*The Times*; City of Portsmouth Records of the Corporation, ed. Gates, Singleton-Gates, Barnett, Blanchard, Windle, Riley)

November 9th

1963: A correspondent in the *Evening News* complained that Milton Locks had become 'a meeting place of rubbish and riff raff'. It was alleged that gangs of scooter and motorcycle riding youths swore and committed acts of hooliganism and that gang fights 'were a nightly occurrence'. The writer said that six scooters were speeding along Locksway Road at 60mph, pursued by a police motor-cyclist, and the pillion riders 'threw explosive fireworks back at the policeman'. (*Evening News, Portsmouth*)

———— ◆ ————

1816: A great gale nearly swept away the new bathing rooms on Southsea beach. The flooding of Southsea Common was a common occurrence throughout the nineteenth century. Four years later, a violent storm wrenched the *Borneo*, an East Indiaman, from her Spithead anchorage over the beach and left her stranded on the Common, and another four years later the ebbing tide took away part of a ballroom. By 1831 it had been resolved to drain and level the Greater and Little Morasses, and work was carried out by convict labour. By 1840, a huge bank of shingle had been put in place as a defence, minimising the risk of flooding. (*History of Portsmouth* by W.Gates, 1900)

November 10th

1884: Eighteen-year-old Beatrix Potter, having arrived in Portsmouth for a brief visit, wrote in her diary:

> In the High Street was a charming bird shop where they had a most incredible number of dormice in two cages. I don't believe they were dormice, too large by three or four sizes. Am considering how it would be possible to convey some home. Only saw one curiosity shop with only old china, which is very interesting to my taste, but not my purse ... dirty old back streets, suggestive of the press-gang. Extraordinary boxes for carrying admiral's cocked-hats, also several shops with curious musical instruments. Quite a flourishing Unitarian Chapel abounding in tombstones opposite the house where Buckingham was murdered.
>
> Quantity of convicts working, several warders on wooden platforms with guns. Scotch soldiers and men of war men ... much sturdier looking and more sensibly dressed than the soldiers, except perhaps the Highlanders.

The next day she wrote: 'Again looked at the dormice. Would they carry in a biscuit canister?' It is not known if she bought any to add to her menagerie of rabbits, frogs, newts, and ferrets which she watched for hours and sketched, developing her artistic abilities. (*Portsmouth as Others Have Seen It: 1790-1900* by M. Hoad, 1972)

November 11th

1907: Kaiser Wilhelm arrived in Portsmouth Harbour aboard the Royal Yacht *Hohenzollern*, accompanied by a squadron of German battleships. The Kaiser was personally greeted by Mayor Ferdinand Foster as he disembarked on the Hard railway jetty.

The *Evening News*, striving to maintain a diplomatic balance, revealed that:

> The Kaiser has the kissing habit but he is not promiscuous in indulging it. As a matter of fact, although Emperor William is the greatest kisser of men among sovereigns of the world, he is also a hearty hand-shaker with a grip that is famous … [he has] a big strong hand with muscles like iron. [This] he reserves for strong men. For the opposite sex he has a hand that is as soft as velvet and a courtesy that is elegant.

Mayor Foster survived this ordeal and announced that His Majesty's visit was an indication of 'the friendly relationships existing between the Royal Houses of Germany and England, which we trust may be long continued to the advantage of the whole world'. A few years later, during the First World War, the *Evening News* suggested that the Kaiser had, after all, been rude during the visit. (*Keep the Home Fires Burning* by J. Sadden, 1990)

November 12th

1900: The *Pall Mall Gazette* reported the 'decided success' of an Automobile Club run from London to Southsea. 'Horseless vehicles' were still a novelty and thousands turned out along the route to wave flags and watch them pass by, some of them carrying brave 'lady passengers'.

The cars were halted at Portsdown Hill to be polished up and, at 4.30 in the afternoon, eighty of the 104 that had set out, drove into Portsmouth under police supervision, to be greeted by thousands of spectators. A civic reception at the Town Hall was headed by Mayor Alderman Emanuel, who awarded a prize for the cleanest vehicle. The festivities continued into the evening at the Esplanade Hotel, and the following day many of the cars took a pleasant spin along the front before returning to London via Basingstoke. (*Pall Mall Gazette*)

———◆———

1912: Petty Officer Thomas Williamson of Portsmouth was a member of a small search party in the Antarctic. On this morning, Williamson and the men came across a snowbound tent and, after summoning up the courage to look inside, they 'saw a most ghastly sight, three sleeping bags with bodies in them'. In his log he recorded, 'The one in the middle I recognised as Captain Scott.' (*The Times*)

November 13th

1948: Lloyd 'Lindy' Delapenha played for Pompey, the team's first black player and the first time a Jamaican had played professional football in England. He made seven appearances for the side, scoring once, and was part of the successful squad that won the League Championship. (*Settlers, Visitors & Asylum Seekers: Diversity in Portsmouth* by P. MacDougall, 2007)

<hr>

1847: Following repeated complaints from the women who wanted their husbands at home, William New, a Rudmore inn keeper, was reported to have been charged with illegally keeping his establishment open out of hours. He was fined £1 with 11*s* costs, and the wives presumably got their husbands back. (*Hampshire Telegraph*)

<hr>

1884: Daisy (Margaret) Scudamore was born, the daughter of Clara and William Scudamore, a Dockyard shipwright. She became an actress and in 1907 married actor Roy Redgrave. Their son, Michael Redgrave, was born the following year. Michael Redgrave married actress Rachel Kempson and the acting dynasty continued with Vanessa, Corin and Lynn and grandchildren Natasha, Joely and Jemma. (www.imdb.com)

November 14th

1832: The poultry house at Great Salterns Farm was broken into, such attacks being one of the problems encountered by farmers who worked within walking distance of the Town. The Great Salterns Estate, owned by Francis Sharp, covered 340 acres on the east side of Portsea Island, three miles from Old Portsmouth. The thieves:

> immediately commenced the work of destruction upon five geese, which they killed, and were about to treat the remainder in the same way, when they were very unexpectedly surprised by a discharge from a fowling piece which although it did them no harm, so frightened them they dropped their booty and made off without further ceremony.

A more serious threat came three years later when a fire broke out in the farmyard which caused £1,000 worth of damage and was found to be the work of an arsonist.

In the early nineteenth century, wheat was prone to diseases, one of the most common being a fungus called smut. This appears to have been a problem that had been solved at Great Salterns in the early 1800s, possibly by soaking the seed in chamberlye (urine). (*Farms and Market Gardens on Portsea Island* by S. Shuttleworth, 1993; *Hampshire Telegraph*)

November 15th

1922: One of the closest General Election results was recorded in Portsmouth (Central) when the Conservative Candidate, Frank Privett, pipped the Liberal candidate by seven votes. (City of Portsmouth Records of the Corporation, ed. Gates, Singleton-Gates, Barnett, Blanchard, Windle, Riley)

———◆———

1976: Portsmouth's new civic offices were opened by Admiral of the Fleet Earl Mountbatten of Burma, bringing together the different departments which had been dispersed throughout the city. Earl Mountbatten was made an Honorary Freeman of the City.

In June 1977, Mountbatten attended a Silver Jubilee civic reception at Portsmouth and, in November, performed the opening of the illuminated Silver Jubilee fountain in the Commercial Road shopping precinct. He returned again in September 1978 to unveil a portrait of himself at the Royal Marine Museum at Eastney.

Less than a year later he was killed, along with three others, in an IRA bomb attack on his fishing boat in Ireland. On the same day, the IRA also ambushed and killed eighteen British soldiers.

Mountbatten had many associations with Portsmouth. He served in the Royal Navy as a midshipman during the First World War. As a young man he was interested in technological developments and joined the Portsmouth Signal School in 1924. (City of Portsmouth Records of the Corporation, ed. Gates, Singleton-Gates, Barnett, Blanchard, Windle, Riley; *Evening News, Portsmouth*)

November 16th

1955: The world premiere of the film *Cockleshell Heroes* was held at the Empire Theatre in Leicester Square. The film was a fictionalised version of a real life commando raid in Bordeaux Harbour in which Major H.G. Hasler led Royal Marine Commandos in canoes (cockles) up the Gironde Estuary in south-west France and damaged several blockade runners with limpet mines.

The secret unit, the Royal Marine Boom Patrol Detachment, was formed in July 1942, and trained at Eastney Barracks and in the waters of the Solent. The frogmen and canoeists achieved their objective on 11 December 1942, destroying vital radar and other equipment that Germany was exporting to Japan. Ten men took part in the raid but only two returned, Major Hasler and Corporal Bill Sparks.

Both survivors worked as advisors on the film. The training sequences were filmed at Eastney Barracks and the Dockyard and Fort Brockhurst railway station are also featured. Written by Brian Forbes, it was directed by José Ferrer (who also starred in it) and included Trevor Howard, Anthony Newley and Dora Bryan in its cast. (*Cockleshell Heroes* by C. Lucas Phillips, 2000; www.imdb.com)

November 17th

1759: The body of General Wolfe, who had been killed leading the campaign against the French in Quebec, was brought ashore at Point with full military honours. The previous year he had written to his mother, 'The necessity of living in the midst of the diabolical citizens of Portsmouth is a real and unavoidable calamity. It is a doubt to me if there is such another collection of demons upon the whole earth.'(*Portsmouth as Others Have Seen it* 1540-1770 by M Hoad, 1973; *History of Portsmouth* by W. Gates, 1900)

———•◆•———

1890: The Local Government Board approved a bye-law forbidding any male over eight years old from bathing in the sea within 50 yards of females. (Bye-laws made by the Corporation of Portsmouth, 1890)

———•◆•———

1813: Martha Chamberlain, who had been convicted of 'pretending to tell the fortune of one Julia Slocombe and taking a sum of money as a fee' was granted mercy. She was imprisoned for a year, but the part of her sentence whereby she was to be set in the pillory every three months during her sentence was revoked. (Extracts from 'Records in the possession of the Municipal Corporation of the Borough of Portsmouth' by Robert East, 1891)

November 18th

1929: Sir George Archdall Reid, a physician whose writings on heredity aroused great interest in the Edwardian period, died.

In 1920, Reid was active in countering Lord Sandhurst's assertion that the incidence of venereal disease was two-and-a-half times greater amongst soldiers in the Portsmouth area than in any other area of the UK. Stating that Portsmouth was 'a model area for the whole country' in prevention and treatment, Reid was backed up by fellow doctors in the *British Medical Journal*.

The example of Clarence Barracks was given, where the Medical Officer recorded, with an average of 2,000 troops, seven cases originating among his men in over two years. The Royal Marine Artillery at Eastney, with 4,000 men, recorded five cases in nine months. This dramatic lowering of the rate since 1917 was attributed to 'the method of carefully teaching men to swab immediately after exposure' with a solution of potassium permanganate. Five hundred bottles were issued to men at the gunnery school on Whale Island with excellent results. This practice of self-disinfection was adopted by Portsmouth Town Council for civilian treatment and soon the dousing of genitalia in the purple solution spread throughout the land. (*British Medical Journal*; *The Times*)

November 19th

1893: Sidney Daniels was born in Bolton Road. His father, Walter, ran the Duke of Devonshire pub in Albert Road. By 1912, Sidney had a job earning 18*s* a week as a steward on board a new liner, the *Titanic*. As she sank, he offered his pocket knife to cut free the last life raft as the icy waters of the Atlantic lapped the upper decks. This raft saved twenty-five crew members, including Sidney.

By 1958, Sidney was a wire-splicer in the Dockyard and one of only twenty remaining *Titanic* survivors. He was invited to the premiere of the film *A Night to Remember* and recalled his experiences.

'We could hear the cries of people in the water around us for hours. I heard them for years afterwards. In the darkness noone spoke. We just said our prayers.' The raft was so loaded that they were sitting in water, and the man next to Sidney died of exposure. 'When I said I wanted to sleep, someone said, "For God's sake don't son, you'll freeze to death".'

When Walter received his son's cable from New York to say he was safe, he kept his pub open after hours to celebrate. (*Evening News, Portsmouth*)

November 20th

1889: Two washerwomen of Havant Street got into an altercation after one told the other's daughter that 'she had the extremely large number of fifty fathers'. This led to an allegation of assault in Grubb's bar involving hitting, spitting and hair pulling. A bundle of hair was offered as evidence for inspection by the Bench. The Bench, however, was not impressed and refused to get involved in a 'washerwomens' quarrel', charging each 4s costs. (*Hampshire Telegraph*)

1916: The Hippodrome in Commercial Road outdid itself in hyperbole. It was, the billboards announced, proud to be showing 'the Eighth Wonder of the World', 'the most stupendous spectacle the brain of man has visioned'. Unfortunately, the visionary brain belonged to D.W. Griffiths, who based his new epic silent film on a novel called *The Clansman*. Renamed *The Birth of a Nation*, the film promoted white supremacy and portrayed the Ku Klux Klan as heroes. The publicity evidently worked. Griffith's racist epic became the highest grossing film of the silent film era. (*Hampshire Telegraph*)

November 21st

1888: Mr Saunders, the sitting magistrate at Thames Police Court, received a letter bearing a Portsmouth postmark. It read:

> Dear Boss,
> It is no good for you to look for me in London, because I am not there. Don't trouble yourself about me till I return, which will not be very long. I like the work too well to leave it long. Oh it was such a jolly job, the last one. I had plenty of time to do it properly, ha ha! The next lot I mean to do with a vengeance – cut off their head and arms. You think it is the man with the black moustache, ha, ha, ha! When I have done another you can catch me; so goodbye, dear boss, till I return.
> Yours,
> JACK THE RIPPER

At around this time, the press reported that an unknown message, written on the shutter of a window in Hanover Street, Portsea, was linked to Jack the Ripper. This, together with the letter, prompted the press to speculate, very briefly, that the murder of a boy in Havant, who had his throat cut, was the work of the Whitechapel killer. (*Blackburn Standard*; *Belfast Newsletter*; *The Star*)

November 22nd

1904: A piece of land on the west side of Fratton Road was bought as a site for a police and fire station for the Fratton District for the sum of £648. At the back of the station, a house was erected for single officers' accommodation and a Bridewell, which was to serve as the main cell block for Portsmouth. Further north, a sub-station at Kingston Cross shared premises with a branch of the public library.

In 1941, the officers' accommodation was moved to Portland Terrace and, in the 1960s, Fratton Police Station was closed, and operations then moved to a new station in Kingston Crescent, which later became the headquarters when, following the amalgamation with the Hampshire Constabulary in 1967, the Portsea Island Divisional Headquarters at Byculla in Queen's Crescent, Southsea was closed. (www.hampshireconstabularyhistory.org.uk)

November 23rd

1781: Following a public meeting, a letter was sent to Lieutenant General Monckton, the Governor of Portsmouth:

> The Town and adjacent Roads are much infested at this time with disorderly People, by whom several Robberies have been very recently committed and many Lamps broken, And as the Road upon the Counterscarp between the Quay and Mill Gates is a great thoroughfare and entirely unprotected Request that your Excellency will be pleased to Order a Centinel in each Redan on the said Road, particularly during the Night; which they presume will be a perfect security to all Persons passing that way and also effectually preserve the Lamps, which at present are frequently destroyed, and the Public thereby deprived of the good Intentions of Government in ordering the said Road lighted.

Two years later, twenty sentinels were appointed and in 1835 it was decided that 'watching' was not enough and thirty constables were appointed to keep law and order. (Extracts from 'Records in the possession of the Municipal Corporation of the Borough of Portsmouth' by Robert East, 1891)

———— • ◆ • ————

1831: Mile End Cemetery was opened, a secure place where the departed could be buried without fear of being 'purloined from their silent abode for sordid gain'. The cemetery was eventually to be lost to commercial development, the site becoming part of the Continental Ferryport in the 1970s. (*Portsmouth in the Past* by W. Gates, 1975)

November 24th

1914: The borough opened its Central Soup Kitchen in St Vincent Street, offering 'the very poor a good meal for a penny'. It was reported that 1,600 pints were served and that 'a very large number of children' were recipients. Ten other soup kitchens scattered around the borough, including St George's Institute (Portsea), St Stephen's (Buckland) and Milton, also appear to have been very busy. During the previous winter, over a quarter of a million pints of soup were served. (*Hampshire Telegraph*)

———•✦•———

1662: Benjamin Burgess, vicar of St Thomas's, refused to bow to royal authority as demanded by the Act of Uniformity in 1662. Burgess maintained that he was accountable to God, not the King, and so was deprived of his living and, along with ninety other aldermen and burgesses, 'expunged from the Corporation' as being 'disaffected to his Majestie and his Government'. He was imprisoned and then released on condition that he left town. The current John Pounds Memorial Church in the High Street evolved from the meeting place for Presbyterians established by Burgess. He died at the age of forty-four and is buried in the cathedral having, presumably, been forgiven. (www.johnpounds.org.uk; *History of Portsmouth* by W. Gates, 1900)

November 25th

1895: Annie Gawn, aged twenty-two, was a barmaid at the Sussex Hotel opposite the Town Hall. One Sunday, Annie visited a Mr Corben's house in nearby Russell Street with two friends, where they had tea. Annie was in high spirits and waltzed around the room. She then fainted and never regained consciousness. At the inquest, on this date, it was revealed that her lower ribs were 'much compressed through tight lacing'. This caused her internal organs to be pushed against her diaphragm, 'encroaching on the chest cavity'. She suffered a brain haemorrhage, a contributory cause being the tight lacing of her corset. The coroner drew attention to 'the foolish custom of tight lacing', observing that it was the second case he had had before him within four months. (*North East Daily Gazette*; *Hampshire Telegraph*)

———•◆•———

1817: A radical Portsea printer, James Williams, was in court charged with libel after printing some parodies which exposed the corruption of those in government. The trial was intended to be a test case before the prosecution of the author, William Hone. Williams was fined and sentenced to twelve months' imprisonment at Winchester. Later, Hone, defending himself with great eloquence against biased judges, was acquitted. (*Diary, Reminiscences and Correspondence of Henry Crabb Robinson*, 1869)

November 26th

1926: The poet and writer Christopher Logue was born in Portsmouth. His father, John, worked for the Post Office and proposed to Florence Chapman on South Parade Pier in 1924. The young Logue attended St Swithun's School and St John's College before settling at Portsmouth Grammar School on the eve of war. He was evacuated to Bournemouth with the school, before joining the Army in 1944.

In the 1960s and '70s, Logue was part of the British Poetry Revival, which reacted against traditional poetry. One of his poems, *Be Not Too Hard*, was put to music and recorded by Joan Baez and Donovan. Logue was a long-term contributor to the satirical magazine *Private Eye*, and has also acted in Ken Russell's *The Devils*, and wrote the screenplay for his *Savage Messiah*. In 2005 he won the Whitbread Poetry Prize for *Cold Calls: War Music Continued*. (*Do Not Pretend* by A.J. White, 2007)

1703: The most severe storm ever recorded on the south coast sank the *Newcastle* at Spithead. The carpenter and thirty-nine men were saved but 193 of the crew drowned. Portsmouth was flooded and when the waters receded a stinking layer of mud, sand, shingle and debris covered the town. (*The Naval Heritage of Portsmouth* by J. Winton, 1989)

November 27th

1874: The photographer, writer and editor, Francis James Mortimer was born in Ordnance Row, Portsea. Educated at Portsmouth Grammar School, he later took evening classes at the local art college. Mortimer won a box camera in a competition, joined the Portsmouth Photographic Society and, in 1904, joined the Royal Photographic Society and wrote widely on the subject. In 1908 he became editor of *Amateur Photographer,* a position he retained until his death in the London blitz. (*Oxford Dictionary of National Biography*)

———•◆•———

1877: PC James Thomas entered the Victoria Tavern in Queen Street and spotted a man who fitted the description of an axe murderer. The constable seized him by the arm and marched him to Portsea Police Station. Under interrogation, the man, an illiterate labourer called James Caffyn, confessed to the murder at Ryde:

> We had a few words in the morning … she aggravated me again and said she would leave me and then I did the deed with the hatchet which was in the room. It was done in a moment … I was very fond of her. I did not want to part with her.

Caffyn argued that he had been provoked, and that it was manslaughter, but the jury disagreed and he was hanged at Winchester Prison in 1878. (*Hampshire Telegraph*)

November 28th

1863: A letter signed 'One of the Inconvenienced' appeared in the press on this day, complaining that soldiers of the garrison were marching, to and from church service on Sundays, four abreast. This meant they were 'occupying the entire passengers' footway' leading to civilians being forced into the gutter and road which was 'wet and muddy'. Perhaps concerned for both their dignity and the state of their Sunday best, 'One of the Inconvenienced' not unreasonably requested that soldiers march in single file on the pavements. This was not the first or last time that the military was accused of acting like they owned the town. (*Hampshire Telegraph*)

1977: Striking firemen, who generally received great public support for their fight for a decent wage, found that an arsonist had burnt down their lean-to used during their picket at Southsea Fire Station. (*Go to Blazes* by P. Smith, 1986)

2005: Born in Ryde in 1909, Malcolm Fewtrell led the Buckinghamshire Police in the investigation of the Great Train Robbery and wrote a popular book on the subject. On retiring from the police, he worked for ten years as accommodation officer for Portsmouth Polytechnic while living at Southsea. He died on this day in 2005. (*The Daily Telegraph*)

November 29th

1762: Edward Gibbon, the famous historian, visited the area while serving with the South Hampshire militia as a twenty-two year old. He grew to dislike military life and the cold discomfort of camps on the Hampshire coast, bemoaning the fact that he was being kept from his books.

On this day, he wrote in his diary:

We went to Portsmouth and crossed the water to Gosport where we relieved Ballard and his officers. My detachment consists of four subalterns, non commissioned officers in proportion and two hundred and fifty men. The officers are relieved every three weeks but the men remain as it is...'

Four days later he went to see a play performed by the Portsmouth Strollers and reported that it was 'miserably acted'.

In July 1761, Gibbon wrote, 'Sailed with Sir Thomas from Pilewell to Portsmouth, dined at Hilsea Barracks, with the Suffolk Militia ... About this time my book became publick.' This is believed to refer to his first book *Essay on the Study of Literature* (in French), which was to distinguish him as a man of letters. The first volume of *The History of the Decline and Fall of the Roman Empire* was published in 1776. (*Gibbon's Journal*, ed. D. Low, 1929)

November 30th

1868: Charles Wright, a homeless man, appeared before the Mayor, acting as magistrate, charged with 'wilfully destroying his clothes' in the vagrant ward of the workhouse. Wright had been admitted the previous evening but in the morning was found to have torn up his clothes and was 'in a state of nudity'. Wright had nothing to say in his defence and the magistrate accused him of destroying his clothes in order to get better ones.

In contrast, the previous day the Mayor considered the case against George Gardner of stealing a coat from a pawnbroker's in Butcher Street. Gardner said he was a boilermaker by trade, but that he could not get any work. He was 'induced to take the coat through want'. The magistrate said it was 'a most impudent robbery'. Both men were sentenced to twenty-one days' imprisonment with hard labour. (*Hampshire Telegraph*)

———— • ◆ • ————

1889: it was reported that an eighty-six-year-old man, who had been found begging in Victoria Road by a police constable, was sentenced to seven days' imprisonment with hard labour. Meanwhile, George Fletcher, aged twenty-three, was charged with having refused to 'perform tasks in the Union Workhouse by not breaking four hundredweight of stones'. (*Hampshire Telegraph*)

December 1st

1855: George James was driving a cart on the Hard. The horse was old and unfit and experiencing difficulty pulling the cart. James was seen striking it several times with his whip under the flanks. The magistrates heard that the horse had been badly beaten before, there being scars and dried blood on its flanks and down its legs. The case was adjourned for a week 'to give the defendant an opportunity of having the horse killed' and 'it was understood that if he did so within that time the case would not be proceeded with'. (*Hampshire Telegraph*)

1823: The *Hampshire Telegraph* advertised an auction of unredeemed pledges, giving an insight into what people pawned when they were desperate: 'To be sold at auction by Mr Patterson at his Auction-room, Union street, Portsea ... a Collection of unredeemed pledges consisting of silver and metal watches, men's, women's and children's apparel, women's and children's shoes, bed linen, bed furniture, household furniture...' On this day six years earlier, across the harbour, Haslar Hospital was selling off dead patients' clothes. (*Hampshire Telegraph*)

December 2nd

1889: 'Telephonic communication was established with Southampton and Winchester.' After persistent efforts by Mr A.W. White, the National Telephone Co. undertook to provide an exchange for the town in 1885. Mr White was also largely responsible for the establishment of the tramway system and also built the Empire Theatre in Commercial Road (later the Coliseum).

The exchange was established over the premises of grocers William Pink & Sons in Commercial Road, and subscribers were charged 12 guineas (£12.60) a year. Discounts were available, saving a guinea (£1.05) a year for a four-year subscription or 2 guineas for ten years. Having taken four years to connect with the Southampton and Winchester, subscribers had to wait a further seven years to connect with London. The 'menacing monopoly' of the private company running this disjointed and slow service was eventually broken when Portsmouth was granted a twenty-five-year licence by the Postmaster General to run a Municipal Telephone Exchange. This was established in 1901 at a cost of £26,000. (City of Portsmouth Records of the Corporation, ed. Gates, Singleton-Gates, Barnett, Blanchard, Windle, Riley)

December 3rd

1889: Major General Drayson delivered a talk at Portsmouth's old Guildhall on 'The Art of Killing', in which he argued that 'the more destructive the weapons that were used in warfare the less was the amount of slaughter'. Drayson maintained that 'the large guns of the present day, the dynamite shells and the torpedoes' were 'life preservers not life destroyers'. (*Hampshire Telegraph*)

———————◆———————

1557: The Governor of Portsmouth, Sir Adrian Poyninge, attempted to abduct the wife of a burgess. This was the low point of the relationship between the lawless Governor and the burgesses of the town.

> he ... sent the sergeant of his bounds restouslye with mo then xl soulders which served under his charge being well weapened with swords billes and other weapens, and caused them to gard and enter into the house of John Holloway with force and arms, Sir Adrian Poyninge being present, caused the chamb dore ... to be broken upp; and one of the companye ... drew his dagger and stroke one Nicolas Walker, servaunte...[Holloway's] wife being forced to enter the kitchen for that feare of the souldiers ... [Poyninge] practiced by all meanes possible to have had her out whereby he might the soner bring his unlawful purpose to passe ...

(*Annals of Portsmouth* by W.H. Saunders, 1880)

December 4th

1883: Dr Conan Doyle, in trying to become established in Portsmouth as a GP, joined the Portsmouth Literary and Scientific Society. On this day he gave a lecture on the Arctic Seas and immediately wrote a letter to his mother:

> The lecture is over – Gott sei dank! And was an unqualified and splendid success ... from the first word to the last the audience (which was a very crowded one) followed me most closely and often I could not get on for the cheering. When I finished there was tremendous applause – a vote of thanks was carried unanimously ... it was quite an ovation. I got about 20 specimens of Arctic birds from a bird stuffer and all my own curios so I had a brave show...'

Doyle closed his letter, 'The great thing is that we are advancing – getting known and quoted and making friends.'

Later, Doyle wrote that, on reflection, his talk had been well received because, upon piling the stuffed birds onto the lecture table, the audience had jumped to the conclusion that he had shot them all, and that this had earned their utmost respect.
(*Arthur Conan Doyle: A Life in Letters*, ed. J. Lellenberg et al., 2008)

December 5th

1805: Several weeks after Trafalgar, a visitor who had been shown around the *Temeraire* in Portsmouth Harbour, recounted an anecdote in a letter sent to future Prime Minister, John Russell:

> The muzzels of the guns often touched in this, I learn, most bloody engagement. ...An English sailor seeing a French one close to the porthole, put out the cannon ramrod with a screw or worm at the end, and fastened it into the Frenchman's breeches and actually hauled (him) by force out of his ship and through our porthole, and said to his Lieutenant, 'Here, your honor, I have lugged in a prisoner through the port.'

(*Early Correspondence of Lord John Russell 1805-1840*, ed. R. Russell, 1913)

———•◆•———

1870: The Elementary Education Act was adopted and Portsmouth's ratepayers were empowered to elect a School Board which could decide on how best to provide elementary education for the town paid for by rates. The first School Board met on 2 February 1871 and decided that school should be compulsory and that there would be no ratepayer funding of denominational schools. The first three schools opened in 1873, Cottage Grove, New Road and Swan Street, followed by Fratton Road, Flying Bull Lane and Kent Street the following year, and Albert Road and Conway Street in 1875. (*Portsmouth's Schools 1750-1975* by P. Galliver, 2011)

December 6th

1862: Mr J. Methvens of the Portsmouth Gas Company enlightened residents as to why they had been kept in the dark the previous evening. This was due, he explained, to the installation of a new and improved larger gas holder, but there had been teething problems as the gas had been contaminated with air. He had, he said, burnt off nearly 100,000 cubic feet of gas so that air would not be delivered to households, but this had not been entirely effective, and residents found they were unable to light their homes on this winter evening.

The Gas Company had been formed in 1823 and its offices opened in Commercial Road in 1877. (*Hampshire Telegraph*; City of Portsmouth Records of the Corporation, ed. Gates, Singleton-Gates, Barnett, Blanchard, Windle, Riley)

———•◆•———

1871: It was reported that Edwin Parkin, a cab driver, had been summoned for having moved too far away from his horse and carriage at a cab stand at St James's Street. The bye-law required cabbies to stay within 10ft of their vehicles, but Parkin was found by a police constable in a pub in Queen Street, 25 yards away. He was fined 15*s*. (*Hampshire Telegraph*)

December 7th

1940: PC Douglas Clarke and PC Arthur Beeson entered a bomb-damaged house in Southsea. The city had experienced five air raids, the King's Road and Stanley Street areas were in ruins, and there had been over 300 civilian casualties. Once inside the house, PC Clarke and PC Beeson helped themselves to a fur coat worth 28 guineas (£30.20) and a cape valued at 8 guineas (£8.40). Shortly afterwards, the Chief Constable received an anonymous letter which asked, 'Are you aware that looting of premises is going on by people who should know better? Perhaps a visit to [PC Clarke's] house might be of interest.'

Three months later, on this day, the two policemen appeared at Hampshire Assizes in Winchester. Summing up, the judge said:

> At the present time when women and children are showing heroism you, who had the opportunity of sharing in the glorious heroism of the people of Portsmouth, have descended to this mean and most wretched crime. I think justice requires that such offences committed under such circumstances should receive condign punishment.

Each officer was sentenced to ten years' imprisonment. (*Looting in Wartime Britain* by T. Gray, 2009; *The Times*)

December 8th

1970: Paulsgrove House, 'one of the finest examples of a centuries old yeoman farmhouse', was demolished to make way for the M275. The house, which dated from at least the seventeenth century, was sited where the traffic lights turn into Port Solent, near the Watersedge Community building. (*Evening News, Portsmouth*)

———◆•◆———

1901: A footnote to the year of Queen Victoria's death took place when the Queen's Hotel burnt down and two chambermaids died, trapped by falling masonry. The fire was discovered in the basement at just after 4.30 in the morning. Fire engines eventually arrived from the Dockyard and Victoria Barracks, by which time the hotel roof was alight. Attempts to direct water into the flames were hampered by a gale. Thirty guests escaped the blaze in their nightclothes.

Seventeen years earlier, a young Beatrix Potter stayed there and recorded in her diary: 'we finally settled at the Queen's Hotel which seems comfortable, a queer old house with mountainous floors'. The current Queen's Hotel was built on the same site and opened in 1903. (*Portsmouth as Others Have Seen it 1790-1900* by M. Hoad, 1973)

December 9th

1898: A 'Portsea character' who went by the name of 'Tip-toe Johnny' was sentenced to two months' hard labour at Portsmouth Police Court. He was one of eighteen men that week to have been prosecuted under a new act which defined a man who lived off immoral earnings as a 'rogue and a vagabond'. The eighteen men were accused of pimping at addresses in some notorious streets, including Primrose Alley, White's Row, Albion Street, Highbury Street, Voller Street, York Place and Rope Walk. Some of the men appear to have shadowed their woman while they were working, presumably as protection. (*Hampshire Telegraph*)

1895: Lancelot Hogben was born in Portsmouth. While a medical student at Cambridge, Hogben became a Socialist and, during the First World War, served in the Red Cross in France for six months, after which he was imprisoned in Wormwood Scrubs as a conscientious objector. In the 1920s he developed the Hogben Pregnancy Test, which was used for many years throughout the world. During the 1930s, he attacked the eugenics movement, the racist theories of which were the basis for Nazi genocide. Hogben is best known, however, as an experimental zoologist and wrote many books popularising science, mathematics and language. (*Oxford Dictionary of National Biography*)

December 10th

1832: Wax modeller Madame Anna Maria Tussaud, who had her head shaved ready for the guillotine during the French Revolution but was reprieved and forced to make death masks of beheaded royals, brought her exhibition to Portsmouth. It was advertised in the local press on this day and the price of admission to the Green Row Rooms was a shilling for adults and sixpence for children. Tussaud was in exile and toured the country with her collection of wax characters before setting up a permanent exhibition in London in 1835. She also appears to have visited Portsmouth in 1815, displaying her Grand European Collection of eighty-three 'public characters' at the Blue Posts in Broad Street. (*Hampshire Telegraph*)

———◆———

1957: It was announced that the Council had submitted a plan for the building of an airport on Farlington Marshes. (City of Portsmouth Records of the Corporation, ed. Gates, Singleton-Gates, Barnett, Blanchard, Windle, Riley)

———◆———

1953: Des O'Connor's name appeared on a Theatre Royal Bill in tiny print below a sea lion and chimpanzee act. (*Evening News, Portsmouth*)

December 11th

1862: The architect, surveyor, civil engineer and 'maker of modern Southsea', Thomas Ellis Owen, died, a month after being made Mayor for the second time. In the 1830s, Owen identified Southsea as a prime area for development, even though it consisted of marshes and tidal inlets. Owen advocated a drainage scheme and, by 1834, had begun building villas and terraces. He bought up 10 acres of land, on which he was to develop a pleasant residential area for the growing number of officers and professional families who wanted something better than what the overcrowded walled town of Old Portsmouth offered. Owen built St Jude's Church to help market his houses, though the Admiralty gave a grant towards the spire, which provided a landmark for ships as they turned to enter harbour. Owen's son-in-law was the first vicar. (*The Houses & Inhabitants of Thomas Ellis Owen's Southsea* by R. Riley, 1980; *Southsea Past* by S. Quail, 2000)

———◆———

1950: Winston Churchill was granted the Freedom of the City in a ceremony on South Parade Pier. In his acceptance speech he recalled how, between 1911 and 1914 when First Lord of the Admiralty, he was at Portsmouth most weekends aboard the yacht *Enchantress*. (City of Portsmouth Records of the Corporation, ed. Gates, Singleton-Gates, Barnett, Blanchard, Windle, Riley)

December 12th

1949: Members of Portsmouth City Council unanimously agreed that the Freedom of the City be granted to the Royal Hampshire Regiment. This gave the right to march through the city with colours flying, to the beat of a drum, with bayonets fixed. The scroll granting the Freedom was awarded on 20 May 1950 on Southsea Common by Lord Mayor, John Privett, who said:

> Portsmouth has long had the proud title of 'Home of the British Navy', but we are equally proud of our associations with His Majesty's Army ... In honouring our county Regiment today we are honouring not only those who are serving, but also those stalwarts of the 37th and 67th Regiments of Foot. We are honouring those who fought at Blenheim, at Malplaquet and at Minden; we are paying tribute to those who fought in the First World War, particularly those at Gallipoli where they effected a landing on V Beach despite terrible opposition. We are paying tribute to the courage, valour and devotion to duty of those who served in the Second World War.

In 1992, the Royal Hampshire Regiment was merged with the Queens Regiment to become the Princess of Wales's Royal Regiment, known as 'The Tigers'. (City of Portsmouth Records of the Corporation, ed. Gates, Singleton-Gates, Barnett, Blanchard, Windle, Riley)

December 13th

1942: The playwright Howard Brenton was born prematurely in Portsmouth. His parents were visiting the city and he was delivered by his aunt. Brought up in Bognor, he picked up the theatrical bug from his father and concentrated on theatre at Cambridge in preference to academic study. His play *Romans in Britain* at the National Theatre notoriously depicted a scene of a Roman soldier raping a Celt. Similarly, the 1985 play *Pravda*, co-written with David Hare, depicted an ogreish press baron attempting to take over the British media. Brenton has written over forty plays and scripted fourteen episodes of the BBC spy-drama *Spooks*. (*The Observer*)

———◆———

1751: Half a ton of lead was stolen from the guardhouse roof at Landport Ravelin. (*Portsmouth 1715-1751* by N. Surrey and J. Thomas; Portsmouth Archives Review, 1976)

———◆———

1953: Sir Adrian Boult conducted the Southern Philharmonic Orchestra at the Kings Theatre in a programme that included Mozart's *Magic Flute*. Reported under the headline 'Spell of the Master', the *Hampshire Telegraph* enthused, 'every signal of his baton, every crooking of his long, thin fingers of his left hand, was alive with crisp significance'. (*Hampshire Telegraph*)

December 14th

1891: This became known as 'Black Monday'. The Portsea Building Society closed its doors to its customers. The society had a good reputation and had Alderman Moody and Councillor Brown amongst its directors.

A few days later, a local newspaper attempted to reassure savers that 'if there has been no wrongful speculation … there ought not to be room for much loss.' After a Christmas wracked with worry, angry customers went along to a Town Hall meeting where the Mayor urged them not to criticise the directors. However, their conduct was described as 'reckless and scandalous' and there were accusations of 'irregular transactions'. A week later it emerged that nearly £180,000 of share capital alone had been 'wasted or lost or embezzled'. A local newspaper described it as 'a deplorable story of wrong-doing, blindness and shameful duplicity'. The 'thrifty poor' had lost most of their savings.

In an age when embezzlement by bankers was against the law, the directors and secretary were charged with larceny, falsification of books, false pretences and conspiracy. It emerged that the secretary's salary had increased from £30 to £750 a year, with £200 expenses for stationery, and they had also personally embezzled £16,000.

Four months later, Mary Ann Wilcox of Ashburton Road, who had lost savings, committed suicide by cutting her throat. (*Hampshire Advertiser*; *Daily News*; *Yorkshire Herald*)

December 15th

1747: A dead man was elected as member for Portsmouth. It was not known that Edward Legg was dead at the time of his election but, when it was realised, another election was organised and a Vice-Admiral with a pulse, Sir Edward Hawke, was chosen. (*History of Portsmouth* by W. Gates, 1900)

———◆———

1894: Women were elected for the first time as members of the Board of Guardians, the body which managed the workhouse. There was considerable opposition but, 'the ladies proved not only their ability to take part in Poor Law administration, but they brought to task a sympathetic understanding which was not a characteristic of exclusive male government. In many ways the poor and the sick are better for the admission of lady members.' Four women were elected, Mrs Proctor, Miss McCoy, Mrs Ward and Mrs Byerling. (City of Portsmouth Records of the Corporation, ed. Gates, Singleton-Gates, Barnett, Blanchard, Windle, Riley)

———◆———

1960: Fletcher's corset factory in Regent street, Mile End, burnt down. During the blaze it was said that blazing corsets were blasted out through the roof and floated down around the area. (*Go to Blazes* by P. Smith, 1986)

December 16th

1899: A new drill hall for the use of the 1st Hants Royal Engineer Volunteers was opened in Hampshire Terrace. (*Hampshire Telegraph*)

———— • ◆ • ————

1813: Elizabeth Harvard and her husband were about to embark as missionaries to Ceylon and India. She had come to Portsea and, while walking to Portsmouth:

> ...for the first time in her life saw the ocean, and heard its rolling waves thundering along the shore – with the self-command of a missionary heroine, she cheerfully expressed the pleasure she felt on being so contiguous to the mighty element which was about to convey us to the unenlightened inhabitants of Asia.

On this date, she sent a last reassuring letter to her parents:

> We shall have four other female passengers besides myself; and twenty soldiers' wives...this morning we were intending to go and see our vessel ... but the sea was too rough for the pilot boat ... I fully expected to be a little frightened [of the sea] but was not in the least. I feel I am in the hands of ... a good God and about to embark in a good cause.

She died at the age of thirty-four as a result of illness attributed to the tropical climate. (*Memoirs of Mrs. Elizabeth Harvard* by E. and W. Harvard, 1833)

December 17th

1970: Portsmouth Junior Chamber of Commerce published a report with advice for 'career girls'. Ambitious young women 'can shine in a senior secretarial post. This can be as a personal assistant to her boss, helping to influence him in his management thinking.' (*Evening News, Portsmouth*)

———•◆•———

1898: It was reported that Frederick and Charlotte Jones of Butcher Street had been summoned for neglecting their four children. Six-year-old Charles, five-year-old Horace, three-year-old Dorothy and Archibald who was only eight months, were found to be poorly clothed, filthy and 'covered in vermin bites'. The home was dirty and 'the stench arising from the bedrooms was almost unbearable'. A doctor said he thought they were all suffering from malnutrition, and the children's appearance in court 'caused quite a sensation'. In the days before Social Services, the plight of the children only came to light because the mother had set fire to a mattress. A fireman contacted the police about the conditions in the house. The parents were sentenced to two months' hard labour. (*Hampshire Telegraph*)

December 18th

1895: Albert Hardy visited the World's Fair at the Drill Hall in Alfred Road. He immediately went to a stand offering the chance to look at 'Foreign Beauties' and paid one penny to look at four reproductions of works of art. Hardy then asked the proprietor if he had 'any others'. The proprietor, Albert Platt, said that for another penny he would show him some 'good ones'. Hardy paid his penny and was shown four 'indecent pictures' of models. Platt was placed under arrest. Hardy was a police constable in plain clothes.

Platt denied the offence at Portsmouth Police Court, saying that the photographs had been given to him by a sailor, and that he had only shown them to two customers to cheer them up, as a joke. He was sentenced to three months' imprisonment. (*Hampshire Telegraph*)

———— • ◆ • ————

1873: Celia Levetus (*neé* Moss) died in Birmingham. She was born in Portsmouth in 1819 of a prominent Jewish family and, with her sister Marion, wrote some of the first fiction ever published by Jewish women anywhere in the world. In *The Romance of Jewish History* and its sequel, *Tales of Jewish History*, they were able to reflect on their own experience of diaspora as Jews in Victorian England. The tales are said to implicitly argue for Jewish emancipation in the Victorian world, and women's emancipation in the Jewish world. (*Oxford Dictionary of National Biography*)

December 19th

1877: It was reported that the Admiralty were conducting 'important armour plate experiments' in Portchester Creek. The 'ironclad' *Warrior* had been launched in 1860, but nobody was resting on their laurels. The object of the tests was to settle the question as to whether steel armour plates were preferable to iron, or whether a combination would be better to 'resist the heavy projectiles which are now in use'. The plates were set up on floating teak frames and fired at with 250lb shot. A 9inch-thick solid steel plate showed least damage.

The use of steel was subsequently adopted in shipbuilding, promising to reduce the thickness, and therefore the weight, of the armour. (*Hampshire Telegraph*)

———— • ————

1939: The first Royal Naval decorations of the war were awarded by King George VI at a ceremony on the parade ground at HMS *Vernon*. During the Second World War, HMS *Vernon* was responsible for mine, disposal and mine countermeasures. Her officers and scientific staff achieved several coups involving the capture of mines and the development of countermeasures.

One of the earliest of these was the rendering safe and recovery of the first German magnetic mine, for which Commander John Ouvry was decorated with the Distinguished Service Order (DSO). (*HMS Vernon* by E. Webb, 1956)

December 20th

1845: Joseph Pinhorn, a Dockyard storehouse labourer, appeared in court charged with having stolen 1¼ stone weight of nails. He had been searched by a police sergeant at the gate, who found his pockets stuffed with new nails. He also had a bag of them, 'apparently constructed for the purpose', hidden under his cap. This 'disclosed a systematic practice of daily plunder'. Mr Pinhorn told the sergeant that he took them from the store to build a pigsty. (*Hampshire Telegraph*)

1913: At 7.25 p.m. a sailor on board a ship lying at the South Railway Jetty spotted a fire in the Semaphore Tower. The alarm was raised but it was too late. The sail loft, rigging house and wooden tower were very quickly engulfed in flames and pensioner Signalman Pook, and Signalman Stewart, who were trapped in the tower, perished. There was speculation that it was down to German spies and suffragettes, but is more likely to have been an accident. Such rumours served the purpose not only of enflaming public opinion but of diverting attention from the Admiralty's apparent lack of concern with fire precautions and the safety of its employees, as the editor of the *Evening News* was not afraid to point out on a number of occasions. (*Keep the Home Fires Burning* by J. Sadden, 1990; *The Times*)

December 21st

1872: The naval corvette HMS *Challenger* set sail from Portsmouth to undertake a historic scientific expedition. Travelling nearly 70,000 nautical miles over four years, the expedition surveyed and explored the oceans, discovering the deepest location on earth, nearly 7 miles deep, and over 4,000 previously unknown species. The expedition is credited with laying the foundations of modern oceanography. (*History of Portsmouth* by W. Gates, 1900)

1959: The Hitchens family took up residence at Cedarwood in Alverstoke. Christopher and Peter Hitchens became award-winning writers and journalists on different sides of the political spectrum. In 2010 Peter Hitchens revisited the area:

> Haunted, raucous, raffish, war-damaged, ugly old Pompey is the nearest thing I have to a home town and it still fills me with mixed feelings. They've tried to tart it up a bit lately, with a fancy shopping mall and a tower, but my memories will always be of bluejackets surging through the streets, dark Edwardian pubs with the strange sweet-sour whiff of Brickwood's allegedly Brilliant ales, yellow funnelled paddle-steamers plying to the Isle of Wight, slum children diving for pennies in the Dockyard mud, the nasty mess left by the Luftwaffe and the large grey warships of a dying empire slipping through the narrow harbour entrance.

(*Daily Mail*)

December 22nd

1964: During a debate in the house of Commons on the abolition of the death penalty, the Conservative MP for Portsmouth West, Brigadier Terence Clarke, said that he 'did not think anyone had 'swung' up to now who had not committed a murder', adding, 'I am perfectly happy if a mistake was made in the odd case.' Whether Brigadier Clarke would have been perfectly happy if he, or a member of his family, was wrongly executed is not known. Brigadier Clarke said he had written to his local Portsmouth newspaper asking people with strong views to let him know what they thought. He said he had received 200 letters saying 'Hang the murderers', many of them suggesting that those who supported the abolition should be hanged too. Clarke described his fellow Conservatives who supported abolition as 'wet'. (*see* also July 22nd, August 28th). (*The Times*)

December 23rd

1940: In the evening darkness, the Luftwaffe dropped a single very heavy calibre bomb near Conway Street, a densely populated area of Landport. The blast was such that whole streets of terraced houses were wrecked up to a quarter of a mile away. Eighteen people were killed and 220 injured. Several Dockyard buildings were damaged.

During the war, 930 civilians were killed in the city, while 2,837 were injured. Many servicemen were also killed (*see* August 6th). There were 80,000 instances of properties being damaged in a city of 70,000 properties, indicating that some were hit more than once; 6,625 were destroyed. (*Battle over Portsmouth* by P. Jenkins, 1986)

1931: One of the principal naval training bases, HMS *Fisgard*, which was made up of a group of Victorian hulks in Portsmouth Harbour, was closed. *Fisgard* trained artificer apprentices. (City of Portsmouth Records of the Corporation, ed. Gates, Singleton-Gates, Barnett, Blanchard, Windle, Riley)

1787: HMS *Bounty* set sail from Portsmouth for Tahiti, under the command of Captain William Bligh. His mission was to pick up breadfruit plants and transport them to the West Indies in the hope that they would grow there and become a cheap source of food for slaves. (City of Portsmouth Records of the Corporation, ed. Gates, Singleton-Gates, Barnett, Blanchard, Windle, Riley)

December 24th

1877: Andrew Nance of Baffins Farm, holder of the record for driving the fastest stagecoach between Portsmouth and London, died at the age of sixty-seven. In 1835, his coach company advertised a 'splendid fast coach', *The Tantivy*, every day at noon from the Fountain Hotel, High Street, to London, in seven hours.

The service was 'horsed all the way through with the best description of horses, and short stages, thereby enabling them to perform the journey with the utmost regularity, without racing'. Stagecoaches in the previous century had taken nine hours, and many passengers made their wills before travelling because of the dangers of highwaymen and pot holes.

In 1839, Nance's competitor, Dick Faulkner, advertised 'the fastest coach to London' called *The Dart*, which left the Bush Hotel, Southsea at the same time as Nance's service. By now, Nance was claiming he could do the journey in six hours, and the race was on. In the event, Faulkner achieved a time of five hours 48 minutes, while Nance pipped him by six minutes. The condition of the passengers upon arrival at London is not known. (*Hampshire Telegraph*; City of Portsmouth Records of the Corporation, ed. Gates, Singleton-Gates, Barnett, Blanchard, Windle, Riley)

1920: John Barron, the actor most famous for playing CJ in the *Reginald Perrin* television series, was born on this day in London. His character's catchphrase 'I didn't get where I am today…' gained popular currency. He attended Portsmouth Grammar School in the 1930s. (*The Daily Telegraph*)

December 25th

1884: Conditions at the Portsea Island Workhouse were unlike anything depicted by Charles Dickens in *Oliver Twist*, on Christmas Day at least, reported the *Hampshire Telegraph*. Dickens would have 'rubbed his eyes in disbelief' at the ward, decorated with holly and the Christmas dinners of beef and plum pudding. The Guardians provided £8 for a special treat of nuts and oranges for the inmates, while wealthy townsmen sent parcels. Male inmates received a pint of ale, females half a pint, and 21lbs and 10lbs of snuff were distributed amongst the 1,300 inmates. The 'rules of discipline were relaxed as far as possible' and 'the inmates were allowed to enjoy themselves to the utmost'. Come Boxing Day, normal service was resumed. (*Hampshire Telegraph*)

———◆———

1890: The Blue Bell, which was later called Barnard's Amphitheatre, the music hall in Old Portsmouth, was burnt down on Christmas Day. Dating back to 1701, the establishment had a colourful history. On one occasion the Mayor, putting aside his civic dignity, was carried across the building on the back of Blondin, the famous tight-rope walker. (*Portsmouth in the Past* by W. Gates, 1975)

December 26th

1875: On this Boxing Day a musketry instructor at Fort Nelson on Portsdown Hill was locked in the guard room. Outside, in the casemates, men were huddled around their blazing fires, continuing their Christmas celebrations.

On the previous evening, Sergeant Carter had reportedly 'drunk somewhat freely' and was arrested for 'an unnatural act' with a private of the regiment and confined to the guard room. As the soldiers celebrated, a shot rang out. Somehow, Carter had acquired a firearm and, according to the subsequent inquest, committed suicide while in a state of temporary insanity. Sergeant Carter was 'a man of whom the officers of the regiment held in high opinion'. (*Hampshire Telegraph*)

———— • ◆ • ————

1794: Thomas Bevan visited Gershon Wolfe's shop on the Hard. Wolfe sold jewellery, was a 'dealer in slops' (seamen's clothing) and acted as a naval agent. Bevan bought six seamen's wills and powers of attorney. The stamps authorising the wills, however, proved to be forgeries, and the relevant duties had not been paid. An official from the Stamp Office visited the premises and Wolfe was arrested. The forgeries were traced to a Solomon Idswell of London. The following summer, Idswell was tried and convicted at the Old Bailey and hanged at Newgate with two other forgers. (Old Bailey Proceedings)

December 27th

1894: Albert Hammond, aged fourteen, a persistent mudlark, was charged with breaking the window of a draper's truck. Hammond had been with a gang of other boys on the corner of Anglesea Barracks when the truck passed by. The gang threw stones at it and Hammond's stone shattered the window. He was described as 'one of the most troublesome boys in the borough' and was sentenced to fourteen days' hard labour. (*Hampshire Telegraph*)

———•◆•———

1914: Frank Graeme Martin was born in St Chad's Avenue. He attended Portsmouth Art School and went on to the Royal Academy Schools, during which time he posed for the central figure of Triton in the Trafalgar Square fountain. During the war he joined the Royal Marine engineers and was twice mentioned in dispatches for bravery during the Anzio landings.

Martin's sculpture, to which he returned after the war, was mostly carved in either stone, or modelled in terracotta clay. He lived with his family at Hayling for many years, and set up the lifeboat station at Sandy Point. In 1952 Martin was appointed head of sculpture at St Martin's School of Art in London, a post he held until 1979. Among the teachers and students he encouraged were Anthony Caro, Elisabeth Frink, Eduardo Paolozzi and Gilbert and George. He died in 2004. (*Oxford Dictionary of National Biography*)

December 28th

1816: The naval ship *Tyne*, commanded by Captain Curran, arrived in Portsmouth Harbour. Up until 1807, when slave trading was abolished, Britain had been the leading slave trader in Europe. Abolition came after a long campaign by Quakers and evangelists like William Wilberforce (whose son, Samuel Wilberforce, was made Rector of Alverstoke in 1840). But, at the time of the *Tyne*'s return, Britain's Navy was working to close down both British and foreign slave traders, the latter largely because it represented unfair competition. Slavery itself was still legal, and continued in the British colonies.

The *Tyne* had returned from Ceylon via Mauritius, capturing several English and French slave vessels and their human cargo of 359 slaves, as well as seizing several empty schooners which were clearly equipped for slave trading. When transferred to the ship, the slaves 'presented a scene of debility and emaciation scarcely describable'. A typical extract of the ship's log reads: 'Fresh breezes, the sea rising, put on the hatches: found four of the slaves dead for want of air.' It was reported that 'the French are more engaged in the trade than any other nation in these seas'. (*The Times*)

December 29th

1888: Emanuel Emanuel, 'one of the most notable makers of modern Portsmouth', died. He first came to prominence in 1825 when, as a seventeen year old, he was charged and fined for assaulting a local pawnbroker. It was, ironically, 'by fighting an image of Portsmouth as disreputable, unruly and unseemly that [he] made his political reputation, transforming the town … beyond recognition'.

In 1844 he became the first Jew to be elected to the Council, and, though he refused to take the oath of office which would have bound him to follow 'the true faith of a Christian', nobody was mean enough to insist that the statutory £500 fine be applied every time he voted.

One of his first acts was to propose the discontinuation of the Free Mart Fair, which 'had degenerated into a fortnight's Saturnalia'. Emanuel recognised the potential for the development of Southsea as a watering place and was instrumental in the construction of Clarence Esplanade, Portsea railway, Victoria Park and Clarence Pier. He also pushed for the water and gas companies to be run by the local authority, rather than by rapacious private companies. (A Tale of Two Port Jewish Communities by T. Kushner, 2002; City of Portsmouth Records of the Corporation ,ed. Gates, Singleton-Gates, Barnett, Blanchard, Windle, Riley)

December 30th

1811: This endorsement appeared in a local newspaper's classified ads, perhaps aimed at those intending to make a New Year's resolution:

> I, John Hillyer, Cooper of His Majesty's Cooperage, Weevil near Gosport was very sorely afflicted with Venereal Disease for Four Years during which I was in St Thomas's Hospital for twelve weeks, in Guy's Hospital five weeks and in the Lock Hospital nine weeks and received no benefit. I came to Surgeon Roberts of 50 St Mary's Street, Portsmouth, reduced to the lowest state of existence, so as to despair of my life, but in less than two months I was restored to perfect health and strength and remain so to this present day.

In contrast, Alexander Rowe of No. 30 Common Hard offered confidentiality with his cure for 'venereal disease which is contracted in a moment of intoxication ... and consequence of juvenile indiscretion'. He challenged 'the approbation of the moralist' by exercising some understanding of the sufferer's plight. His medical credentials, however, were undermined by his reference to 'solitary vice' inducing the disease. (*Hampshire Telegraph*)

December 31st

1835: The first council meeting comprised of members elected by ratepayers took place. Previously, the borough 'had been in the power or control of one family for nearly fifty years'. The new council included six gentlemen, five surgeons, four merchants, three grocers, two druggists, and two pawnbrokers as well as innkeepers, brewers, a banker, an attorney, a solicitor, a Lloyd's agent, a wine merchant, coal and corn merchants, a painter, a butcher, a hatter, a staymaker, a tanner, a cordwainer, a sailmaker, and a farmer.

One of the first resolutions to be passed was for the formation of a police force 'for the due preservation of Order, Decency and propriety, and for the protection of Property within the Borough'. (*Borough Government in Portsmouth, 1835-1974* by S. Peacock, 1975)

———•◆•———

1847: The last message by semaphore from Portsmouth to London was sent. The system of signalling over long distances was established in 1795, and consisted of revolving shutters set in a frame. The first was on Southsea beach, the next on Portsdown Hill and there were twelve others on heights between the town and the Admiralty. On a clear day, a message could be transmitted in five minutes. (*The Old Telegraphs* by G. Wilson, 1976; City of Portsmouth Records of the Corporation, ed. Gates, Singleton-Gates, Barnett, Blanchard, Windle, Riley)